Will Rogers

Will Rogers

THE COWBOY WHO
WALKED WITH KINGS

CATHEREEN L. BENNETT

Published by
Lerner Publications Company
Minneapolis, Minnesota

ACKNOWLEDGMENTS: The illustrations are reproduced through the courtesy of: pp. 5, 6, 8, 12, 14, 20, 36, 39, 50, 54, 56, 72, Will Rogers Memorial, Claremore, Oklahoma; pp. 22, 44, 47, 61, 62, 64, Museum of Modern Art, Film Still Archives; p. 66, Independent Picture Service; p. 70, Wide World Photos; front cover, Independent Picture Service; back cover, Will Rogers Memorial.

We are especially indebted to Mrs. Paula Love, Curator of the Will Rogers Memorial, for her kind assistance.

International Standard Book Number: 0-8225-0704-8
Library of Congress Catalog Card Number: 71-128806

Second Printing 1972

Contents

1 Birth of a Cowboy 7

2 A Taste of Freedom 15

3 The Cherokee Kid 23

4 A New Home 30

5 "Kinder Nervous" 37

6 A Hollywood Career 45

7 Ambassador of
　 Good Will 51

8 "Can't Help Being
　 Funny" 55

9 The Last Trip 67

A statue of Will Rogers in the
Will Rogers Memorial, Claremore, Oklahoma

Will as a student at the Kemper Military Academy in Missouri

1   Birth of a Cowboy

Will always was happiest twirling his rope aboard a quick-moving horse. He began riding not long after he started walking, and he had his own horse at the age of five. Nearly every day of his life he practiced twirling his lasso and catching objects with his loop. As a young boy, he learned every well-known rope trick and invented many of his own. A keen interest in roping and riding came naturally to him, as it did to all boys who grew up in the range country of the Midwestern prairie.

Will's home was near Oolagah, Indian Territory, which later became part of Oklahoma. Both his mother and his father were part Cherokee, and he always took pride in his Indian blood. He was born November 4, 1879, on his father's ranch, 12 miles north of the town of Claremore. The baby boy was christened William Penn Adair Rogers, after a prominent Indian chief who was a friend of his parents. At his birth, Will's mother began hoping that he would become a minister. His father just wanted him to "amount to something," and as Will grew up, Clem Rogers often shook his head, angry and puzzled at his son's carefree ways. Will was not an industrious boy; when he should have been doing chores, he could usually be found in a shady place playing with his rope. He spent most of his free time racing his pony with his friends instead of reading school books.

The birthplace of Will Rogers, near the town of Oolagah

Will began his education in a one-room school house in the Cherokee Indian Nation, but from the beginning the restless boy found it difficult to concentrate on his ABCs. It was not that Will lacked intelligence; he was bored. He preferred activity to study, and he hated being confined indoors with good sunshine going to waste. Roping fence posts was more exciting than history, and swapping ponies was the only kind of arithmetic that interested him. Will's teacher worried about his lack of interest and talked to the boy's parents about it. His father became exasperated with the poor quality of Will's school work. Hoping that the boy might settle down to his studies when he was away from his horse and his fun-loving friends, Clem Rogers sent his son away to school to learn to be a minister.

Will's mother talked earnestly to him about the importance of education, trying to instill in the youth a desire for book learning. She realized that Will had long ago decided that what a cowboy needed to know could not be found between the covers of a book. Besides, Will could not see himself dressed up in a black frock coat trying to tell other folks how to live. He liked people pretty much as he found them. But for his mother's sake he promised to try to do well at his new school.

Will did try. He was good-natured and not deliberately mischievous. He made friends easily and soon became a favorite with the other students. They enjoyed his stories of ranch life and greatly admired his roping skill.

A year after Will went away to school, his mother died of typhoid fever. Will was deeply saddened by her death. All his life he never forgot her kindness and understanding. The next fall he returned to school, this time to one a few miles from the ranch. Here Will's roping skill proved to be his undoing. Lacking hens, dogs, fence posts, and his father's cows to lasso, Will had to find a substitute. A lone statue stood tall and tempting in the school courtyard below his dormitory window. The lure of the statue, a perfect target for his rope, was too much for Will to resist. One night he shook the cobwebs from his coiled lariat and slipped down the stairs. Moments later he flung his rope. Then he watched, helpless and horrified, as the heavy statue slipped from its pedestal, plunged from atop its high perch on the stone fountain, and shattered on the paving stones below.

Will's father scolded him thoroughly and paid for the broken statue. A shamefaced Will vowed to keep his lariat out of the courtyard, and the incident was smoothed over. One afternoon a few weeks later Will was practicing with his loop in what he thought was a safely deserted spot by the side of a building. Unfortunately, it happened that one of the teachers was out for a leisurely after-dinner stroll. As the teacher calmly rounded a corner of the building he found himself caught and thrown in the dust like a range cow. Immediately Will helped the shaken man to his feet, freed him of the rope, and attempted to explain and apologize. The red-faced teacher refused the boy's stammered explanation and had him dismissed from school.

His father ignored Will's pleas to stay on the ranch and sent him to another school, a seminary in Missouri. In this school, as in every one he attended, Will was extremely popular. He could turn any situation into a joke, and he enjoyed entertaining his friends. Although he had a quick mind and a good memory, he could never take schooling too seriously. There was too much else to do to have fun.

When Will was about 16, his father sent him to a military school, hoping that the discipline would tame him. Sadly, Will traded his chaps and high-heeled boots for a snug-fitting, high-collared cadet uniform. At first he enjoyed the military academy; he liked to shine his rifle and parade in the school ground. But after a few weeks his lighthearted personality was

Will (center) with two of his school friends

smothered under the strict routine. He good-naturedly but unsuccessfully tried to fit his shambling walk to the smart military drill required of him. Worst of all, Will was forbidden the use of his beloved rope. He felt the loss keenly and sighed frequently over his books. Will spent two long years at the academy before his spirit rebelled completely. He slipped away one dark night, deciding to "quit the entire school business for life."

Will as a young man

2　A Taste of Freedom

Not wanting to face his father and determined to prove himself, Will made his way to Higgins, Texas, where his ability with horse and rope won him a job on a nearby ranch. Years later a Congressman from Oklahoma told of working on this ranch with Will. He said that he noticed a cowboy perched on a corral fence fiddling with a rope and cracking jokes. He asked the ranch owner why he kept Will on, since he had never seen him doing any work. The man laughed and said, "In the first place, he's so funny I can't let him go, and in the second place, I'm just wondering if he can do anything." Will later said that he was about 28 percent effective as a working cowboy.

However, Will could work hard when he wanted to. The ex-schoolboy did a man's work when the ranch hands drove a herd of cattle to Kansas. In spite of his youth, he was shown no favors and asked for none.

This was the life he had dreamed of when he had lain sleepless in his bed at school. In Will's opinion, the tiresome bawling of the cattle and the bone-weary ache in his body were small prices to pay. The hours on the trail were long—sunup to sundown. In addition, Will had to stand his turn at night watch. But he reveled in his freedom. He cheerfully rode day after day in the choking cloud of dust raised by the moving herd and slept contentedly under the stars, using his saddle as a pillow. Each morning he rose happily to eat beans and boiled coffee for breakfast.

When Will received his wages in Kansas, he bought a horse and headed south to Amarillo, capital of the Texas Panhandle. Like Will, this lusty, sprawling town was young but had grown up fast. It was the railhead of northern Texas. All the business for the huge ranches and farms in that part of the country was conducted in this dusty town. After three days of wandering around Amarillo, broke, hungry, and homeless—sleeping on the prairie at night with his horse—Will talked his way into a job as a horse wrangler. His outfit moved to Panhandle City and then to Woodward, Oklahoma, where Will helped with the roundup.

Next the young cowboy's restless spirit led him to take a job tending a trainload of cattle bound for San Francisco. One night after Will had arrived in

California, his companion blew out the gas light in their hotel room without turning off the gas. All night the poisonous substance seeped into the room. In the morning both boys were unconscious and close to death. After many hours they were revived, but they still were very weak. Will went home to recuperate.

When he arrived in Oklahoma, his father, as usual, had plans for his future. Surprising plans. The Chief, as Will called his father, had moved into Claremore, and he wanted to turn the ranch over to Will to run as his own. Clem Rogers was a well-to-do man who was very influential in that part of the country. For years he had been a senator in the Cherokee Nation, and now he was working to obtain statehood for Oklahoma. With Will to run the ranch, the Chief could devote his time to this task and also to the bank he had started in Claremore.

Will took ranching as seriously as he had his schooling. The first thing he did with his new author-ity was to arrange for the building of a wooden dance platform. During his travels Will had become an excellent dancer and had won many prizes. Cowboys and fiddlers drifted on and off of the ranch as word spread that Will was back home and holding "open house." When Will was not dancing he was organizing roping contests and running the fat off the calves.

Before long his feet started itching, and he traveled as far as Springfield, Missouri, over 100 miles away, to try his hand in steer-roping contests.

About this time Will got his first taste of show business. Later he said that it ruined him for life as far as actual employment was concerned. When he entered a steer-roping contest in St. Louis, Missouri, he met Colonel Zach Mulhall. The Colonel worked for the San Francisco Railroad but spent his free time staging riding and roping contests. He had two daughters who could outrope and outride most men. The Colonel was putting together a cowboy band. He hired regular musicians and dressed them in chaps, boots, spurs, and broad-brimmed hats. Then he looked around for some honest-to-goodness cowboys who knew horses and roping. Will signed up and was given a trombone that he could not play a note on. He just held it to his lips.

The band went on tour through the Midwest, appearing at state fairs. When a sizeable crowd had gathered at the bandwagon Colonel Mulhall would challenge the onlookers to produce anyone who could beat his boys at steer roping. Deceived by the talent of the musicians and the newness of their Western clothes, members of the crowd would eagerly meet the challenge and make their bets. Then Will and a fellow cowboy, Jim O'Donnell, would saddle up.

In those days steer roping was rough work. The animals were full-grown, half-wild range steers, not the calves that are used in rodeos today. The cowboy had to keep his rope tied to his saddle until the steer had a good 100-foot lead. Then the flag was dropped, and the roper had to untie his coiled lariat, make a loop, rope the steer, throw him to the ground, and tie his four legs. The contestant who did all this in the best time won.

Will enjoyed his work with the cowboy band. The pay was not regular, but the company was good. At the state fair in San Antonio, Texas, he met a tall Texas cowboy named Tom Mix. Tom and Will soon became good friends. Although Tom was a year younger than Will, he was better traveled; he had been to China and also had fought with Teddy Roosevelt in the Spanish-American War. Like Will, Tom had been bitten by the show business bug. The next place the two men would meet was Hollywood, California. Tom Mix became one of the country's most famous motion-picture cowboys.

When Will returned to Oolagah he discovered that during his absence the sleepy cow town had been brightened by a new arrival. Blonde, blue-eyed Betty Blake had come from Arkansas to visit her sister. As

Betty Blake (center) performs in a school play at about age 17. In just a few years, she was to become Mrs. Will Rogers.

Will's friends watched excitedly, the two young people fell in love. Will lost his heart the first time he saw Betty walking down Oolagah's dusty board sidewalk.

Will courted Betty earnestly. He took her riding in an open buggy, showing her the places he loved—the stream where he caught his first fish, the huge shade tree under which he had practiced his roping as a small boy, and the now abandoned little school house on the Indian Nation. But before the young couple made any serious plans, Will began another exciting adventure.

Will twirls his rope in Australia.

3   The Cherokee Kid

Will's conversations with Tom Mix had given him a new curiosity. The Oklahoma cowboy began to yearn for faraway places. When he had raised enough money from selling the ranch's cattle he set out to satisfy his new longings.

Will had heard a lot about the Argentine country, and with his pockets full of money he decided now was a good time to go take a look. He teamed up with another footloose cowhand, Dick Parris, and together they went to New Orleans to get a boat to South America.

The charming Southern city at the end of the Mississippi River provided a wide variety of delight for sophisticated tastes. Its shops were filled with costly European imports and its architecture was varied and elaborate. The evening air was pierced by the strange, melodious chant of Creole fishermen selling their day's catch in colorful stalls along the crowded, cobbled streets. Although the city had much to offer, it proved a disappointment to Will and Dick. The harbor was busy with the traffic of many boats, large and small, but not one could supply the boys' needs. New Orleans had no commerce with her South American neighbors. Disappointed but determined, the adventurers made their way north to New York, only to learn that they had missed the yearly boat to Buenos Aires, gateway to the Argentine. Their hearts were set on a sea voyage, so they decided to ship passage to England and to make their way from there to South America.

Will had never before traveled on the water. A Western saddle horse had always been his chief means of locomotion. Even before the ship had cleared the New York harbor, Will felt a slight twinge. He lasted on deck just long enough to envy the Statue of Liberty its solid mooring in the watery expanse. The Oklahoma cowboy spent the entire trip across the North Atlantic groaning and tossing in his bunk, miserably seasick. Will was certain that the heaving ship underneath him was more lively than any bucking horse. He landed in England determined to stay "until some enterprising party built a bridge back home."

Will and Dick were greatly impressed with London and toured the city tirelessly. Preparations were being made for the coronation of Edward VII, great-grandfather of Elizabeth II. Will was amused by the bright-colored uniforms and the tall fur hats of the guardsmen at the gates of Buckingham Palace, but he concluded that "different nations have different ideas of humor."

Will's memory of his agonizing boat trip dimmed during the passing weeks. Still anxious to see the Argentine, he and Dick boarded a boat for Rio de Janeiro, capital of Brazil. Will had the same unhappy experience on this voyage. Unable to eat, weak and dizzy, he spent most of the trip below deck, while Dick strolled topside, thoroughly enjoying the voyage and eagerly answering the dinner gong. Twenty-three days later the ship docked, and Will, his suffering over, happily set foot once again on dry land.

After the boys had traveled from Brazil to Argentina, their money was nearly gone. Suddenly Dick developed a serious case of homesickness. There was just enough money to pay for one fare home. In a typical act of generosity, Will let Dick take the money and return. Will remained behind to punch cows for $7.50 a month, United States money.

Will traveled the length and breadth of the Argentine cattle country for five months, never staying long in one place. Argentinians speak Spanish, and Will's only language was the ungrammatical English of a Western cowhand, but his obvious friendliness and good humor overcame the language barrier.

Will was itching to display his Western roping technique to the gauchos, the Argentine cowboys, until he witnessed the amazing skill with which they handled their bolas. A bola is a rawhide sling four to six feet in length, weighted at the ends with stones or iron balls. Gauchos throw their bolas with remarkable accuracy and are able to bring down a running cow instantly. Will later insisted that they could throw a bola as far as he could shoot a Winchester rifle.

While in Argentina Will heard tales of the Boer War in South Africa and decided to try his luck on the other side of the Atlantic. The thought of another boat trip was not a welcome one, but he swallowed his reluctance and went to the harbor stockyards to look for work. A steamer bound for Africa was taking on a load of mules. The gauchos were having difficulty roping and loading the terrified animals. Will could not make himself understood when he asked the foreman for work, so when he spotted a gaucho in trouble with a particularly cantankerous mule, he uncoiled his lariat and caught the rearing animal. Immediately he had a job roping mules for $.25 apiece.

It turned out that an Englishman owned the

steamer with its lively cargo, and he hired Will to help tend the animals on the crossing. Will fared a little better on this trip. The mules were accompanied by a few cows with calves, and caring for the animals kept Will so busy that he did not have time to be seasick. Much to his surprise, Will discovered that he still had his appetite. Unfortunately, he was not getting enough food to satisfy it. He began tying up the calves at night and milking the half-wild cows. Then he traded the milk to the ship's cook for food. The cook was delighted to get fresh milk at sea and kept Will well fed during the month-long crossing.

When Will reached South Africa he found that the authorities would not allow anyone to go ashore unless he had at least $500, or £100 in British money. Will had only his wages, so he waited until no one was looking and quietly slipped off the boat. Once on shore, he had no trouble finding a job. At first he went to work on the Englishman's ranch, and then he began breaking horses for the British army. However, the Boer War ended a short time later, and the British army went home.

Out of work, the homeless cowboy drifted north. In Johannesburg, South Africa, he discovered a Wild West circus. Will was overjoyed; it was like finding a piece of home in that alien land. He joined up and was in show business once more. Besides doing rope tricks and riding broncs, Will played a clown and did a blackface song-and-dance act. He wanted his audience to know that he was a real Western cowboy, so during the year that he toured with the show he called himself The Cherokee Kid. At the year's end Will considered himself a true circus performer, and he wanted to join an even bigger circus. He also began to feel a strange longing for seasickness about the same time. After Texas Jack, the owner of the show, gave Will a letter of introduction, the restless cowboy shook the dust of South Africa off his boots and sailed for Australia.

Texas Jack's letter got Will a job with the Wirth Brothers Circus in Sidney, Australia. This time, Will devoted his act to horse and rope. He soon was a big hit with the circus fans. The Australians were great horse lovers, and they recognized and appreciated young Will's skill and daring. One afternoon when the circus was not playing, Will entered a racing meet and tried a new trick. Urging his horse to a full gallop, he hooked his toes around the saddle horn and flung his body backward. With the galloping hooves just inches from his head, Will snatched three hankerchiefs from the ground with his teeth. The crowd yelled its delight.

Australia's governor general was in the stands watching the performance. He sent a man over to ask Will to repeat the trick. "Tell him I'll do it again for $150," Will said. The governor's man was shocked at this demand, but Will could not see that he owed the governor any special favors. His face split with the wide, easy grin that was to become so famous, and he drawled, "You tell the governor general if he'll do it cheaper, I'll loan him my horse and handkerchiefs."

After touring Australia, Will and the circus went to New Zealand. When that tour was over, Will took a boat to San Francisco and then a freight train to Oklahoma.

4 A New Home

Back home at the ranch in familiar Oolagah County, Will decided to take a rest after his long journey. (Will Rogers considered himself "one of the most accomplished resters on earth.") The young cowboy had traveled around the world in nearly three years and had covered more than 50,000 miles. Home looked mighty good to Will; the faces were friendly and the meals were regular. Best of all, there was no heaving ocean to turn his stomach upside down.

Will had learned many things in his travels. Most important was what he had learned about himself. The fun-loving cowboy from Oolagah had left the United States caring more about riding and roping than anything else. He returned feeling much the same—with one change. Will had discovered that it was a lot more fun to "punch cows" in front of an audience than on a dusty trail, and besides, it paid better.

The townspeople of Claremore had become accustomed to the abrupt arrivals and departures of their favorite cowboy, so Will's homecoming did not surprise them. They greeted him warmly, happy to have him back among them. But Will did not stay long. He received word that his old friend Colonel Mulhall was getting together a Wild West show. Will said a hasty good-bye to his friends in Claremore and rode a train north to join the Colonel in his new venture. The show played at the World's Fair at St. Louis in 1904. Lucille, the Colonel's daughter, was all grown up now and one of the show's main attractions.

When the fair closed, Will left the Colonel's show to try his luck on the stage. He picked Chicago as the place to make his debut in vaudeville. Theaters were springing up all over the country, especially in the larger cities, to accommodate this new kind of entertainment. The shows at these theaters were not new to Will, however. The main difference between a vaudeville show and Texas Jack's Wild West Circus in South Africa was that the actors performed on a board stage in front of footlights instead of on the dusty, uneven ground of an arena.

At first Will had no luck getting a job. No one was anxious to try out an unknown personality who did rope tricks. It was quite by accident that Will finally found work. He was buying a ticket at the box office of a Chicago theater when he heard the manager talking on the telephone about needing an act. Will's luck held. The theater manager was so desperate that he hired Will without an audition. Will dashed to his hotel to get his ropes and was on stage in 10 minutes. When he finished his act he was engaged for the rest of the week. During one performance a trick dog got loose backstage and dashed across the footlights in front of Will. The cowboy threw his rope quick as lightning and lassoed the unsuspecting dog. The audience loved it.

Will left Chicago after the week was over and returned to the Oklahoma ranch. There he staked out a piece of bare, hard-packed ground the same size as a stage and began training his horse Teddy to work in that limited area. Will decided that if what people really liked was seeing him catch something with his rope, he would be happy to oblige them.

After working out for weeks in the small arena, Will left the ranch and agreed to join Zach Mulhall once more. The Colonel was on his way to New York's Madison Square Garden. Mulhall's Wild West Show had made it to the top of the ladder. Only the best shows appeared at the Garden, and Zach knew that Will was the best roper anywhere around. His one complaint about Will was his lack of neatness. Neatness was very important to the Colonel, and he always wanted his performers to look trim and tidy. He never really succeeded with Will. Even when Will had recently showered and shaved and dressed, he somehow looked unkempt. The moment the grinning cowboy put on his clothes, no matter how carefully pressed or sharply creased they were, they immediately assumed a slightly slept-in look.

During one of the night shows at the Garden, a steer used in a roping act got loose from the riders, jumped the arena fence, and ran up into the grandstand. A thousand pounds of wild steer rampaging through a tightly packed crowd is a fearsome sight. The terrified people screamed helplessly when the animal, as frightened as they were, plunged among them. Will did not hesitate. He ran up the aisle to head off the steer and threw his rope. He then swerved the steer down into the arena, where other cowboys were able to bring it entirely under control.

The next morning the newspapers published detailed accounts of the courageous action of the quick-thinking cowboy. Will Rogers was front-page news. The shy cowboy was embarrassed to learn that he was a hero. As far as he was concerned, it was just another piece of roping. Will scratched his head and grinned, figuring that these New Yorkers were just a little bit crazy. The newspaper stories did give Will an idea, though. He decided that when the show left town he would not go with it. He would stay in New York and put his roping act on the stage.

There was no demand for single cowboy acts in vaudeville. In fact, they were practically unheard of. But Will kept trying, faithfully making the rounds of the theaters. Disappointed but never discouraged, he wore his boot soles thin walking the sidewalks. Will's determination won over one theater manager's skepticism, and he hired Will to do a supper show. These acts were always considered unimportant because they played between six and eight o'clock in the evening, when most people were eating dinner. Even though Will was playing for only a small and scattered audience, he was content.

In the first few years of his vaudeville career, Will used a horse and rider. The horse was Teddy, the same one he had practiced with on the ranch. Teddy was small and quick with a placid disposition. He was not bothered by the confinement of the theater, the bright footlights, or the confusion backstage. As nonchalant as his owner, Teddy performed like a veteran. Will had felt galoshes made to cover Teddy's hooves so that he would not slip on the smooth waxed boards of the stage. Will had developed a trick of throwing two ropes, one with his left hand and the other with his right. He caught the horse with one loop and the rider with the other. Although the theater audiences enjoyed Will's roping skill, he did not make a big hit at first. It did not take the cowboy long to realize that audiences enjoyed comedians the most.

For years Will had been amusing his friends with his droll humor, but he dreaded trying to talk to the sea of unknown faces that made up a theater audience. While on stage, Will often made wisecracks to other performers and to stagehands in the wings. The performers saw the value of his lively wit and began to persuade him to use it to introduce the tricks in his act.

Little by little Will started talking on stage, and he was pleased by the response to his drawled remarks. His popularity with the vaudeville audiences grew. The restless, rope-throwing cowboy from Oolagah had launched his career.

Will on stage at the Ziegfeld Follies

5 "Kinder Nervous"

Success did not change Will as it has changed many people. He never forgot his cowboy friends or lost his restless spirit. And he never tired of traveling. In 1906 Will went to Europe. On this trip he was a performer, not a wandering, footloose cowboy, as he had been before. He played successfully in many countries, but he had one bad experience in Germany. When he roped a fireman standing in the wings the audience was offended, not amused. Will said that the German people had cultivated everything except a sense of humor.

When Will became a star attraction on Broadway and in Europe, earning good money, he began to think longingly of the lovely girl he had met back in Oklahoma. Although Will made many new friends in New York, several of them beautiful show girls, he never forgot Betty.

Betty and Will were married at Betty's home in Rogers, Arkansas, and then the couple went to New York. Betty became Will's partner and business manager, as well as the mother of his three children. Will declared, "She's the luckiest thing that ever happened to me." He considered roping Betty the star performance of his life.

Will became even more successful in the years after his marriage. The audiences enjoyed his stories and wisecracks so much that Will began to appear on stage without his horse. He just twirled his rope and talked. In 1912 he appeared at the Victoria, one of New York's largest theaters.

In 1915 Will joined the Ziegfeld Follies. Florenz Ziegfeld was one of the greatest showmen on earth. He filled his show with beautiful girls, gorgeous costumes, and elaborate stage sets. Only the best acts played in the Follies. Ziegfeld also introduced a midnight show to Broadway and Will became its star. Each night the homely, soft-spoken cowboy entertained one of the most sophisticated audiences ever gathered under one theater roof. Men and women traveled miles to see New York's finest show. Many of the same people came back two and three times to hear Will. Knowing that he was often playing to repeat audiences, Will began worrying about his jokes.

While performing in the Follies, Will lived on Long Island. He spent much of his free time riding and roping.

He did not have a set routine as most comedians did; he preferred to talk about something different each night. Betty suggested that Will talk about what he read in the newspapers. It was his habit to read several papers each morning, and he sometimes commented on what the politicians were doing. As usual, most of Will's remarks were humorous.

Betty's idea took hold, and Will had a never-ending supply of fresh material for his act. He thought that the United States Congress was funnier than anything anyone could make up. He liked to wisecrack about the actions of important people, but Will never kidded a person publicly unless he considered him "on top."

One night in Baltimore, Maryland, just before he went on stage, Will learned that President Woodrow Wilson was in the audience. At this time the United States was having trouble with Mexico. A bandit named Francisco Villa, or "Pancho" Villa, as he was better known, had tried to take over the government of Mexico. At first the United States supported his action, but when stories of Villa's brutality reached President Wilson in Washington he changed his mind and sent an army to stop the bandit. Pancho Villa was enraged at the change in government policy, and his men began murdering United States citizens wherever they found them. The two armies chased each other back and forth across the border.

This particular night Will had planned to comment on the troubles the United States army was having. In spite of his popularity, Will considered himself nothing more than an ordinary cowboy "who had learned to spin a rope a little and who had learned to read the daily papers a little." Now he was expected to go out on the stage and kid the President of the United States. Will later said, "Well, I am not kidding you when I tell you that I was scared to death."

They had to push the comedian out on the stage. Will slowly made a loop and began twirling his rope. The first thing he said was "I am kinder nervous here tonight." This remark was so obviously true that it charmed the audience. Will then made a few remarks about a former presidential candidate, and President Wilson laughed. This gave Will courage to start talking about the trouble in Mexico.

Watching the President anxiously out of the corner of his eye, Will said, "I see where they have captured Villa. Yep, they got him in the morning papers and the afternoon ones let him get away." Again the President laughed. Will relaxed a bit and joked about the army's lack of preparation for war, saying that it would have to borrow a gun if it ever wanted to fight a battle. Then Will said that the soldiers chased Villa into Mexico but were forced to come back because they ran into a lot of government red tape. Each time Will made a remark he watched to see the President's reaction.

President Wilson enjoyed Will immensely and laughed hardest at the jokes about himself. Wilson even repeated one of the jokes in a speech he gave in Boston. Will said later that this was the "proudest and most successful night" of his stage career.

This was Will's first contact with an important world figure. In the following years he counted among his friends many famous people. England's Prince of Wales became one of his favorites. Cowboys or princes, laborers or millionaires, Will treated them all alike. He could talk to anyone because he was everyone's friend. Will accomplished many amazing things in his life, but he is probably best remembered for saying "I never met a man I didn't like."

He soon gained a reputation for kindness and generosity that was unsurpassed among the people in show business. His fellow workers admired his common sense and often sought his advice. An out-of-work actor could always count on Will to help him over a rough spot. The assistance Will gave Fred Stone is a good example of his unselfishness. Fred was starring in a musical comedy at the Knickerbocker Theater in New York. He needed some rope tricks for a new show he was rehearsing, and he had hired an Oklahoma Indian to teach him a few simple tricks. But before Fred could learn the tricks, the Indian went back home.

When Will heard about the young star's predicament, he offered his services. Fred was delighted to have the opportunity to learn from a master like Will. He quickly picked up the rope-spinning tricks he needed for his act and regularly used them as part of his routine. Will's kindness launched a friendship that lasted many years. It never occurred to Will that he might hurt his own chances by sharing his roping know-how with another performer. His unfailing generosity brought him the love and respect he enjoyed all his life.

Will in the silent movies

6   A Hollywood Career

Once Will mustered the courage to talk to an audience while spinning his rope he became a sensation. In 1919 he accepted an offer from Samuel Goldwyn to make motion pictures in Hollywood. Will went to California and learned to be an actor. Unfortunately, the film industry had not yet discovered how to put sound in moving pictures. Will had to rely on his appearance and actions to tell the story. He enjoyed making films. He once remarked, "It's the only business where you can sit out front and applaud yourself."

Most of the pictures Will starred in were Westerns. On a movie lot one day a director was telling Will about a scene that required him to ride a horse. The director said that a stunt man made up to look like Will would do the riding. Having someone else ride for him did not sit very well with Will, but he did not argue. Certain that action would speak louder than words, he looked around and saw a stagehand leading a saddled mare. Will took the reins in his hand, leaped into the saddle, and galloped across the lot cowboy style. The director instantly realized that he had made a mistake in thinking that Will Rogers was a "Broadway cowboy."

Another time, Will was doing a scene that required him to be thrown from his horse into a creek. He was supposed to mount the horse in a corral and ride him to the creek. Each time Will tried the scene the half-broken horse threw him before he got out of the corral. He finally became exasperated, and when the director complained Will offered this suggestion: "Listen, if you want me to do this scene, you get a corral that's nearer the creek; or better still, find some creek that's nearer a corral."

Will made 13 silent films before returning to the stage. Here are some of his comments about motion pictures:

"Moving picture audiences are just like an old gold miner, they will keep on going and going for years hoping against hope to eventually some day strike a picture."

"What is the salvation of the Movies? I say run em backwards. It can't hurt 'em and it's worth a trial."

"Pictures are getting so long that the life of a moving picture fan is four features."

Will liked the warm California climate so well he decided to make the state his permanent home. He built a ranch in Santa Monica and equipped it with roping corrals and a polo arena.

The Rogers' ranch in Santa Monica. Today it is preserved as a state park.

He spent three years working in Hollywood before he returned to the New York stage. He told his friends in New York that it was good to be back where he could be using his brain instead of loafing around a movie lot. "You know," he said, "you've got to exercise your brain just like your muscles."

One night after a performance in New York Will was visited by the president of the McNaught newspaper syndicate, who had realized that Will's humorous comments on political happenings would make choice newspaper copy. When the newspaperman suggested that he write a regular column, Will said that he did not know anything about writing, but "he'd try."

Will's articles were an instant success. He wrote just as he talked—in the homely speech of a prairie cowhand. Critics were soon referring to Will Rogers as a humorist and philosopher. Every day for over 20 years Will pecked out "a piece for the papers" on his typewriter. His column was widely read, and it made him one of the highest paid writers in the newspaper business.

A few years after Will started publishing his newspaper articles, he began a series of lecture tours across the United States. He visited many of the smaller cities, giving his shrewd, witty talks to people who had never before seen him in person. He was able to reach the people he loved, the ones he considered the heart and backbone of the country—the small rancher and farmer, the unskilled laborer and miner. Will said that these people had more "savvy" than any of the well-dressed theater audiences. When he took his act to Sing Sing state prison, the prisoners applauded his jokes so heartily that Will began to wonder if maybe the wrong people were locked up in there.

Will talks with the captain of the *Leviathan* in 1926, on the way to Europe.

7 Ambassador of Good Will

In 1926 *The Saturday Evening Post* persuaded Will to take a world tour. The Oklahoma cowboy found himself an honored guest wherever he traveled. He interviewed kings and dictators and attended formal banquets in England, Italy, Spain, and other European countries. He became friends with many world political leaders. They enjoyed Will's shrewd observations about the events in their own countries as well as in the United States.

Will furnished articles to the *Post* relating his experiences as an unofficial ambassador for President Calvin Coolidge. The articles, called "Letters of a Self-Made Diplomat to His President," were read everywhere the *Post* was sold. Many people suspected that Will's trip was more official than was told. His reports did show that he had a good understanding of the current state of world affairs. Will worried when he discovered that the United States was not liked by many of the foreign countries he visited. He reported to President Coolidge, "We don't stand like a Horse Thief abroad . . . Whoever told you we did was flattering us. We don't stand as good as a Horse Thief."

The First World War had been over for eight years when Will visited Europe. He had hoped to find the countries on friendly, peaceful terms with one another, but he discovered that their relations were far from cordial. He wrote a colorful description of some of Europe's troubles. "France and England think as much of each other as two rival gangs of Chicago gangsters. . . . Russia hates everybody so bad it would take her a week to pick out the country she hates most." Will told the President that what Russia needed was more of a sense of humor and less of a sense of revenge. Many of Will's remarks are as true today as they were during his time. He described Switzerland as the most independent country in the world. "They have neither imports nor exports. Its sole commodities are conferences and neutrality." Will called Switzerland "the Blind Tiger of Europe." This was and is an appropriate label for the small snowbound country that opens her borders to all nationalities and carefully ignores the problems of her neighbors.

Back home the people read about Will's trip and felt as if they were traveling with him. Will was one of

them. The working people of the United States believed that he was their personal ambassador. He
represented their way of life and their kind of thinking.
He scorned fancy clothing; he toured the world and
visited its dignitaries dressed in the comfortable clothes
and battered hat that were as much a part of him as his
ungrammatical Western drawl. Will attended formal
dinners wearing his worn blue serge suit and a friendly
smile. He represented the heart of the country in a way
that no one else had done before or has done since.

Will is named honorary mayor of Beverly Hills.

8 "Can't Help Being Funny"

When Will returned from his trip he found that the people of Beverly Hills, California, had made him honorary mayor. There was even talk of nominating Will for President, but he never took that seriously. Will figured that he was better suited to kidding a President than being one.

As much as Will loved visiting strange places and meeting new people, he liked being at home best. In spite of his busy schedule he spent many happy hours on the ranch in Santa Monica in the company of his three children. All of Will's children learned to ride very young. Will once described his two-year-old son Jim as "the youngest cowboy in the world": "If you want to start a Civil War, just try to take him off that pony. He eats there."

Will depended on his wife's good judgment and rarely made an important decision without talking it over with her. He often would read his news articles

The Rogers family. In front, Betty Rogers and Mary; in back, Will Jr., Will Sr., and Jimmie

to Betty before he sent them to be published. If there was something she did not understand, he would change it.

Once in an interview Betty was asked if Will were funny at home as well as in public. "Of course he is!" she replied. "Will can't help being funny wherever he is. His humor isn't the artificial kind that you can put on and take off like a coat. He doesn't try to be funny. He just is."

Will never tired of practicing his rope tricks, and he took special pleasure in teaching many of them to his children. In California he took up a new pastime, polo, that allowed him to spend many hours in the saddle. He formed a team with his wife and children and became an expert polo player. Will loved the competition of the game and the thrill of riding a fast horse in pursuit of the small wooden ball.

On one of his cross-country lecture tours of the United States, Will developed a pain in his middle that he described as a "bellyache." He was rarely sick and was proud of his good health. He had appeared almost daily on the stage for 20 years without ever missing a performance. After a brief visit to the ranch in Oolagah, Will arrived in California a sick man. His description of the events that followed shows how he could find humor in any situation:

"We were primitive people when I was a kid. There were only a mighty few known diseases. Gunshot wounds, broken legs, toothache, fits, and anything that hurt you from the lower end of your neck down was known as bellyache. . . .

"I don't remember when I first had it, but I sure do remember one of my dear old Mother's remedies for it. They just built a fire in the old kitchen stove and heated one of the old round flat kitchen stove lids—the thing you take off the stove if you want what you're cooking to burn. Well, they would heat it up—not exactly red hot, but it would be a bright bay. They took it off, wrapped it up in something and delivered it to your stomach with a pair of tongs. Well, the heat from one of those stove lids burned you so you soon forgot where you were hurting. It not only cured you but it branded you. . . .

"Well, the bellyache hadn't shown up in years, until one spring on my tour of national annoyances. . . .

". . . When I got home they called in a doctor. He gave me some powders. The pain just thrived on those powders. I never saw a pain pick up so quick as it did when the powders hit it. Instead of setting around like most people do, I would take a stool or chair and arrange myself over it something like this: My head and arms would be on the floor on one side and my knees and feet on the floor on the other side. My middle was draped over the seat of the chair. Finally, my wife called in Doctor White, a famous physician.

"'What part of your stomach hurts?' he asked.

"'Practically all of it, Doc'. . . .

"'. . . It's the Gall Bladder—just what I was afraid of.' Now you all know what that word 'afraid of,' when spoken by a doctor leads to. It leads to more calls. . . .

"He then says, 'We operate.' My wife says, 'Operate?' And as soon as I came to enough I says, 'Operate?'

"'Where's the phone?' he asked.

"I didn't know whether he was going to phone for knives, the hearse the ambulance or what. The wife pointed to the phone kind of dumbfounded. . . .

"Well, the household was up bright and early the next morning to get old Dad off to the hospital. The whole place was what the novelist would call agog. Even the chauffeur—part time— had the old car shined up. This going to the hospital was a new thing to me. Outside of those stove-lid episodes I had never been sick a day in my life. . . .

"There was a kind of a little balcony up above the operating room floor where people with a well-developed sense of humor could sit and see other people cut up. It must be loads of fun. But there wasn't a soul in there for my operation. I felt kind of disappointed.

"I thought, 'Well, here I am maybe playing my last act, and it is to an empty house'. . . .

"Next thing I knew I heard the nurse on one side and my wife on the other saying, 'Lay perfectly still, you're all right. You are fine now. Just relax.'

"Finally this ether got to leaving me and I sort of remembered what the operation had been for. I asked them, 'Did you get any gallstones?'

"Yes, they had got some. A couple of sizable dimensions, but nothing in any way approaching what could be used for exhibition purposes. I felt right then that the operation had been a failure. . . .

". . . Now what causes the stones to form? Well, there are various reasons. Republicans staying in power too long will increase the epidemic; seeing the same endings to Moving Pictures is a prime cause; a wife driving from the rear seat will cause Gastric juices to form an acid, that slowly jells into a stone as she keeps hollering.

"Of course I will always believe that mine was caused by no sanitary drinking cups in the old Indian

Will played the title role in *A Connecticut Yankee* (1931).

Territory where I was born. We used a gourd, raised from a gourd vine. Not only did we all drink out of the same gourd but the one gourd lasted for years. . . ."

In 1929 Will received another offer from Hollywood. Sound projection had proved a success, and films were no longer silent. The head of Fox Studios, who was a good friend of Will's, persuaded him to return to California and try his hand with the "talkies."

Will was an immediate success. He made 19 features and numerous short comedy films. With sound on the film Will had a chance to show his real ability. He gave fine performances as a happy-go-lucky tramp, a country doctor, a hog-raising farmer, and in *David Harum*, a banker and horse trader. Will had an extraordinary ability to make people forget that he was a

One of Will's last movies was *The County Chairman* (1935).

comedian. The sincerity with which he played his various roles was remarkably convincing.

Will never lost his easy-going manner in the artificial, make-believe world of Hollywood. Although he became the highest salaried movie star of his time, he always kept his simplicity and genuine friendliness. He wandered around the movie set in overalls, high-heeled boots, and an old sweater, looking more like a working cowboy than a Hollywood star.

When he was at the movie studio Will used his car as a dressing room and office. He rarely used the luxurious dressing room that the studio provided for him, preferring to keep a change of clothes, as well as his typewriter, in his car. When things were quiet on the set and Will was not needed in front of the camera, he would pull his typewriter out of the rumble seat and sit down on the running board. Balancing the machine on his knees, he would tap out his piece for the papers.

Visitors to the movie lot always asked to see Will Rogers first. He entertained more important people than any other star of his time. When President Calvin Coolidge came, Will received him in the studio dressing room. This was one of the few times Will used it. He decided that he should give the President a comfortable place to sit.

Will types his "piece for the papers."

Will had one more outlet for his boundless energy and talent. Radio was fast becoming the chief source of news and entertainment in the United States. Almost every parlor proudly displayed one of the heavy wooden radio cabinets that were the style of the day. The radio brought Will's soft Oklahoma drawl into most of the homes of the country.

In all his radio programs, lecture tours, and newspaper articles Will told the people what they liked best, the truth. He told them the truth about the nation's politics, its public organizations, and its social habits. He ridiculed what was false and pompous and showed the people that their leaders were men just like themselves, with the same faults and weaknesses. Will talked to the people in a language they could understand, and he brightened their days with his infectious chuckle.

Will Rogers—humorist, movie star, philosopher

9 The Last Trip

One of Will's close friends was an airplane pilot named Wiley Post. Early in his career Will learned to take advantage of air travel. The airplane was still a new invention, and many people thought that it was dangerous and foolhardy to fly in the flimsy planes of the time. But airplane travel suited Will's restless nature and love of speed. At every opportunity he praised the skill of the pilots who flew the mail planes, and he probably did more than any other individual to promote flying as a sound and profitable business. He had a special government permit that allowed him to fly in any mail plane. He was the number-one air passenger of the United States, flying over 500,000 miles during his lifetime.

The plane ride that really sold Will on flying was one with Colonel Billy Mitchell, the maverick army flyer who in the 1920s outraged his superior officers with his demands for a fighting air force independent of the army and navy. Mitchell took Will up on his last flight before he was demoted from Brigadier General to Colonel. Will was also well acquainted with Charles Lindberg, who in 1927 made the first nonstop solo flight across the Atlantic Ocean.

One of Will's ambitions was to become "the world's airplane reporter." He wanted to spend his time flying to the troubled areas of the world and recording the news as it happened. He never learned to fly because Betty asked him not to. Instead Will depended on the skill of his friend Wiley Post to pilot the plane.

Wiley was one of aviation's most skillful and daring masters. He grew up in Oklahoma, and when he was very young he gained a reputation as a good man with machinery. He lost his left eye in an accident in the Oklahoma oil fields and always wore an eye patch. Wiley logged over 700 hours of flying time before he got his pilot's license. He improved his vision until it was better with one eye than it had been with two.

In his plane the *Winnie Mae,* Wiley set many world records for both speed and endurance. He also flew as a test pilot for the Lockheed Aircraft Company, and he later was a commercial pilot for Transcontinental and Western Airlines. In 1934 Wiley designed a rubber flying suit that could supply oxygen and maintain constant pressure at high altitudes. His experiments in high-altitude flight provided aeronautical engineers with information that led to the development of the pressurized cabins used in modern aircraft. The *Winnie Mae* was later placed in the Smithsonian Institution alongside Lindberg's *Spirit of St. Louis*.

In the early days of flying, pilots had to fly by the "seat of their pants." Without instruments and in open cockpits they were entirely at the mercy of the elements. They often followed telephone poles, flying low enough to see the ground clearly. Many emergency landings were made in farm fields or in any available flat open space. (Will was once forced down in Wyoming in a chartered airplane.) The planes had no radios, and airfields were very scarce.

Will had long wanted to fly across the "roof of the world," over the Arctic Circle to Asia. He and Wiley had discussed it often. The idea grew, and in 1935 Wiley started building the plane that would take both men on their last journey. The plane was designed for long-distance travel and equipped with a powerful Wasp engine. It also had fixed landing gear that could be fitted with wheels, skis, or pontoons for water landings.

Will and Wiley Post stand on the airplane which was to take them on their last ride.

Wiley and Will took off from Seattle and flew to Alaska, where they visited the pioneers in Matanuska Valley, near Anchorage. Will walked around the valley, talking with the hardy men who had come to this wilderness to make their home. One man gave Will some cookies he had baked. Will thanked him and said jokingly, "If Wiley has trouble getting the plane off the ground, I'll throw these out first."

These tough pioneers were Will's last audience. The next word anyone had of Will was a tragic radio message from a lonely outpost at Point Barrow, the northernmost tip of Alaska. An Eskimo who had seen the plane crash ran 15 miles with the news of the two men who were inside. He described them as "man with rag over sore eye and a big man with boots."

The world was stunned by the loss of its beloved humorist. Although Will's restlessness had brought his life to an untimely end, it was fitting that he should lose his life in his endless search for new sights and new faces. The rope-throwing cowboy from Oolagah had lived each minute of every day to its fullest. The lives he touched were enriched by his warm presence.

A statue of Will Rogers outside the Will Rogers Memorial in Claremore

Soul Surgeon

Becoming a Healer of Wounded Hearts

✳ I am deeply indebted to the many individuals who have given me the privilege of hearing their story and being part of God's process in their lives. Personal accounts shared in this book are fictitious, though they may be loosely based on common experiences shared by many individuals. In those cases, names, locations, and other details have been changed to protect the innocent and offer mercy to the guilty.

Cheryl Lynn Shea

PUBLISHING

Belleville, Ontario, Canada

Soul Surgeon
Copyright © 2007, Cheryl L. Shea

All Scripture quotations, unless otherwise indicated, are taken from the New Revised Standard Version of the Bible. Copyright 1983, 1985. Published by Holman Bible Publishers, Nashville, Tennessee. Used by Permission of the National Council of Churches of Christ in the United States of America. Scripture quotations marked The Message are taken from The Message version of the Bible. Copyright by Eugene H. Peterson, 1993, 1994, 1995. Used by permission of NavPress Publishing Group. Scripture quotations marked NIV are taken from the New International Version of the Bible. Copyright 1973, 1978, 1984. Scripture quotations marked NIVI are taken from the New International Version of the Bible Inclusive Language Version 1995, 1996. Used by permission of Hodder and Stoughton, a member of the Hodder Healine Group. Scripture quotations marked GNT are taken from the Good News New Testament, Fourth Edition. Copyright 1966, 1971, 1976 American Bible Society. Scripture quotations marked NLT are taken from the *Holy Bible,* New Living Translation, copyright 1996. Used by permission of Tyndale House Publishers Inc., Wheaton, Illinois 60189. All rights reserved.

Library and Archives Canada Cataloguing in Publication

Shea, Cheryl, 1958- Soul surgeon / Cheryl Shea.

Includes bibliographical references.

ISBN 978-1-55452-207-1 1. Spiritual healing. 2. Faith. 3. Self-actualization (Psychology)–Religious aspects–Christianity. 4. Christian life.

I. Title. BT732.5.S457 2007   248.4   C2007-904932-X

Essence Publishing is a Christian Book Publisher dedicated to furthering the work of Christ through the written word. For more information, contact: 20 Hanna Court, Belleville, Ontario, Canada K8P 5J2.

Phone: 1-800-238-6376. Fax: (613) 962-3055.
E-mail: info@essence-publishing.com
Web site: www.essence-publishing.com

To my mom, Frances,
who chose to give me the gift of my life,
and in memory of my stepdad, Bill,
who adopted me as his own
and walked with me as best he could.

If you get rid of unfair practices,
quit blaming victims,
quit gossiping about other people's sins,
If you are generous with the hungry
and start giving yourselves to the down-and-out,
Your lives will begin to glow in the darkness,
your shadowed lives will be bathed in sunlight.
I will always show you where to go.
I'll give you a full life in the emptiest of places—
firm muscles, strong bones.
You'll be like a well-watered garden,
a gurgling spring that never runs dry.
You'll use the old rubble of past lives to build anew,
rebuild the foundations from out of your past.
You'll be know as those who can fix anything,
restore old ruins, rebuild and renovate,
make the community livable again.

Isaiah 58:9–12 The Message

This is not to say the heart is only swirling emotion, mixed motives, and dark desire, without thought or reason. Far from it. According to Scripture, the heart is also where we do our deepest thinking. "Jesus, knowing what they were thinking in their hearts," is a common phrase in the Gospels. This might be most surprising for those who have accepted the Great Modern Mistake that "the mind equals reason and the heart equals emotion." Most people believe that. I heard it again, just last night, from a very astute and devoted young man. "The mind is our reason; the heart is emotion," he said. What popular nonsense. Solomon is remembered as the wisest man ever, and it was not because of the size of his brain. Rather, when God invited him to ask for anything in all the world, Solomon asked for a wise and discerning *heart* (1 Kings 3:9).

Our deepest thoughts are held in our hearts. Scripture itself claims to be "sharper than any double-edged sword, it penetrates even to dividing soul and spirit, joints and marrow; it judges the thoughts and attitudes of the heart" (Heb. 4:12). Not feelings of the heart, the *thoughts* of the heart. Remember, when the shepherds reported the news that a company of angels had brought them out in the field, Mary "pondered them in her heart" (Luke 2:19), as you do when some news of great import keeps you up in the middle of the night. If you have a fear of heights, no amount of reasoning will get you to go bungee jumping. And if you are asked why you're paralyzed at the thought of it, you won't be able to explain. It is not rational, but it is your conviction nonetheless. Thus, the writer of Proverbs preempts Freud by about two thousand years when he says, "As [a man] thinketh in his heart, so is he" (Proverbs 23:7 KJV). It is the thoughts and intents of the *heart* that shapes a person's life.

—John Eldredge in *Waking the Dead,* pg. 44–45

Table of Contents

Acknowledgements 11

Part One: Understanding the Problem 15

1. Reality Check 27
2. The Diagnosis 39

Part Two: Getting Ready. 53

3. Preparing for Surgery. 57
4. Why We Hurt Each Other 81
5. The Healing Process. 103
6. Walls and Boundaries 135
7. Confession and Forgiveness 155
8. Family Foundations 171

Part Three: Understanding Wounds. 187

9. Overcoming the Fear of Abandonment and Rejection 191

10. Freedom from Shame.................... 217

11. Acknowledging Our Powerlessness.......... 243

12. Betrayal.............................. 269

13. Sexuality, Intimacy, and Identity............ 293

14. Putting It All Together 315

Mood Disorder Symptoms Checklists................. 319

Style of Relating Questionnaire..................... 327

Suggested Reading................................ 335

Endnotes...................................... 339

Appendix A..................................... 343

ACKNOWLEDGEMENTS

❋　❋　❋

Many people have played a part in my life, my healing journey and growth as a Christian, and therefore in the writing of this book. This list could go on for pages! You loved me, sometimes when I was difficult to love, and for that I am forever indebted.

Specifically, my deep appreciation goes to the following people:

To all the community at the Mars Hill Centre, Edmonton: Thank you for walking with me in this journey and believing in the gifts God has put in this clay vessel.

Margey, Louise, Dorothy, and Heather: You started this whole thing by covering for me when I was on sabbatical.

Louise: You continue to stand with me and speak the truth into my life.

Andre: Thank you for running with the new ministry areas so that I can concentrate on this book.

Cheryl: You are my letter of recommendation!

And everyone who is part of our Mars Hill Centre community: I thank God daily for you all.

To pastors Rick and Nell Vanderwark: This would never have happened without your friendship and investment in my life.

To Jim, Quinn, Trudie, Alma, Dan, Grant, and many others who were used by God to counsel, heal, and deliver me: You are a gift of God to a broken world. Keep walking in your anointing.

Lissa—who now wears toe rings: Your friendship is a foundation stone in my life.

Don Brown, who has been enjoying heaven for many years: You were my first pastor, but more importantly, the first man I was not afraid of. Ruth: You were a mother and friend when I really needed someone.

Shelley and Mary Charlotte: What a gift we've been able to enjoy over these last ten years mentoring and encouraging each other. You too, Eve!

To the congregation of my home church, Christian City Church, Edmonton, and my "feels just like home" churches—Strathcona Baptist Church, St John the Evangelist Anglican, and Old Strathcona Vineyard Christian Fellowship: Thank you for your partnership in sharing the gospel.

Jessie S.: My deep appreciation for helping me turn pages of typing into a book! I know the eye of God is upon me.

Angie: It feels great to get a star from a former junior-high English teacher. Thanks for proofreading and checking my grammar and for your encouragement in this project.

And to all my friends who have encouraged me and prayed for me to get this book done: Honestly, you wouldn't be reading this page if it wasn't for you!

Part One

Understanding the Problem

Everything looked different. I had no idea that saying a few words to Jesus would have had such a profound effect on my life. The colours in the hallway looked different. Compassion stirred in my heart toward people I had previously despised. I felt such a deep love in my heart. I felt like I was finally okay and that somehow life would turn out that way too.

I know that not everyone has such a dramatic conversion experience, but my encounter with Christ at the age of seventeen rocked my world and set me on a new path. I knew that everyone needed this, and so I and my new friends set out to tell everyone we could.

From day one in my Christian life, my desire was to see people change. I carried around a little Bible with me and told everyone who would listen—and even those who didn't want to listen—what Jesus had done in my life and how they needed Him in their lives, too.

As the years progressed, my fervour continued. My friends and I went to the streets and city parks to tell people about Jesus. I was in prayer and Bible study groups as a participant and leader. We'd see people come to faith in Christ on a regular basis.

I did notice a little problem, however—people would make a choice for Jesus, but often their commitment didn't seem to stick. They'd hang around for a while; then they would drop out. Being the mature young adult I was, I assumed it was simply that they weren't trying hard enough, reading their Bibles enough, or that somehow, unlike me, their desire to follow Christ was lukewarm.

Specifically, I remember a young-adult Bible study group. We were studying a passage in the New Testament that spoke about the need to put off things that were ungodly and put on things that were of God.

"How do you do that?" asked one of the group participants, named John.

As one of the group leaders, I answered, "Well, you just stop doing things that are displeasing to God and start making other choices."

He responded, "So, how do I do that?"

I replied, "Just stop doing those things and start doing the things that are godly. Pray, read your Bible, and follow the Holy Spirit, and He'll show you how to do that."

At that point we continued discussing the Scripture passage. John melted into the background. I really didn't know what other answer to give him. A fairly new Christian myself, I had seemed to be able to pick up on all the things that I wasn't supposed to do as a good Christian in that era. I didn't drink; I didn't smoke cigarettes (or anything else, for that matter). I read or watched only "wholesome" books or movies, and I tithed and was in church whenever it was open.

John was a recent ex-con. Our College and Career group had connected with him and his wife through a weekly Bible study in the nearby federal penitentiary that was led by a group from my church. I didn't know what had landed this twenty-year-old man in a federal penitentiary, but it had to be something significant to warrant a minimum two-year sentence. I knew that John and his wife struggled with the temptations of alcohol and drugs on a regular basis. I knew that he and others in that prison Bible study group had made sincere commitments to Christ.

As a church group, we continued to pray with and for John and his wife, helped them read the Bible, and helped them out in practical ways, such as providing food and household items. We all assumed that, with their sincere commitment to Christ, Bible study, prayer, and our good words, John and his wife would make it.

But they didn't. Eventually they stopped coming to church, and then they stopped returning phone calls. We didn't know what else we could do, so we did nothing. We suspected that John had fallen back into alcohol and drug addiction, and our suspicions were correct. Almost twenty years later, I bumped into his wife in a grocery store and heard that John had dropped out of her (and her daughter's) life years ago. It was not what I wanted to hear.

The story that I've just related is not a new story. Change the names and the faces, the locations, and the length of time a person has been a Christian, and the central fact remains: well-meaning Christians drop out of the Christian journey, discouraged by their inability to conquer the bad habits of the past. And well-intentioned church leaders seem helpless to stop the drop. It's a story repeated day after day in churches, small groups, and pastors' offices around the world.

This book is written to give you some basic tools that you can use to help stop the drop. It will help you identify foundational life truths that are often not established in early childhood. You will see how these unstable foundations become masked as addictions and other behaviours. Most importantly, you will be given tools to help you to be part of the process of restoring the foundations.

This book will address heart issues—or emotional issues—rather than intellectual ones. Time after time, I have found that intellectual assent does not propel people to change. If you doubt this, think of your own conversion experience. Personally, I intellectually believed Jesus was the Son of God years before that truth had an impact in my life on a heart level.

Discipleship is the process of someone becoming a sold-out follower of Jesus. While the Church acknowledges that this is a matter of character development, the keys to the process are often limited to prayer and Bible study. Churches are discovering that leading someone to faith in Jesus is now much more complicated than praying with someone and leading him or her through a six-week "New Believer" class.

In reality, many of these people are wounded, struggling with baggage they're bringing from their previous life experiences. Increasingly, our society is built of such individuals. They have been wounded in relationships, and now they're looking for new relationships that will help them recover from these wounds.

Unfortunately, most people in the Church still do not understand the basics for helping people find freedom from bondage and healing for deep emotional wounds. While there is a growing understanding of counselling and support-and-recovery group ministry, Christian leaders still tend to relegate these individuals to the category of "Extra Grace Required" and shuffle them off to someone else's care. Or, equally destructive, they miss the opportunity to correctly apply God's Word of truth to the everyday wounds we all experience. Christian counselling and inner healing and deliverance ministries still struggle to be acknowledged as a valid and important part of the Body of Christ. In many cases, these ministries are disconnected from the Body of Christ. Because of this, the church continues to be ineffective in discipling wounded people.

This book intends to build a bridge of understanding to those in all levels of leadership in the Body of Christ. By reading it, you will develop a fuller understanding of the key emotional issues that everyone must wrestle with in order to become what we are meant to be in Christ. These issues are wounds inflicted in the past—wounds caused by abuse, abandonment, and dysfunctional families—which result in fear and mistrust.

You will also gain knowledge of the key skills required to help bring healing to those in your care. These skills include developing relationships in a safe environment, applying confession and forgiveness in emotional healing, and developing specific ways of applying the process of emotional healing to the faulty foundations that we all struggle with.

Healing is what Jesus did in His ministry here on earth. Over and over again, people wounded in body and spirit came to Him, and He did not turn them away. He touched them and made them whole. They became committed followers of Christ, doing great things in His name. Today, the Church *is* the Body of Christ, called to bring healing to

19

those wounded in body and spirit so that they will follow Him forever.

There are broken foundations that need to be repaired in each one of our lives. It is what we are called to do as the Body of Christ. We are not merely to slap some paint on the surface, but we are to be *"rebuild[ing] the ancient ruins...rais[ing] up the age-old foundations...Repair[ing]...Broken Walls, Restor[ing]...Streets with Dwellings"* (Isaiah 58:12, see also Isaiah 61:4 NIVI).

As you read and learn, you will also, of necessity, look at your own life, and you will likely discover areas that need healing. This book shares anecdotes of leaders who have done so and lived to tell the tale. Learning about yourself, and growing through the process, will help you to become a better counsellor and leader for those in your care.

What God Taught Me About Freedom

You may wonder who I am and why I am qualified to write this book. Twenty-five years ago, I was sure I had all the answers. I knew the power of Christ had changed my life, and I was sure that it would do the same for others.

But, underneath that veneer of assurance, I had my own personal struggles with change. You see, my experience was like many others: after the first few months, the shine had come off the new Christian glow, and I had fallen back into the personal bondages of overeating, perfectionism, and control—I'd even acquired a new bondage: religion.

As I continued on in my Christian life, John's story and others like it lingered in the back of my mind. They posed unanswered questions, which I mostly managed to avoid. Eventually, I tired of street ministry, moving on to a new city, a new upwardly mobile career, and a new suburban middle-class church. For a time, the questions surrounding John left my conscious mind.

I worked hard at my career, making good money and a good name in the industry. Then, a series of events started to awaken my heart to a call to full-time ministry that I had abandoned years earlier.

By this time, God had used a serious of events to start me on my personal healing journey. Part of this journey for me included meeting with a Christian counsellor on a regular basis for about two years. In addition, during this time, I became part of a smaller, less "religious" church that helped me "stay real" and not fall into the trap of over-spiritualizing my healing journey. At the same time, returning to seminary to complete my master of divinity degree helped to put an academic framework on my internal process. And it was during this time that God began nudging me to establish a ministry for people with wounded hearts who were looking for spiritual answers but wary of established churches.

Now somewhat more emotionally and spiritually healthy, I began offering groups for women who had been sexually abused or molested as children. These groups were offered through our church but met in a community setting. Much to my delight, women came—some were believers, some weren't, but, by the end of twelve weeks, they and I had changed![1]

I had offered the first group in order to meet my ministry "field experience" requirements. While it was a positive experience, I was looking forward to graduating and moving on to more "spiritual" pastoral endeavours like preaching, leading Bible studies, training church leaders, and the like. However, God had other plans.

Women kept coming to me and asking when I would lead another group. Now, over ten years later, I have had the privilege of helping hundreds of women find true healing and wholeness in Christ. The Mars Hill Centre began in January 1995 with the focus of using a support-and-recovery-group model to reach out to those who are interested in emotional and spiritual healing but wary of traditional churches. This continues to be our primary model for ministry. What was started reluctantly, over ten years ago, has grown beyond the scope of my time and abilities. Various staff and volunteers offer weekly groups for men and women victims of childhood sexual abuse, adults with mental illnesses such as depression or schizophrenia, and a variety of other groups, geared to help apply the truth of the power of the resurrection to broken hearts and lives.

THE CHURCH: THE SOLUTION OR PART OF THE PROBLEM?

As I entered into this ministry, I started to notice a disturbing trend. Many of the people who participated in our groups or came for counselling had some type of church background. (Probably two-thirds of the people who access our ministry fall into this category.) In fact, many of these individuals had, at one point in their lives, been regular church attendees and participants. Yet their Christian foundations had not prevented them from becoming emotionally broken.

When I honestly reflected on my own life, it became apparent that "the church"—meaning pastors and lay leaders in my local church—was ill-equipped to help me address issues in my own life. Because I was "functional" and not involved with drug or alcohol addictions, I think we all (myself included) thought I was fine. At those moments when the truth about my depression, insecurity, or fear became apparent and I looked for help, I was encouraged to pray and read my Bible more. Good things, but, sad to say, they never seemed to get to the root problem.

I've seen this pattern repeated over and over again in the lives of many Christians. I recall one couple who, upon seeking help, were given a list of Scriptures to read and instructed to spend more time praying together. Since this couple was highly functional, the pastor had no idea that the husband was an alcoholic. Through my own experience, and by seeing countless similar encounters, I came to the conclusion that the Church is often in denial about the emotional health of its members or can't even identify those who are ill.

I believe that facing the truth about emotional health in the Body of Christ is essential. In his book *The Emotionally Healthy Church,* author Peter Scazzero states, "It is not possible for a Christian to be spiritually mature while remaining emotionally immature."[2] What I came to realize in my own life many years ago and saw repeated in the lives of others is that spiritual maturity is hampered by lack of emotional maturity.

It's impossible to set out on a journey if you don't think you need to go anywhere. So I began to identify the problems I was seeing and also discovered possible solutions.

First, I came to understand that emotional maturity is our ability to handle our emotional life in a God-honouring way. God, after all, gave us emotions. Jesus, while on earth, expressed human emotions. If you doubt that, read the Gospels. Unfortunately, most of us do not handle our emotional life in a way that honours God. We struggle with anger, insecurity, fear, or envy. These emotions are often amplified, not by a present situation but by some experience in our past.

Next I observed the reality that emotional and spiritual healing and growth can only happen in the right environment. It's impossible to bring someone to a place where you haven't been. I discovered that, as leaders, we need to re-establish churches as sanctuaries of hope. These safe places begin not with policies and procedures but within our own hearts. In this context, all emotional and spiritual healing must happen in community.

In the context of relationship, we will look at the key issues individuals must address in order to become whole. These issues are the same whether the initial wound is sexual, physical, or emotional abuse, neglect, addiction, divorce, or a variety of other traumas.

This is a not a book about another Christian counselling technique. In my experience, we need a variety of approaches to address the variety of ways we, as humans, are created in God's image. Different approaches work for different people. A resource list is included at the back of this book.

Nor is it a book about a *specific* area of emotional wounding, such as sexual abuse, growing up as a child of divorce or in another dysfunctional family setting. I have observed that, no matter how the emotional wound is inflicted, the wound is the same. For example, people experience shame whether they have been emotionally, physically, sexually, or spiritually abused. Likewise, the deep wound of emotional abandonment can be caused by being raised in an alcoholic family or in an emotionally detached family.

Medical emergency wards have begun the practice of having patients seen by a triage nurse, who assesses them before they are seen by a doctor. As a pastor or lay leader, you are the emotional triage nurse for the people under your care. This book will help you assess the patients' wounds and provide some basic first aid, and, if required, give you some confidence to refer people to the necessary "heart" specialist.

Before we get there, however, we need to take a reality check.

Chapter One

REALITY CHECK

✳ ✳ ✳

It's finally becoming apparent to North Americans that the middle-class dream that many esteem—one house, two cars, 2.5 kids—just isn't working for everyone. The nuclear family is under severe stress. For example, in 1969, the divorce rate in Canada was 14 percent (or 1,367 divorces per 10,000 marriages).[3] By 1979, 32 percent of marriages ended in divorce. The end of the 1980s saw the divorce rate reach 40 percent, and the rate has remained there, or slightly higher, for the last decade. Of the close to 8 million family units in Canada, 47 percent are blended families, 11.5 percent are common-law families, and 14.5 percent are single parent families, leaving 27 percent of all families in Canada as traditional nuclear families.[4]

These statistics aren't listed here to make anyone more depressed! Rather, they are to remind us all of the absolute woundedness of the world in which we live. If we are to bring people hope, we need some understanding of what it is that makes people so hopeless, overwhelmed or driven.

If that's not enough for the average church leader to

deal with, there's more. The Public Health Agency of Canada, tells us the following:

❑ Mental illness indirectly affects all Canadians at some time, often through a family member, friend or colleague.

❑ 20 percent of Canadians will personally experience mental illness in their lifetime.

At Any time In Canada:

❑ Approximately 8 percent of adults will experience major depression at some time in their lives.

❑ About 1 percent of people live with bipolar disorder or manic depression.

❑ Schizophrenia affects 1 percent of the population.[5]

If you add up those numbers, this means that 10 percent of the population struggles with a mental illness. And if, as a pastor, your church is a cross-section of the population, you can expect that 10 percent of your people live with a mental illness. A large study sponsored by the World Bank stated:

Major depression ranked forth worldwide in combined disability, outranking heart disease, stroke and AIDS. In fact, the only conditions that outranked depression were those experienced mainly by Third World countries including infections, diarrhoeal disease, and perinatal (i.e., both before and after childbirth) mortality. This study also estimated that depression will rank second worldwide by 2020.[6]

Now let's look for a moment at the tragic reality of sexual abuse in our society.

Twenty years ago [circa 1980], no reference was made in most psychology programs to child sexual abuse. If it was discussed at all, it was mentioned in passing, as an aberration, even though a number of studies existed reporting incidence rates consistent with current data...Now it is generally accepted that at least approximately one out of every four women and one out of every six to ten men have been sexually abused during childhood...These are considered conservative estimates. Other studies suggest a higher incidence...as many as one out of every three women has been sexually abused...[and] anywhere from 11 percent to 47 percent of sexual abuse victims are males.[7]

What all that means is that when you look at a group of 100 people, 25 to 33 women were sexually abused as children, as well as a similar number of men. Sobering thought.

From a business perspective, the day-to-day stress we live under is taking its toll too. A report by Chrysalis Performance Strategies states that stress costs Canadian business over 16 billion dollars a year.[8] This includes direct and indirect costs due to absenteeism, lost productivity, health claims, short- and long-term disability claims, and workplace accidents.

This is not to say that the current generation experiences more relational trauma than at any other time in history. Family units disintegrated generations ago, too, albeit in a different—yet not any less traumatic—manner.

The average life expectancy of males in 1851 was about forty years, compared with forty-two years for females. This had profound implications for children. In 1851, the average first-born child would have been a maternal orphan at the age of seventeen, while the last-born child would have been a maternal orphan at the age of six. Today, males and females are living much longer...In the mid-nineteenth century, only 6 percent of couples would have lived long enough to celebrate their fiftieth wedding anniversary, compared with 39 percent today...nearly 98 percent of all marital dissolutions in 1921 were caused by the death of one parent, compared with 1986 where the primary cause of marital dissolution was due to divorce or separation.[9]

Over the years, I've spoken with many individuals whose mother or father died when they were young. The pain they have experienced as a result of the change in family system is as wounding and tragic as that of divorce. And these wounds, unless they are healed, will have an impact on succeeding generations.

My dad fought in the Second World War. When he died, we discovered that he had enlisted in 1939 and stayed for the duration. He never talked about it. Dad, in fact, never communicated about much. When, on one occasion, we were able to have a brief discussion about God, he told me that what he experienced in the war made him think that there could not possibly be a loving God. That was the only thing he ever shared with me about his war experience—or life experience, for that matter. Although he had been orphaned at a young age, he never talked about it. My father's scars affected him and so also had an impact on his parenting. Thus, his emotional scars had an effect on me.

And those scars must have been formidable. In war, families lost brothers, fathers, uncles, sisters, aunts, and mothers. What was called "shell shock" is now recognized to be the serious condition Post Traumatic Stress Disorder (PTSD), which can have profound negative effects on victims and their relationships. Many men who returned from war suffered emotional flashbacks and nightmares, and, while they may have been able to function in life, many were left emotionally wounded and had difficulty entering into meaningful relationship.

> Most World War I and II veterans who suffered from PTSD kept their problems to themselves or drowned them in alcohol. If it is not considered manly to admit inner turmoil today, it was even less so in the past. As a result, numerous World War II and Korean War veterans still suffer from nightmares and other symptoms of PTSD.[10]

However people are wounded—through sexual, physical, emotional, or spiritual abuse or neglect; divorce; loss of a parent, spouse, sibling, family member, or close friend; or traumatic incidents such as war or physical or emotional trauma—deep soul scars remain long after the incident has ended.

This is the world we are called to reach. And many churches are reaching out. But what happens when these wounded people walk through our doors?

Enter the New Believer

It was the best of times. It was the worst of times.

That's how I remember the first year or so after becoming a Christian. I remember the great peace in knowing that God loved me and had some purpose for me being here. Coupled with that, I remember being confused. Had I just joined some cult? I understood why drinking too much was a bad thing but never did "get" why you couldn't play cards. It was, in fact, the only thing, other than watching TV, that my family really did together.

About six months after becoming a Christian, I found my way into a small Pentecostal church. My friend and I were the youth group. But it didn't really matter, because what we both needed were fathers and mothers. I wasn't aware of it then, but she came from an alcoholic family. My emotionally abusive and neglectful family was outwardly less dramatic but inwardly distressing to me.

In that small group of believers, we found men and women who became our spiritual parents. My friend drifted off from that group to another fellowship, but I stayed, primarily because of the spiritual mom and dad I had found. Looking back, they were far from perfect, but they managed to put something into my life that was missing.

Another positive in my first year as a follower of Jesus was that I discovered that a few of the gals I hung around with were actually Bible-believing Christians themselves. So, I had a ready-made discipleship group. With some others, we started a Bible study group at our high school, which grew to about twenty people. As far as we knew, it was the first such group established in our school.

Intermixed with these highs were periods of doubt and

frustration. I wondered at times if I really had gone off the deep end. When I had told my mother of my decision to follow Christ, she said, "That's nice, dear, but don't get too involved." Maybe my mom was right.

Every week I actively participated in a midweek Bible study with my church and in my high school Bible study, while also attending church twice on Sundays. I grew in spiritual knowledge but, as I would only realize years later, remained emotionally stunted. (Over the years, it appears that we have changed the format, but we still tend to disciple new Christians in the same way I was—lots of Bible, which is good, but not a whole lot of practical life application.)

It was a good thing, reading my Bible and learning to pray. I'm convinced that it kept me from going over the edge. I've heard enough people's stories to know that it is the same with many others, too. The vast majority of sincere believers I have spoken with over the years who were involved in our ministry recovery groups or counselling share a common story. Whether they came from Christian, pleasantly pagan, or downright evil homes; whether they were "nice" people before they "got saved" or had been "bad" sinners who drank, smoked, used drugs, and slept around—they knew that something was missing in their lives. Spiritual disciplines kept them alive, but, without a complete package that included emotional healing and other life skills, they have struggled to live the abundant life that Jesus promised to His followers.

Call it *backsliding* or some other theological term, the truth is that many Christians give up their commitment to follow Christ. It's not always because they're lazy or not committed enough, either. Could it be that new believers do not always receive the grounding they need to stay put—in church and with God?

When new believers stumble, we often encourage them to do more of the same thing they have been doing—more Bible reading, more prayer, join a small group, get more fellowship. For some, it helps them to hang on for a few more years. Others quickly drop by the wayside.

Have you heard the definition of *insanity* used in the Twelve Step movement? Insanity is doing the same thing over and over and expecting a different result! We don't like to think of ourselves as insane, but the Body of Christ does sometimes appear that way. We keep doing things the same way but somehow expect different results. Perhaps we need to acknowledge that new believers with wounded hearts need new tools to help them grow.

Exit the "Experienced" Believer

Author, pastor, and church planter Peter Scazzero describes his realization that his emotional life was affecting his spiritual maturity. This realization came the day his wife said she was leaving him. A successful church planter and pastor, he discovered only then that she was unable to deal with the stress and physical and emotional absence of her husband. She could no longer trust his leadership, his inability to confront difficult people, his long working hours, and his deafness to the truth of her warnings.

He states in his *book The Emotionally Healthy Church:*

Embracing the truth about the emotional parts of myself unleashed nothing short of a revolution in my understanding of God, Scripture, the nature of Christian maturity, and the role of the Church. I can no longer deny the truth that emotional and spiritual maturity are inseparable...It is not possible for a Christian to be spiritually mature while remaining emotionally immature.[11]

Unfortunately, untold others have lost marriages and careers because they were in a spiritual home that did not allow them the privilege of addressing their emotional wounds. I have known of married couples who were told that the whole problem in their marriage was based on the wife's non-submissive character. So, the wife tried harder. And the husband continued on in what he was doing—working long hours, being emotionally absent, hiding addictions. Nothing improved simply because they tried harder.

I have known men to struggle for years with an addiction to pornography. Despite their desire to stop, they have been unable to break the pattern on their own, often too ashamed to admit the truth to anyone in the church family.

Others have had perhaps less overt wake-up calls that alerted them to their emotional bankruptcy.

David Eckman, in *Becoming Who God Intended,* writes about an encounter he had after leaving what he had experienced as a "wonderful, exciting, interesting and stimulating" seminary class.

I was walking downhill...Coming toward me was an attractive blond. The young woman's face was covered with one of the happiest expressions I'd ever seen—simply glowing with joy. The thought leaped into my mind: "Ask her why she's so happy!" Instantly another thought jumped out: "I wish I was as happy as she is." With that another one popped out: "You should be as happy as she is, because you are a Christian, especially since you just left a great theology class." A quick shot of shame went through me as I recognized I envied her. I'm not a shy person, but now I was embarrassed. If I asked why she was so happy, I would be asking to find out for myself how I could become so happy. "I'm a Christian," I told myself. "I'm supposed to be happy!" I did not want to admit that a happy stranger with a wonderful smile could so quickly reduce me to a state of envy.[12]

Whatever their background—whether as new Christians or ones who've been in God's kingdom for years—many people within the Church are trying to build a new emotional and spiritual structure on a faulty emotional foundation. Biblically speaking, it is the man building his house on sand instead of the solid rock (see Matthew 7:24–27). This is not a wise thing to do, but as church leaders we are not immune from this practice ourselves, and we help others to do it every day! Why should we be surprised when they wander away from our church, from Christian fellowship, or from Christ Himself? We promised them an abundant life but haven't delivered.

As church leaders, we want to see people's lives change. If we didn't, we would be in some other life occupation or volunteer position. But often we are hindered in our ability to help, simply because we have never been healed from some of the emotionally wounding issues in our own lives. We can hardly rescue someone else from drowning when we have a hard time keeping afloat ourselves.

This book has been written for pastors, counsellors, and church leaders who are helping those with wounded or broken hearts. The reality is that God has chosen us to be His instruments for binding up the broken, wounded hearts of our world and setting captives free (see Isaiah 61:1). He does want all of His children to experience abundant life. The beginning for any leader is to look at his or her own life. If something describes you, please use this book first to help you understand yourself and your own emotional wounds.

Part 1 of this book continues to look at the problem we face in this world: how wounded we have been by our sin and the sins of others. Part 2 suggests some of the prerequisites for emotional healing, and part 3 describes the common wounds we all experience and how to work with God to bring healing to a wounded heart.

Keep in mind that God has given some of us a general knowledge of a subject, and others He has made specialists. In examining your own life or walking with someone else, don't be hesitant to seek the help of a trained Christian counsellor.

Chapter Two

THE DIAGNOSIS

❈   ❈   ❈

W hen Jesus told the story of the sower who went out to sow his seed (Matthew 13:3–23), He was talking not only to Israelites of His time but to the modern Church as well. When we sow the seed of God's Word, we're hoping that the seed will find rich ground, be well watered, and grow to bear abundant fruit. But the reality is that some seed falls in rocky or weed-infested soil. It germinates and springs up, but unless the farmer provides better conditions for the tender seedling, it will die. And this happens in our ministries too. As we've seen in chapter 1, there are many ways Christians can fall away. Sometimes, as in the parable, it's worldly temptations or shallow commitments that extinguish God's spark of love.

The seed, God's Word, is sown not so much in our intellect—though that is part of it—as in our heart. We have a common understanding in our culture that "our heart" is at the core of who we are. "Our heart" includes our emotions, will, intellect, and personality. It contains everything outside of our spirit and body that makes us human.

When our "heart" is wounded, our soil ceases to be good soil. As spiritual leaders, we are responsible for cultivating the soil and providing better conditions so that the plant can grow strong and bear fruit. But often past wounds have turned people's hearts into bad soil, and no amount of skilled exegesis or gifted communication can make it anything else. While we desire to apply the Word of God well, wounded Christians, just like you or me, sometimes don't "get" it. I remember times when a preacher was saying something very important, something that should have had implications for my life, but for some reason I just didn't "get" what he was talking about. The preacher may have been a gifted communicator, but there wasn't a place of reference for the Word inside of me. My life experience didn't provide me with the reference points I needed to understand and apply what the preacher said. In that area of my life my heart was rocky soil and there wasn't a place for the good seed to settle in my heart. Though I could give intellectual assent to a Biblical truth, emotionally my heart was rocky, shallow ground.

This chapter will explain why wounds from the past cause such havoc—why all the preaching, Bible study, and prayer may not reach the wounded heart and bear fruit. And we will also look at why the church is often inept at providing means of healing.

MY OWN STORY

My own story is an example of the ineffectiveness of traditional "church" practices in effecting real change. Early in my Christian life, my experience with emotional or inner healing had consisted of having someone pray with me at an altar service. Things were "broken off," emotional wounds were "healed," and I spoke forgiveness (though never directly) to people who had hurt me in the past. That night and the next day I felt great. But, while I felt a temporary release from my sadness, fear or anger usually returned within the week. To the best of my ability, I continued to read, memorize, and recite Scripture. I prayed and asked others to pray for me, but little seemed to change.

While I continued to do the right things, I seemed incapable of sustaining the inner peace that I so earnestly desired. Soon, to deal with my sense of failure, I began to shut down my emotions and build a thick wall around my heart. I struggled relationally, had no self-esteem, and was judgmental. My inner turmoil manifested itself in the socially acceptable addictions of workaholism, churchaholism, codependency, and food addictions. My Christian life was difficult and disappointing.

One day about fifteen years ago I heard a sermon that changed my life. In the late '80s I had moved from my home city, and I was attending a large suburban church. On my most recent job performance review, my employer had praised my hard work and long hours and said that I was "upwardly mobile." I continued to regularly attend church twice on Sundays and dropped into a home group when I wasn't out of town on business. Life seemed to be going well.

That particular Sunday night, the youth pastor was speaking about the issues teenagers need to resolve in their lives in order to grow into healthy adults—issues like understanding who they are, emotionally separating from their parents, and forgiving their parents. He challenged us as a church family to reach out to youth spiritually and emotionally. It was a good sermon, but halfway through I began to feel that ache in my chest that comes when I know God wants me to hear more than the words. As the youth pastor shared about these adolescent issues, it became painfully clear to me that I had not resolved any of them. And I was in my early thirties!

It took me a year to get up the courage to go see a Christian counsellor. I was afraid that once someone saw into my heart I would be declared "unclean" and a sham as a Christian. It felt like my character was only skin deep. Any prodding would expose me as shallow and defective. Fortunately, years ago I had begun writing down my thoughts in a journal. As I reread these old words and wrote new ones, I began to understand that the Holy Spirit was directing me to seek out professional help. I knew I couldn't fix things, and neither could those around me. I could begin to see that while I was now alive in my spirit through Christ, my soul was still damaged goods.

UNDERSTANDING THE IMPORTANCE OF EMOTIONS

As mentioned earlier, the good soil (or bad soil, for that matter) is found in our hearts. Our hearts are so important that the writer of Proverbs says we are responsible to *"above all else, guard [our] heart"* (Proverbs 4:23 TNIV) because everything we do comes out of it. The Message puts it this way: *"Keep vigilant watch over your heart; that's where life starts."*

Later on, the writer of Proverbs reminds us that how we look on the outside, what we do, how we think, what our relationships are like—in other words, the harvest of God's Word scattered in our lives—are merely reflections of what's in our hearts. *"As water reflects a face, so a man's heart reflects the man"* (Proverbs 27:19 NIV).

The North American Church has done a good job at apologetics, at helping us know—or at least know where to find—the right answers. It is, of course, important to know our core Christian doctrine, but there is more.

Emotions have generally been relegated to the bottom of the pile in terms of mentoring and discipling young Christians. In the Christian world, we often speak of behaviours instead of root attitudes. For example, we might instruct a young Christian to get control of his physical outbursts of anger that escalate to the point of a fist fight. However, few people would place a decade-long cold disdain in the same category, even though a cold disdain that produces distance in relationship, born out of childhood wounds of neglect, is as sinful as anger that ends in a brawl.

Many people who struggle to control their temper attend "anger management" classes. These can be a good thing. Unfortunately, these courses may only provide management tools while not addressing the root of the problem. If they do not identify and bring healing to the core wound that birthed the anger, they keep our hearts full of rocky, shallow soil. The inward anger, left untouched by behavioural change, is a foothold for the enemy of our soul (Ephesians 4:26–27).

It is unfortunate that many Christians believe that emotions are small factors in determining our success in the Christian life. But even Jesus experienced emotions (John 2:13–17;11:33–36; Matthew 8:10, among others), and God is said to be grieved (Ephesians 4:30), full of compassion (Exodus 22:26–27), angry (Numbers 11:10), and overjoyed (Isaiah 62:5). Since we are created in the image of God, it only makes sense that God wants to heal and renew our emotional cores, too.

BUILDING ON FAULTY FOUNDATIONS

Think of it like this: take a large glass jar and place some large rocks from your garden in the jar until it is full. But is the jar really full? Well, no, not really—there are still gaps between the large rocks. Go to your yard again and collect some smaller stones and dump them into the jar. You'll have to shake the jar around to get these stones to the bottom. Now the jar is full, right? No, not yet...there are still visible gaps between the small stones and big rocks.

Back to the garden you go. Scoop up some sand and gravel and add it to the mix. Once again, shake the jar around. But there are still microscopic gaps of air around each sand particle. So grab a watering can and add some water. Now the jar is truly full, with no air pockets remaining.

We all construct a picture of our lives. Like the jar, there are significant foundation stones (like the large stones we first put in the jar) that must be set in place early in our lives. These are tangible life experiences that form the foundation of how we understand our world and ourselves. These foundational experiences are instrumental in developing a sense of security, of knowing who we are, with a healthy identity, a healthy sexuality, and the ability to trust others—along with many other things. When these emotional foundations are not laid in our childhood years, we end up struggling in our adult lives. We are trying to build an "adult" house on a nonexistent or weak emotional foundation. And it is a messy job to build these foundations later.

Usually we try to keep our jars in order and simply try to ignore the fact that some of the foundation stones are missing. Fortunately, God doesn't like to leave things unfinished, so from time to time He comes along, tips over our jars, creates a mess, and begins the process in us of replacing the missing foundations.

And what happens if you leave the full jar on a bookshelf, ignoring it for a few months? That's what I did. Then, one day, it caught my attention and I noticed that green slime (and a few other interesting colours) had started to appear in the jar. Even tipping over the jar and making a mess, then putting it back together again, doesn't guarantee that all will now be well. The jar needs tending and vigilance and periodic cleanup work.

Much of what we do in pastoral care and counselling is working with the Holy Spirit in the cleanup job when people's jars get tipped over. God wants to heal their hearts so that their lives can truly be a reflection of Him.

Restoring those emotional foundation rocks is a messy process—often messier the longer the jar has been left untouched. It cannot happen any other way. That is also why the process takes time and patience. And, because we have been created as relational beings, this process must happen in relationship.

THE NECESSITY OF HEALTHY RELATIONSHIPS

As the Holy Spirit began to bring deep transformation to my soul through the counselling I received, He rebirthed a call into full-time vocational ministry. Wanting to help others enter into the process of heart healing, I asked the Holy Spirit to show me a better model than what I had experienced so far in my life.

I learned that if there is going to be any real healing in their lives, people with wounded hearts need to find that healing in the context of caring relationships. They have been wounded in relationships, and now they're looking for new relationships that will help them recover from these wounds.

It is important to note that in each of Jesus' physical healing miracles He did not worry about social norms of "touching not" certain people or even not being with them. No doubt even in His touch and presence people gained hope. He was willing to risk touching them and loving them.

How did Jesus deal with deep emotional wounds, like the kind of damage done when a person is sexually abused? Jesus' manner in addressing people's heart wounds was quite different from the prescriptions of the time. He spent time with them. He entered into relationship with them. We see Jesus spending time with people who were sexually broken, like the woman caught in the act of adultery and other women who were prostitutes. Jesus entered into relationship with these women. Mary Magdalene changed from a woman carrying the weight of shame to the honoured first witness of the resurrection.

Many models for emotional healing come from an understanding of physical healing that primarily centres on the Gospel accounts. Jesus prayed for people, and they were healed of leprosy, hemorrhaging, or paralysis or they were raised from the dead. This pattern continues in the New Testament Church, where in the Book of Acts people are healed of disease (Acts 3:1–10;9:32–41, and others). The power of God was so strong that only Peter's shadow needed to fall on people and they were physically healed

(Acts 5:15). A simple piece of Paul's clothing led to physical healing in others (Acts 19:11,12).

As I thought about these healings, I soon became aware that there was more happening than simple physical healing. In fact, *all the physical healing miracles recorded in the Bible had the effect of restoring people to relationship and community.* For example, lepers were social outcasts. Levitical law required that they be separated from the rest of society (Leviticus 13:45–46), and they were relegated to leper colonies, where a few caring and brave individuals delivered food and provisions. Lacking our current medical understanding, fear and superstition entered, leading many to believe that others would catch their disease merely by touching them or having them in the vicinity. Obviously, healing would restore a leper to relationship and to community.

A woman had been hemorrhaging for twelve years (Mark 5:25–34). It would have been like having a menstrual period for 144 months. According to Levitical law, she was unclean (Leviticus 15:25–28). Anyone who touched her, or even brushed against her clothes, became unclean. Consequently, it is likely that she was divorced or had never married. Certainly she shouldn't have even been in the crowd. Imagine the number of people who had been made unclean simply by bumping against her that day. When Jesus healed her, He did more than stop the bleeding. Jesus said to her, "*Go in peace, and be healed of your **trouble**"* (Mark 5:34, emphasis mine, GNT). He restored this outcast woman to community.

Demonic activity in an individual had the potential to exclude them from relationships. Often this was because the demon manifested as an illness. In the most dramatic account of the demon-possessed man in the territory of

Gadarenes (Mark 5:1–20), the separation from relationship was most obvious. People were terrified to come anywhere near the young man. In fact, such was his torment that he even despised relationship with himself—slashing his own body. When Jesus healed him, he was restored to his right mind and was no doubt welcomed back into his immediate family and his community.

Even the man with a withered hand (Matthew 12:9–14), while perhaps able to earn a living, would have been socially outcast due to his physical deformity. Today, in our society, any form of physical deformity still has the potential to place relational barriers between individuals.

Our struggle in discipling a wounded generation is that the New Testament gives us wide brush strokes, not the particular understanding needed to help someone move from brokenness to wholeness. Generally, the Epistles provide a much better model for emotional and spiritual healing. While not providing the "how-tos" of discipleship, they provide a framework for the issues people need to face.

The Bible teaches that emotionally healed people

❑ are rooted and grounded in love (Ephesians 3:17)

❑ are able to love others (1 John 4:20–21)

❑ are able to forgive (2 Corinthians 2:5–11)

❑ have a healthy understanding of sexuality and who they are (1 Corinthians 5 and 7)

❑ are free from fear (2 Timothy 1:7; 1 John 4:18)

❑ are free to use their spiritual giftings appropriately (1 Corinthians 12–14)

❑ are able to walk in faith (Hebrews 11)

When talking with my friend John, the ex-con mentioned in the introduction, I didn't understand that addictions were mere symptoms of the wounds and sins of his heart. With any type of addiction, we do need to challenge each other to stop the ungodly behaviour and start doing things that are pleasing to God and beneficial to us. However, I could not help John, because I did not understand how feeling abandoned, shamed, powerless, betrayed, or ambivalent about our sexual identity can keep us from being disciples of Jesus and truly living an abundant life. Since I did not understand or appreciate the underlying issues, I could not walk with John down a healing path.

He would never be able to put off his addictions without the informed emotional support of his friends. I needed to help him to be *rooted and ground in the love of God,* not merely to do the right things. Since I had not received this myself, I could not hope to pass it on. My love was based on doing things right, not on a grace-filled friendship. The very thing that can bring healing—relationship—was blocked by my own woundedness, which was manifested in self-protection and other "acceptable addictions." The things flowing out of my own wounded heart—religiosity, control, shame, and others—were as damaging to my soul and my relationships as John's addictions were to his.

For the emotional damage in our lives that occurred in relationships to be healed in relationship, we must be able to give and receive love. Religious rights and wrongs simply do not work. They end up isolating us. It is not enough to say, "I love God." *"Those who say, 'I love God,' and hate their brothers or sisters, are liars; for those who do not love a brother or sister who they have seen, cannot love God whom they have not seen"* (1 John 4:20).

WAYS OF BEING THE CHURCH

A last stumbling block that stands in the way of an effective ministry to wounded Christians is the practice of traditional but faulty ways of being the Church, the Body of Christ. Being a group of wounded Christians ourselves, we have created wounded systems that keep us in our socially acceptable sin, and we have invited others just like us to join us. Those who don't like the way we do things are told directly or indirectly that they do not fit, so they should move on. And they do. However, there are so many faulty church systems that we soon find one that's just right and settle in!

The Church of the Right Answers

Sometimes, the church or church leaders mistakenly believe that they need to provide a definitive answer to every problem that's presented to them, even if they're not qualified to give answers. When people come to them with problems, pastors who have received hundreds of hours of instruction in Biblical theology and only one or two short courses in counselling may think they need to fix the problems with solutions. No wonder these answers just don't work.

The Church of Continual Victory
(No One Suffering Need Apply)

Other churches may teach that Christians always conquer all their problems. Not to do so means that the believer just hasn't tried hard enough or asked with enough faith. So just how much faith are we supposed to need? Right, a little tiny mustard seed (Matthew 17:20)!

The Church of Continual Victory forgets that the Bible teaches that we are living in the last days; not everything is completely fulfilled—and won't be until Christ returns. *"What we see now is like a dim image in a mirror; then we shall see face-to-face"* (1 Corinthians 13:12 GNT). Additionally, these churches deny that there is a Biblical place for suffering, even though Christ learned through what He suffered and Paul looked at his sufferings as badges of honour (2 Corinthians 11:16–31) and a way to complete the suffering of Christ (Colossians 1:24).

The Instant Church

Unlike the Church of Continual Victory that allows people some time to "exercise their faith," in the instant church there is no such thing as a problem that can't be overcome in a relatively short period of time. Recite the correct Scripture verse, read the right book, attend the next great conference, and everything will be swell! There is little concern for spiritual or personal discipline, because if we do the right thing we'll be better!

The Happy Face Church

Just put on a happy face! Tinkerbell told Peter Pan—who then told others—to think good thoughts and then he could fly. The Church of Positive Confession relies more on making sure we say right things to change us than on the power of the resurrection.

Not that we should walk around being messengers of gloom, but really, if everything is so great, why are we still here? Their theology implies that there is little need for Christ to return, because here and now—and completely—we can be the total, complete kingdom of God! No exceptions.

The Authoritarian Church

As its name implies, this church believes that, if we would just all get in line the way we were meant to, everything would be fine. Here, authority is not about giving direction and safety to relationships; rather, it is about knowing who is in charge. The assumption is that if, and only if, the authority structure of the church, marriage, and other relationships is in order, then everything is fine.

While a Biblical understanding and use of authority is paramount to having an emotionally healthy church and relationships, it is not the only determining factor.

The Ostrich Church

Really, all churches—even healthy ones—have a measure of this. It's called living in denial. We'd rather stick our heads in the sand and pretend that there are no problems. If we work harder, try another program, pray more, give more—do something—then everything will be fine. We fail to see that the problem is—us!

MAKING OUR CHURCHES PLACES OF HEALING

Unfortunately, we all live with a good measure of denial. Denial is part of the human condition. Even the apostle Paul reminded us that right now we, at best, see a distorted image (1 Corinthians 13:12). That's why we've taken time to determine what the problem really is. The problem is, not only are people wounded but the Christian community is, as well. And, as a result, we need to acknowledge our own woundedness and create a community of healing in order for others to be healed in our midst.

Part Two

GETTING READY

✹ ✹ ✹

Now that we have better defined the problem, it's time to make sure we are well equipped to assist the Holy Spirit in the healing process. As with most areas of life, some people will have more of a natural or spiritual gift in this area, but that doesn't mean you can't improve on what you have.

So, what are the prerequisites for becoming a "Soul Surgeon," a healer of wounded hearts? Will years of graduate counselling courses get you to that point of qualification? They may be helpful, but they might not, as many of the prerequisites have to do first with the condition of your own heart.

Before we even begin, we must acknowledge that it is only God who call heal a wounded heart, bring joy out of sorrow, and replace grief with gladness. While some have the spiritual gift of healing, miracles, or mercy, it is the power of the Holy Spirit working through us that makes anything happen at all. Lose this perspective and you become merely a secular guru, advocating amazing, yet powerless, truths. If the emotional healing process is devoid of the internal working of the Holy Spirit, nothing much changes. Make your pastoral counselling job easier by learning to rely on the real-time revelation of the Spirit.

Additionally, as a Christian leader, the place to start is in your own life. As you read through this book, looking for ways to help others, pay close attention to areas you struggle with, too. And don't hesitate to ask for help if you have struggled in an area without receiving healing or a change in behaviour. Just as a student is not above his teacher (Matthew 10:24), the reciprocal is true: you can't take someone to a place you haven't been yourself.

And now, on to the next step. What does it mean to prepare to become a Soul Surgeon? What does it take?

First, it takes the ability to create a safe environment for God to work. This is so much more than having a comfortable meeting place; it is about you! Are you the kind of leader people can open up to? Do people share their personal lives with you? If they don't, it might be that you are missing some key components in your leadership. Perhaps shame and control filter in at times when you talk with people. Or maybe you are fearful and operate out of a program-based mentality rather than a relational framework for ministry. The chapter "Preparing for Surgery" will help you examine these issues.

To help wounded people, we must be able to offer them some understanding of the age-old question "Why do bad things happen to good people?" Granted, there is no perfect answer to this question, but the chapter "Why We Hurt Each Other" should be helpful in understanding why abuse and neglect happens.

In "The Healing Process," you will begin to understand the journey. I would never go on a road trip without a road map. I wish I had had a road map for my healing journey, too. This healing process chapter is a key to understanding the internal shifts that must happen to restore health to our wounded hearts. In this process, we move from reacting to the world, acknowledging that we have been wounded, to taking responsibility for our own lives instead of blaming others. We must recognize wounds that need to be healed, in order to ask God to heal them; and we must acknowledge the way we have reacted sinfully to the wounds we have experienced, in order to be forgiven

Personally, I never really understood the power of confessing my sins to God and asking for His forgiveness. It wasn't that I thought I was perfect. It was that I couldn't identify what was really wrong with me in order to ask God to come into that broken place and restore it. I might have cried repeatedly about not loving God enough, but I had no understanding of what I had done to shut off my heart. Without that revelation, without the words to ask for help, I was unable to move on. And years ago I certainly would have never confessed my deep, dark, dreadful sins to another. Neither did anyone else then, but now there has been a shift in the evangelical church, and we are beginning to understand and practise the healing discipline of confessing our sins to another and praying for our healing (James 5:16).

In the context of these more intimate relationships, we need to make sure we have healthy boundaries. Often, out of fear, many leaders have erected walls instead of boundaries. Sometimes labelled "a professional distance," walls are ineffective ways of protecting our hearts. Godly personal boundaries keep the bad out while letting the good in. We can all do with more good inside of us.

Who we have become (who those you minister to have become) is to a large measure influenced by "family." Intuitively we know this. How many young people have said of a comment by their mother or father, "I'll never say that to my children," only to find their parent's words coming out of their own mouths? Our relating styles, how we deal with conflict, and how we understand the world are influenced by our families.

The following section deals with foundational understandings that you need in order to be God's instrument to bring healing to a wounded heart. In surgical terms, think of it as the pre-surgery scrub down. If you miss this section, it would be like having a surgeon operate on you without disinfecting his hands, instruments, and garments. Cut down on the possibility of cross-contaminating someone with your own sin. Get ready; closely examine these attitudes in your own heart first.

Chapter Three

PREPARING FOR SURGERY

✳ ✳ ✳

I am both honoured and surprised when people inter-
ject in a recovery group or counselling session "I've
never told anyone this." The surprising thing is not the
trauma the individual suffered or even their response to it.
Time and time again I am surprised to be the first person
who has heard of the horrors they have suffered in their
lives. Most of these people are Christians; many have been
in "the Church" for years. Nevertheless, no one really
knows the tragedy of their lives.

I've often wondered why they choose to share the com-
pleteness of their story with me. I used to flatter myself by
thinking that it was some super-special anointing of God.
Perhaps it is partly that—but not entirely! As I would talk
further with these individuals, I would often ask them why
they had chosen now, and me, to share their story. While
the words were different for each person, the theme was
the same. They felt safe.

Sometimes that meant that they knew I would listen and
not judge them. Or it meant that I would listen and not give

them the five things to do to feel better. Sometimes it was because they felt more comfortable talking with a woman. But in all of these cases it boiled down to one reality—they felt safe.

In our ministry, we have come to realize that one of the things God has gifted us to do is to create a safe place for people. In the midst of that emotional, physical, and spiritual safety, they feel they can finally open up and share the pain, fear, and anger in their hearts. As people feel the acceptance that comes when they share their deepest shame with us, they change.

We may wonder why safety is so important. Perhaps that is because most days we take our safety for granted. Most days, most of us are relatively free from danger or injury. We live in a peaceful country, and we expect it to remain that way.

But then we face the reality of insecurity in this world. It may be that we are in a car accident, or we are exposed to unexpected violence that shakes up our feelings of security. A good friend of mine recently witnessed a shooting at work in which two youths shot at a security guard using a flare gun. All who witnessed the incident were shaken, and some were so emotionally distraught that they had to go home. When we no longer feel safe, our perception of the world changes, along with how we understand ourselves, others, and God.

The Kingdom of God Is a Safe Place

Safety is a promise of God's kingdom. God promised Israel that, in the Promised Land, there would come a day when there would be no more enemies. *"But you will cross the Jordan and settle in the land the LORD your God is giving you as an inheritance, and he will give you rest from all your enemies around you so that you will live in safety"* (Deuteronomy 12:10 NIV).

Prophecies of the coming Messiah and the coming kingdom speak of safety, too.

"The days are coming," declares the LORD, "when I will raise up to David a righteous Branch, a King who will reign wisely and do what is just and right in the land. In his days Judah will be saved and Israel will live in safety. This is the name by which he will be called: The LORD Our Righteousness" (Jeremiah 23:5–6 NIV).

In this passage God declares that a true sign of the coming Messiah is the safety that will envelop the land. These were words of hope to people who were in the midst of a siege by the strong nation of Babylon.

The psalmists also recognized that being safe could only come from being in God's presence.

I will lie down and sleep in peace, for you alone, O LORD, make me dwell in safety (Psalm 4:8 NIV).

"Because the poor are despoiled, because the needy groan, I will now rise up," says the Lord; "I will place them in the safety for which they long" (Psalm 12:5).

God communicates to His people through the prophet Ezekiel about the characteristics of a good shepherd, the good shepherd He will be to His people. He promises His weary people safety.

They shall no more be plunder for the nations, nor shall the animals of the land devour them; they shall live in safety, and no one shall make them afraid (Ezekiel 34:28).

In reality, those who were most vulnerable in Israel's society had special promises of God's protection.

Father of orphans and protector of widows is God in his holy habitation (Psalm 68:5).

You shall not wrong or oppress a resident alien, for you were aliens in the land of Egypt. You shall not abuse any widow or orphan. If you do abuse them, when they cry out to me, I will surely heed their cry; my wrath will burn, and I will kill you with the sword, and your wives shall become widows and your children orphans (Exodus 22:21–24).

The church, as the Body of Christ, the representation of Jesus here on earth, is meant to be that safe place for people. There's an older song I recall that goes something like this: "You're the only Jesus some will ever see." It's true. We are to be that safe place for people.

THE UNSAFE CHURCH

Is the church a safe place today, a place of refuge where hurt people can be heard and find solace? Unfortunately, enough evidence exists to show that many churches are not safe.

Throughout the last decade, both Canadians and Americans have watched news reports in disbelief as allegations of sexual abuse by Catholic priests became horrendous leading news stories. In many cases these men were multiple offenders; in some cases, it appears that the administration of the church was aware of the incidents but had not reported them to the appropriate civil authorities.

Other headlines report the hidden secrets of residential schools. These schools were part of a plan by the federal government to assimilate aboriginal people into mainstream Canadian society. Beginning in the late 1800s, children were removed from their homes and taken to residential schools. For many, this was their first time away from their families and their first exposure to non-aboriginal society. The federal government contracted with several church denominations to operate these schools. While there were, no doubt, many genuinely caring people employed at these schools, the setup of the schools seems to have made it easy for children to be abused. First Nations people of Canada, and Canadian citizens as a whole, were appalled to hear of the reports of rampant physical, emotional, and sexual abuse by lay leaders and clergy within the now-defunct residential school system in Canada. In addition to being punished for speaking their own language, children were physically disciplined to the point of abuse and sexually abused. On a much broader scale, residential schools contributed to the complete breakdown of aboriginal society; in many families, three generations of individuals were raised in these schools and therefore grew up with no concept of family.

Is it any wonder that a large majority of aboriginal people find Christianity bad news? While there were many notable exceptions, the people who claimed to bring the gospel brought only shame, not good news. Within Canadian society as a whole, this has provided many skeptics with further proof that Christians are not to be trusted.

In the 1980s the Christian Church was rocked by the sexual, financial, and overall moral failure of key leaders, many of whom led TV or radio ministries and portrayed themselves as godly men and women.

I remember a seminary professor telling me that in the 1950s and 1960s it was not uncommon for the local daily newspaper to carry the sermon of a prominent evangelical minister, word for word, in Monday's paper. In contrast, today the Church is fortunate to get any positive newspaper coverage outside of paid advertising. The postmodern world is much more interested in looking for answers, if there are any, outside of existing societal structures like the Church.

In *What Canadians Think*, authors Darrell Bricker and John Wright summarize a variety of surveys conducted that reflect what Canadians think. In relation to trust and respect of various society leaders, they comment that there has been

> an increasing erosion of deference to traditional institutions and people in power...It isn't just politicians and lawyers who are taking the hit—most people have expected these groups to play loose with the truth for many centuries now...But how about CEOs, journalists, bankers, judges, clerics, royalty, police officers and other authority figures of the past? They're increasingly being looked at sideways in today's world.[13]

The study ranks firefighters as the most trusted vocation (94 percent), followed by pharmacists (91 percent), nurses (87 percent), and doctors (85 percent). "Religious figures" (35 percent) come between TV and radio personalities (36 percent) and auto mechanics (33 percent).[14] All these factors contribute to a wariness of our churches. Consequently, many people faced with dealing with any disclosure of deep pain and shame would choose a New

Age practitioner rather than any type of church leader. Since many people do not see a minister as someone they can trust, neither do they see our faith communities as safe places.

SAFETY BEGINS WITHIN US

Many Christian groups have done much to increase the physical safety of those within their walls. In fact, most denominations have set policies for this. Sunday school classrooms have inside windows, as do the offices of most pastors. In some children's groups, a teacher is not allowed to take a child to the washroom on her own; two adults must take the journey with the child. In most churches there are fewer dark, secluded places where a child can be physically hurt.

Unfortunately, many churches and Christian leaders have missed the point. Gaining people's trust and being a safe place are not simply a matter of installing a few new windows. While these actions and safeguards are necessary and important, they are only the beginning. Many of us have reduced safety to an aspect of building design; but providing a safe place begins, instead, with who we are. Safety begins with our internal world. In attempting to provide safety for people and reduce the risk of lawsuits, some people have missed the point altogether.

While we do need to be wise, we don't need to strain out gnats and swallow camels (Matthew 23:24). Physical, sexual, or emotional abuse of any kind does not happen simply because the physical environment is unsafe. People are hurt and trust is broken when we are emotionally and spiritually unsafe people.

North Americans have learned the harsh reality that things that appeared safe and secure, like steel office towers, when put under extreme pressure crumble and fall. For many, our illusions of safety have been shattered. Likewise, physical safety measures alone can crumble when the underlying emotional structure of its leaders is put under pressure.

I suspect that, physically, the homes of most adult survivors of any type of childhood abuse would have appeared physically safe. Outside doors were locked at night. Strangers were not allowed in. Nevertheless, children were harmed, in spite of the physical security measures taken.

These individuals were abused not because their physical environments were hazardous but because the individuals who lived there—fathers, mothers, brothers, sisters, aunts, uncles, or other extended family and friends—were not safe. Emotionally, they were exposed to people who were not safe. As children, or even as adolescents, they were unable to do anything to protect themselves from these dangerous people. Either they had not developed the skills they needed in order to acknowledge that this was not a safe situation or they did not have the power to do anything about it.

UNSAFE PEOPLE AFFECT OUR ABILITY TO CHOOSE SAFE PEOPLE

Growing up in this continual emotional or physical trauma has devastating effects. Among other things, it impairs a person's ability to trust others. Is it little wonder that many people are not able to trust us with their life stories?

Shauna remembers being screamed at by her father from an early age. At times her father would become so agitated that he would pick her up from her seat at the kitchen table and throw her against the wall. Her mother sat nearby, seemingly indifferent to the chaos of her home. When the abuse began, Shauna was a toddler, and it didn't end until she left home.

She continues to struggle with the idea that there can be any safety in her world. When she's honest, she doesn't believe that God will protect her. After all, if He didn't do this for her when she was a child, why would He do it now? As a result, she struggles to understand what is a safe situation and what is not. She continues to put herself in dangerous situations.

Despite her distrust of God, she has a deep desire to follow Jesus. She is an evangelist, eager—sometimes too eager—to tell others about Jesus. One day, she told me about going to a shabby hotel, in a bad part of town, with a man she had met on the street. She knew he was lonely, and she wanted to tell him about Jesus. They talked in his room. While she told him about Jesus' love, he tried to seduce her. She never realized how close she came to being raped. She still has a hard time understanding that that this was an unsafe situation.

She continued to look for a positive father figure, someone she could trust. Until recently, she would gravitate toward male ministers whose counselling techniques bordered on manipulation and control. These individuals would often use guilt to try to get her to think right thoughts. Shauna has clinical depression. Even with medication she struggles to maintain thought control. This is not simply mental laziness. One of the symptoms of clinical depression is the inability to control thoughts; it is not simply feeling sad, as many people think.[15]

Since Shauna could not consistently control her thoughts and take mental victory, she was an open target for condemnation. She felt it from herself, from others, and from the Evil One. The individuals that were working with her could not seem to understand that encouraging Shauna to try harder to memorize more Scripture verses simply was not going to work. And Shauna, looking for a daddy, continued to try to do it right and earn their approval.

I doubt that these men knew, or understand today, that they were not being safe people for Shauna. Though in her thirties, she was like a little girl and was unable to distance herself from the strong guidance of these men. What they were saying was quite correct for many people but at that time not godly counsel for Shauna. Their counselling technique was merely confirming to Shauna that, no matter how hard she tried, nothing was going to change.

Wounded people who come to us are generally unable to set safe boundaries for themselves. Therefore, it is mandatory that we be safe people for them. Being a safe person is not about knowing the latest Christian counselling technique. Ultimately, it is about who we are inside. It is imperative that we become safe people so that others will know that the Jesus we talk about is someone they can trust. We are the only "Jesus" they may see.

The lack of emotional, spiritual, and physical safety in many people's life experience leads to a deep confusion and desperation. Intuitively, people who have been abused know that what happened to them was not right. However, most often the abuse came through someone who was supposed to be a safe person, such as a parent, coach, or relative. This confusion over who is safe and who isn't leads to bewilderment, rage, and fear.

UNSAFE PEOPLE AFFECT OUR ABILITY TO TRUST GOD

People who have been wounded in their childhood have always known the reality that life is not safe, that things that seem safe are sometimes not. They wonder why people say that families are important to the stability of society, when their family has self-destructed, leaving broken souls and broken bodies in its wake.

Jesus said, "*Would any of you who are fathers give your son a stone when he asks for bread? Or would you give him a snake when he asks for a fish?*" (Matthew 7:9–10 GNT). To this question, the victims of childhood or adolescent abuse or neglect would reply, "Of course a father would give a son a stone or a snake. My father always did."[16]

Experience has taught them that their parents are not able to provide for their basic needs, let alone protect them. They have grown up knowing that the world is an unsafe place at the best of times, and people—especially those in authority—are not to be trusted.

So, in summary, if we hope to create a place for restoration to begin, we need to remember these important concepts as we prepare to bring healing to wounded hearts:

❑ The kingdom of God is a safe place.

❑ The church is often regarded as an unsafe place.

❑ Safety is not first of all a matter of policies and procedures; safety begins within, with who we are.

❑ Experiences with unsafe people affect our ability to choose safe people.

❑ Experiences with unsafe people affect our ability to trust God.

All of us want to gravitate to the "ten easy steps"—better yet, "five easy steps"—to freedom. But that is the law. And as Christians we know that the law brings death. We'd like to find a pattern that will give us control over life and make sense of it. God's pattern is that healing of past soul wounds must come through relationship.

If people with wounded hearts are to experience God as a safe person and find healing, they won't find the answer in mere programs and techniques, helpful as they are. *They must first experience that safety in us.* And that brings us to the most important principle of all as we prepare for soul surgery.

BE WHAT JESUS IS—A SAFE PERSON!

It is a good thing to do what Jesus did!

It is a better thing to be what Jesus is!

Good actions from wrong motives are not good at all. Even worse, wrong motives can lead to the damage and destruction of our lives. That's why the writer of Proverbs stated: "*Above all else, guard your heart, for it is the wellspring of life*" (Proverbs 4:23 NIVI).

Jesus knew who He was, He knew who His Father was, and He knew what He was sent to do. With this security deep in His heart He could continue to radically minister to men, women, children—sinners who knew they were sinners, and sinners who did not. He was a safe person, even though the ministry opportunities that came His way sometimes were not.

Jesus was a safe person. He called people to follow Him in a radical way. He challenged them to acts of repentance, service, and faith but left the door open for them to make a choice. He went to them in public places and private ones. We can glean, from Jesus' recorded interactions with people, ways to be a safe person—just like He was.

1. No Pride, No Shame
Jesus and Zacchaeus (Luke 19:1–10)

During a walkabout in Jericho, Jesus noticed a short man perched in a tree, craning to see Him. We don't really know Zacchaeus's motivation to see Jesus. Crowd curiosity? Perhaps. When he was shopping for groceries, had he seen a picture of Jesus in the *National Jewish Enquirer* and wanted to see this miracle worker first hand? By this time in Jesus' ministry, He had healed the sick, turned water into wine, cast out some demons, and fed a few thousand people from one boy's lunch. Curious indeed, Zacchaeus just needed to see this man.

Zacchaeus was a chief tax collector, a contract employee of the occupying Romans. Whether or not he had ever been teased because of his height, he was definitely spurned for his occupation. He was wealthy because of the thievery of his associates and himself. Think of Zacchaeus as the local businessman in your neighbourhood who has recently been charged with, and convicted of, embezzling a few million dollars. Probably not someone you would strike up a conversation with on the street, let alone invite to your backyard barbecue. Zacchaeus was a wounded heart, for sure.

Jesus knew all this, yet not only did He publicly acknowledge Zacchaeus, he went as far as to invite Himself to Zacchaeus's house. And it wasn't just a short visit; Jesus insisted that He must stay at his house.

Because Jesus was secure in who He was and secure in His relationship with His Father, He didn't care what others might have thought. He didn't care if onlookers were shocked. Pride of status had no place in Jesus' heart. Equally important, Jesus would have felt no pride in His graciousness to this sinner. Early in my Christian walk, some friends and I would head to the absolute worst part of town to go street witnessing. I look back on this time and realize my mixed motives in it all. Yes, I wanted people to know how much Jesus loved them. Of course, I wanted these people in the inner city to be free from drugs and alcohol. Unfortunately, I also liked the boost it gave to my ego. People in our church praised us. And in my insecurity and woundedness I thought it had earned me some extra favour with God. There was none of this in Jesus' heart. He simply loved Zacchaeus. Nothing else was important.

In ministry, we must guard our hearts so that we are not motivated by pride or by the flip side of the same coin, insecurity. Some of the most proud people I know are also the most insecure. Flaunting their ministry accomplishments— even veiled in the Christianeze "Look what God did"—is merely a prop to their wounded security. The kingdom of God is based on Jesus' example of grace. He gave His life freely for us with no personal gain attached.

Equally important, we must also be like Jesus in our avoidance of the use of shame as an instrument of change. Public shaming, or even private shaming for that matter, had no role in Zacchaeus's repentance. It's interesting to note that in this account Jesus doesn't seem to challenge Zacchaeus about anything! And Jesus, who certainly knew all about Zacchaeus, could have come up with many things that needed correcting. "Zacchaeus, you need to tithe properly." "Zacchaeus, you have taken too much money from the people." The account records simply that after

Jesus invited Himself to Zacchaeus's house, Zacchaeus was moved to repentance.

In our hearts, most of us know our shortcomings. Even though we are masters at cover-up, we know that what we have been doing, or thinking, is against the principles of the kingdom of God. Jesus did not use shame to elicit a response from Zacchaeus; rather, Jesus' unconditional acceptance of Zacchaeus provided a way out of the shame Zacchaeus carried in his heart. Never use shame tactics or emotional manipulation to bring repentance.

Early in my own recovery process, God brought along a man who has become a dear friend and true brother. He was (and still is) my pastor, and he loved me unconditionally (which I'm sure was very hard to do on some days). God's grace and mercy flowed out of him to me. Through his acceptance, I was able to put down my religious, perfectionist shield. My rage came out. My deep shame bubbled to the surface, no longer contained by my pride and judgment. I began to truly see the sin in my heart; I began to truly be free in Christ. With this man's Christlike love, which had no room for pride and shame, and with the guidance of a Christian counsellor, the shackles on my life began to break.

2. Respect, Not Fear
Jesus and the Woman at the Well (John 4:1–42)

The disciples left their teacher, Jesus, beside a dusty well outside a town in Samaria. It was approaching midday, so most women, desiring to avoid the midday heat, had already come for water. The disciples went to town looking for some food, leaving Jesus to rest at the well. He was tired and thirsty. A woman approached. She was on her own.

And she was a Samaritan. Given the societal norms of the time, Jesus should not have had any interaction with her. But He did. The conclusion of the story was that she became an evangelist to her town; many came to hear Jesus because of her testimony, and many believed.

In today's Church world, this interaction would never have happened. Many Christians, and church leaders themselves, distrust their male leaders' ability to set sexual boundaries. In some circles this is compounded by a lingering—unspoken—belief that women are dangerous seductresses.

Let me give you an example. At a leadership conference we viewed an excellent video about how sexual abuse can happen in a church setting. In this case, the minister, a single man, had emotionally and then sexually seduced three women in his congregation. The video clearly showed the dynamics of how the man took advantage of these women's vulnerable points to seduce them into a relationship that was beyond the role of colleague, friend, or pastor.

After the video was finished, we broke into discussion groups. I was the only woman in my group. As things progressed, the discussion began to centre only on prevention through setting: never meet with a woman unless your wife is present, never give a ride to any woman if you are alone in the car, etc. Not one person commented on how the character of the minister in the video had ultimately led to the abuse of these three women. While being alone with a woman in a counselling session or in a car may provide the opportunity, it is the lustful condition of a man's heart, and the misuse of the authority he holds, that allows it to happen.

Clearly, Jesus was not afraid to be with women. In addition to His very private encounter with the woman at the well, He was a close personal friend of Mary and Martha (John 11:5), associated with prostitutes, and allowed a woman to wash His feet with her tears—a very intimate moment (Luke 7:36–38). Women were a part of Jesus' entourage, even supporting Him with their own money (Luke 8:1–3). Jesus respected these women; fear of them and how they might contaminate His ministry had no place in His heart or life.

Since Jesus was fully God and fully man, we should assume that He had all the desires any thirty-year-old man would have had. *"For we do not have a high priest who is unable to sympathize with our weaknesses, but we have one who in every respect has been tested as we are, yet without sin"* (Hebrews 4:15). Jesus would have had desires for emotional intimacy and physical intimacy that could have put Him in a compromising situation. But it didn't happen. Why? Jesus dealt with His own desires in a healthy and godly manner. Consequently, not only was He not afraid to be with women, but He was also not afraid of what others might think.

As the Body of Christ, the biggest mistake we make in establishing sexual boundaries is to assume that physical boundaries alone provide safety from adultery and sexual abuse. They do not. The only truly safe boundary line is the one that runs firmly and clearly through our hearts. In order to establish it, we must, men and women, acknowledge that we are created as sexual beings. God made us that way. There is nothing inherently wrong with these desires for sexual intimacy. What is wrong is how they are expressed. It must be decided in our hearts and minds that we will steer clear of all forms of sexual immorality. We must be like Jesus, with respect for (and without fear of) the opposite sex, to give people a safe place to heal.

If, when you examine your heart, you need to work on these issues, there is more information for you in chapter 13 on setting sexual boundaries.

3. Belief, not Condemnation
Jesus and Peter (Matthew 16:13–28; Matthew 26:31–35; John 21:15–19)

Peter knew, because the Spirit revealed to him, that Jesus was the Christ, the Son of the living God (Matthew 16:16–17). It was a bold statement. And Peter, who had a few short chapters earlier experienced walking on a storm-tossed sea, said it with conviction. I imagine Peter standing a little taller after the "You're the Son of God" statement. He had, of all of them, figured it out. Now with the skillful use of a play on words, *Petros Peter* and *Petra Rock*, he believed he was being called "a rock" and given sole use of the keys of the kingdom!

Jesus, knowing everything about all of us, knew that Peter would have an attitude correction soon enough (Matthew 16:23). Can you imagine what it would have felt like to be called "Satan" by someone who had just praised your revelatory abilities? Despite this lapse, Peter was still a witness to the transfiguration and other amazing events before he denied Jesus in his time of emotional need.

I don't know about you, but I'd be hard pressed to call someone a rock who I knew was going to betray me when I needed him. Jesus saw in Peter more than what was obvious from his current behaviour and attitude. If we are to be safe people, we must be able to see beyond the surface and see into people's hearts.

Sometimes that requires taking a risk. I think of the people who have done that for me. Because they believed in me, I began to be able to believe in myself. Then I was truly able to allow the Holy Spirit to direct my life. Prior to that I had limited what God could do through me, because I didn't really think He could, or would, work through me. Jesus saw people's hearts and risked His love on them.

4. No Program; Relationship
Jesus and the Pharisees (John 3:1–21)

Does it come as a shock to you that Jesus loved the Pharisees? He did. While he openly and publicly rebuked their religious practices, He desired that they come into a true relationship with God.

In John chapter 3, Jesus receives a nighttime visitor, the Pharisee Nicodemus. His dialogue with Nicodemus is different from any discussion he has had with anyone else. He talks with Nicodemus on a fairly abstract, theological level about the workings of the Holy Spirit. And then He challenges Nicodemus to be born anew, or born again, by the Spirit.

This is the only place in the gospels where Jesus used the phrase *born again*. It was an illustration specifically shared with Nicodemus so that he could understand and come into the kingdom. Why is it, then, that we tend to use that phrase with everyone? While everyone needed a relationship with God, the words Jesus used to call each person were different.

One of the most striking things about the recorded ministry of Jesus is that every encounter was unique. Granted, the Gospels are only a synopsis of all that Jesus said and did, but still they show us a principle. Jesus treated each person as an individual. He respected them enough to not resort to routines or methodologies to address their need.

Too often the Christian Church becomes a place of methodology, not relationship. We hear a preacher, listen to a teaching tape, read a book, and seem to assume that this newest revelation is how things must be done—as in the case of my friend Shauna: the Christian counselling method used on her was not wrong, just not right for her at this time in her life.

If we are to honour people the way Jesus did, we must learn to listen, just as Jesus did to Nicodemus. Everyone's story is different. We do them a disservice when we try to fit everyone into a predictable little box. We force them into a mould that was never intended for them. We, then, are unsafe people.

To be a safe person, we are called to be like Jesus:

❑ with no room in our hearts for pride or shame

❑ treating those of the opposite sex with respect, not fear

❑ seeing the belief and not condemn the mistake

❑ focusing on relationships, not programs

DEVELOPING A SAFE ENVIRONMENT

If we are convinced that we need to be safe people and practise principles of safety like Jesus did when we work with hurting people, then we will also work hard at the practical task of developing a safe environment physically, emotionally, and spiritually. Many resources are available for creating a physically safe environment. For the sake of this discussion, we will look at constructing an emotionally and spiritually safe place for people.

Since 1994, the Lord has given me the privilege of facilitating recovery groups for adult survivors of sexual abuse. If there was ever a need for a safe place in which to be real, it is in that group. Drawing on others' experiences, and our own, we have developed something at the Mars Hill Centre that seems to work. I'd like to share my experiences with you so that you can do the same in your ministry.

In this chapter, I'd like to share two important components of our group interactions. When I talk with others involved in small group leadership, I am surprised that they do not use a similar process to facilitate safety in a group setting. Ultimately, the group must be structured so that the characteristics of being a safe person we discussed earlier are encouraged, not discouraged, in this setting. Confidentiality and respect are the keys.

It is important that we meet with each person before the group starts. This gives the group leader an opportunity to see where the potential group member is at, ensure that the group is the right place for them, and let them know the kind of "place" we expect to be.

Every potential group member must sign a contract that says they agree to the way the group will operate. The key point is for each group member to understand is that everything said in the group is confidential. No one, not the group facilitator nor any group member, may share what is said outside the group unless specific permission is given to do so. (A detailed example of the group confidentiality covenant is found in appendix A.)

We have three exceptions to the rule; these also reflect our concern that all members of the group are safe.

1. If the group facilitator believes an individual is suicidal, she must report this to the proper authorities.

2. If the group facilitator becomes aware of ongoing child abuse or if she is concerned that a group member would physical endanger someone else, she will report these concerns to child services or the local police.

3. If the group facilitator is concerned about something that was shared in the group or how a situation could have been handled better, she may share this with her supervisor.

We did not specifically address the issue of confidentiality when we looked at Jesus as a model of a safe person. Nonetheless, I believe He was someone who could keep confidences. We have no accounts of Jesus saying publicly, or even to the disciples, what had happened in His encounter with an individual. And Jesus' encounters with others, as we have seen, were based on respect for every person as a unique individual.

Each of us must decide what level of confidentiality we will live with. If you are married and share everything with your spouse, the people in your care need to know this. And you need to ensure that what is shared with your spouse stays with your spouse!

In groups and congregations, it is important that confidential concerns do not leak out as "prayer requests." We have a committed group of prayer intercessors. One of the main criteria for being an intercessor for this ministry is an agreement with the concept of confidentiality. Even so, they are not given specific details of a person's situation unless we have received specific permission to do so. Imagine how a young woman felt after returning to her church after a two-week absence. She had attempted suicide, and somehow it had been circulated through the church via the "prayer chain." She was ashamed of what she had done and deeply hurt over the gossip that had circulated around her church home. It took her years to come back to church.

Confidentiality is critical if people are to be able to trust us with the pain of their lives. It is important that we do not assume that everyone understands the concept of confidentiality. I have known people who, without malicious intent, shared with another person what someone had told them. They thought they were doing a good thing, perhaps even enlisting someone's help in prayer. However, if the individual has not given permission to share his story, we have no right to do so.

Being a safe person takes work. One of the results of the fall is that this world is no longer intrinsically a safe, life-giving place. Sin in each of us continues to cause us, often despite our best intentions, to be unsafe people and create unsafe environments. With Jesus as our model, and with His power at work in our lives, the Body of Christ can once again be the place of restoration it was always meant to be. The kingdom of God is a safe place for the healing process to take place.

Chapter Four

WHY WE HURT EACH OTHER

❋   ❋   ❋

I had been meeting with a lady for a few months, helping
her walk through a challenging situation. She had been
sexually abused as a child, and, while she had previously
seen a counsellor, this was the first time she had looked at
the pain in her life from a Christian perspective.

We didn't begin by talking about the childhood abuse she
had experienced, but it became evident that the challenges
she was currently facing were related to it. As an adult, she was
struggling relationally because of the ways she had developed
to cope with sexual abuse that masqueraded as intimacy. We
spent some time looking at unhealthy ways she was using to
protect herself from rejection, as well as at her personal
strengths. In the midst of this difficult conversation she
shrugged her shoulders, shuffled in her chair, and pro-
nounced, "Well, I guess I should thank God for the sexual
abuse, because it's made me a stronger person." She had,
after all, been taught to give thanks to God in all things.

I couldn't let that statement go by without comment.
"Sexual abuse is evil. We are never to thank God for evil. We

can thank Him for sustaining us, growing us, keeping us alive, and bringing us new life, but we are never to thank God for evil!"

This woman went on to ask a question many Christians struggle with. "If God is all-powerful, loving, merciful and just, why do bad things happen to good people? And why did this evil happen to me?" It is one thing to grapple with this question in a Bible college class; it is another thing altogether to wrestle this through with an adult who was abused or neglected as a child. The woman I was talking with had been sexually abused from the time she was four years old. Why didn't God intervene?

We ask the same question when landslides bury villages, tsunamis kill more than 100,000 people, famines destroy the lives of innocent children, and more. But the question becomes even more personal when traumatic incidents happen to people at the hands of people in their community or their families. Why didn't God stop it?

In many people's sincere desire to defend God, they put forth some disturbing answers to this question. These answers either place the blame solely on the victim or paint God as an impotent cosmic ruler. As Christians, our desire to defend our belief in a loving and powerful God can lead us to some confusing conclusions about why there is evil in the world and what we are supposed to do about it.

IT'S *NOT* THE VICTIM'S FAULT

Listening to anyone tell you their story of childhood sexual abuse is not easy. The first time someone told me her story, I remember feeling a mixture of disgust, rage, and disbelief. I could hardly imagine that a parent could do such a thing to a young child. I'm not alone. Most of us would rather turn our eyes away from gazing upon the life ravaged by evil.

I've heard numerous victims of childhood sexual abuse try to explain how the abuse began by saying they were "too sexy" or "seductive" for their fathers to resist. They felt that, as three-, four-, five-, or six-year-olds twirling around in the living room with skirts flaring, they were too much of a sexual temptation for their abusers to resist.

I hope you are appalled by the last paragraph. You should be. Unfortunately, even more appalling is the reality that victims of sexual abuse (and other abuse or neglect) are often made to feel responsible for what happened to them.

And sometimes the churches, or sincere Christians, increase the pain with their misguided responses. Once, someone said to me that sexual abuse happened to children because they didn't pray and ask God to stop it. This individual went on to say that if the children had prayed, God would have intervened and stopped the abuse. In contrast, most victims I have spoken with share that at some point in their childhood they *did* ask God to stop the abuse. When the abuse didn't stop, they either assumed they "deserved it" or that God really didn't care about them. As adults, even as Christians, they are haunted by these unanswered prayers and doubt that God really does love them. I've talked with hundreds of adult survivors of childhood sexual abuse, and I know of only one person whose abuse stopped after she prayed. Does that mean God loved this one child more than all the others or that somehow she got the prayer right? That it's the child's own fault that she was abused? Of course not.

"God Is Watching Us—From a Distance"

Others, anxious to defend God's love and mercy, imply that He is an all-powerful God who has merely set the universe in motion. He does not interfere in the affairs of mankind. He has a kingdom, but His authority doesn't extend beyond the throne room. He has set up the universe and established its operating rules, and now He sits back and watches how things develop.

Many assume bad things happen to seemingly good people because God does not meddle in day-to-day human life. These people would say that it is our responsibility to intervene, stop, and punish evil in this world. This removes any notion of God being "with us" and creates a God who merely watches us from a distance.

Neither explanation—"it's the victim's fault" or "God is a hands-off deity"—adequately answers the question of why evil happens. Nor do they provide hope for a survivor of horror. It does not work to blame the victim or to make God an impotent, distant sovereign. The reality is that it is a complex question that incorporates an understanding of sin, authority, and the kingdom of God.

If we are to effectively minister in a fallen world, we have to give an answer to those who are asking us "Why?" No answer will ever be complete. My attempts at providing some direction in the discussion are no doubt lacking in some areas. Nevertheless, we must attempt an answer to this difficult question if we are to understand how to minister to wounded people in a sinful, wounded world.

Defining "Garden Variety" Evil

What's your picture of evil? Did you come up with a name of someone, present or past, whom you would consider the personification of evil? I'm sure that without too much thought you could come up with a list of ten or more names of evil dictators or serial killers. It's not hard to do. What is harder to see and understand is the everyday variety of evil that impacts our lives. To understand that more fully, we need to go back to a time before evil existed.

In the beginning God created a perfect world. When man and woman were created, it went from being a good place to a very good place (Genesis 1:26–31). It was a paradise that our limited human minds can hardly fathom. There was no death, no nine-to-five daily grind, and no difficult relationships—at least for a time.

God was so intimately involved in creating man and woman that He got down and got His hands dirty. With only His words He created land, water, sky, fish, and animals, but He got down in the dirt to first create Adam and then create Eve (Genesis 2:7,21,22). It's the first picture of God's desire to be intimately involved with humanity.

In addition to this special intimacy with their Creator, Adam and Eve enjoyed living in idyllic surroundings. It was a sensually pleasurable place. There were trees that were not only good for food but also pleasant to look at (Genesis 2:8–10).

Man and woman were given the maximum freedom and authority of any created being. They were given authority over every created thing in the Garden of Eden (Genesis 1:28). There was only one rule to follow: Don't eat from the tree of the knowledge of good and evil. "*The Lord God commanded the man, 'You may freely eat of every tree of the garden; but of the tree of the knowledge of good and evil you shall not eat, for in the day that you eat of it you shall die*" (Genesis 2:16,17). Only one simple rule! Think of how may rules and regulations we must deal with simply to drive to the mall. Speed limit 50. No right turn on red. "Stop" signs, "Yield" signs, and unsigned rules of the road. They only had one rule—stay away from that tree.

God's intent was that we would never have knowledge of evil. His desire was for us to feast on fruit from the tree of life.

In two short chapters, the course of humanity changed. If we were directing a Hollywood blockbuster, we would indicate the dramatic change of events by the changing music, diminishing light, and other visual clues. But there are no special effects to soften the paramount change in humanity recorded in Genesis chapter 3. Spurred on by the serpent, Eve eats from the forbidden tree and then encourages her husband to do the same. He willingly participates (Genesis 3:1–6). Nothing will ever be the same again. Evil has entered our world.

What Is Evil?

Eating fruit from a tree is not, in and of itself, an evil act. First and foremost, it was evil because it was an act of overt rebellion against the Creator of the universe. Most of us understand that such rebellion is evil. However, in addition, consider that evil should be defined by the outcome of the act. Evil (or *sin,* as it would come to be called) always has two outcomes as it works its way out in human life:

> Evil results in the breakdown of an intimate,
> open relationship with each other
> and
> Evil results in the breakdown of an intimate,
> open relationship with God.

No longer would Adam and Eve trust each other. Rather, they would consistently refuse to take responsibility for their actions and blame someone else. Says Adam, "It wasn't my fault—Eve made me do it" (see Genesis 3:12). Eve responds, "It's not my fault—the serpent made me do it" (see Genesis 3:13). And he tries to pass the blame on God too. They were no longer trusting co-regents of paradise.

No longer would Adam and Eve trust God. They were afraid of Him, and they hid (Genesis 3:8).

It wasn't God who broke relationship with us; it was humanity that broke relationship with Him. God created people with free will, and, with that free will, humanity has chosen the wrong way. In spite of that, God did not abandon Adam and Eve but reached out to His disobedient children. We may be separated from God, but He is not separated from us. He loves us intimately and unconditionally. And He showed this by entering into the mess of evil we created. God the Father sent His son Jesus to experience first-hand the worst abuse anyone could experience. It is through His suffering, His death, and His resurrection that relationship with God has been restored. He took the initiative to remind us that He desires relationship with us.

The reason any act of evil or sin against another separates us from God or from each other is because it creates a barrier in a relationship. When someone sins against us, in our hearts we, generally speaking, come to one or both of two conclusions. The first is, "This person has hurt me, and to protect myself from further pain I will put up some type of wall of self-protection." The second is, "God is not loving, because He allowed this to happen to me."

That is the destructiveness of sin and the reality of the human heart. When we are sinned against, we put up a wall of self-protection between us and the other person and God. This wall of self-protection keeps us from having the type of relationship God intended us to have with others and Himself.

EVIL IN ACTION

Most of us can easily describe evil acts that are a direct rebellion against God's written laws. God's recorded laws, the Ten Commandments, and other laws elsewhere in the Old Testament in most cases give clear moral directives. As Christians, we understand that doing evil, or sinning, is choosing not to obey God's moral code. On the other hand, we are often unable to see how acts that may not be seen as evil in and of themselves are by definition evil because of their effects on the victim.

In his book *People of the Lie,* author M. Scott Peck recounts various experiences of "garden variety" evil or the everyday evil (or sin) that is active in each of us.[17] In one incident, he was meeting with parents who were concerned about the behaviour of their son. Their older son had recently committed suicide by using one of his father's hunting rifles. For the first few months after the suicide, the younger son had been grief stricken but otherwise coped fairly well. Then, shortly after his birthday, his behaviour became erratic and rebellious.

When Peck met with the son, he discovered that for Christmas the parents had given him a hunting rifle. It wasn't just any rifle; it was the same rifle his brother had used to kill himself. The son interpreted this to mean that his parents wanted him to end his life too. Upon questioning the parents, they informed Peck that they had given him the rifle as a gift because they were short of cash. They had no understanding of how this was interpreted by their younger son. Some would say this was merely bad judgment on the parents' part. The truth is that it was an act of cold, albeit ignorant, evil. But then, many evil acts are not perceived as evil by the perpetrator.

Evil acts recounted throughout the Bible, as well as in present-day events, continue to have the same effect of separating us from each other and from God. Any act of sexual abuse is evil because it is, in and of itself, a violation of God's laws as recorded throughout Scripture. In addition, it is evil because it sets the stage for the victim to become separated from God and others.

Sexual abuse is a particularly graphic example of the work of evil, because of how it affects our souls. It shuts its victims down from having an open heart with God and with others. A child intuitively knows that what has happened to him is not right. It continues to happen, and the child begins to wonder if there is a God who loves him. He projects his anger on himself, feeling deep shame and contempt for his body and even for his godly desire to be loved. As he grows, his anger toward his abuser intensifies and is directed at other authority figures. The evil act of sexual abuse connects with the sin in his own heart and closes down his heart to loving others and loving God. When any evil act occurs to us—whether it be a car accident, abuse or neglect by parents, an unexpected death of someone we love and need in our lives, or any break in relationship—the evil (or sin) in our own hearts quickly takes root.

Evil happens because there is sin in the world. People choose to commit sinful acts against others. And when others sin against us, we often, because of our own sinful nature, choose to respond by shutting down our hearts to God and to other people.

The effects of evil can multiply over time. For instance, in dealing with an abusive relationship it is often essential to maintain a physical distance. Abused spouses, or children, need to seek a safe physical place. This both protects them and makes a clear statement to the abuser that their behaviour is unacceptable. Unfortunately, in distancing ourselves physically from abusive people, we often shut down our hearts, not only to the abuser but also to others who remind us of the abuser. An adult who was physically abused by her father as a child will often maintain a relational, or heart, distance not only from other older men but also perhaps from all men or all authority figures. Our own sin nature reacts to the sinful act committed against us in a sinful manner that in turn hurts others. This is why a key part of the healing process is being able to take responsibility for our own actions.

Misuse of Authority

Our concept of evil can get entangled with our beliefs about Biblical authority. Biblical authority is a difficult concept to grasp. Our concept of authority structure is generally based on a hierarchical system such as the military or many business models. Flow charts have a top and a bottom.

Often, our understanding of authority defaults to a discussion of "who is in charge."

Adam and Eve are given *dominion* over the earth, a word that carries a sense both of reigning over and bringing under submission (Genesis 1:26–30). However, the second chapter of Genesis paints a different picture of this dominion. *"The Lord God took the man and put him in the garden of Eden to till it and keep it"* (Genesis 2:15). This is a picture not of a harsh, controlling, or demanding dominion but of a nurturing, protective authority.

In a New Testament example, Paul is very clear with the Corinthian church that the authority he has been given is *"for building up and not for tearing down"* (2 Corinthians 13:10, see also 2 Corinthians 12:19).

We are created beings with authority and under authority. God has given all of us authority in our own lives and, for most of us, authority in someone else's life. We are called to submit (or submit that authority) to each other as a way of honouring Christ (Ephesians 5:21; Philippians 2:3). There are other relationships outlined in Scripture where God has delegated authority. Unfortunately, our sinful nature often sabotages the godly use of our authority. Rather than protecting, nurturing, and building up under the sphere of our authority, we may use our authority to sin against others.

Evil happens in this world when authority is misused or neglected. All abuse or neglect is the intentional or unintentional misuse of authority delegated to us by our Creator and heavenly Father. As a general rule, God does not interfere in the use of authority He has delegated. That is not to say that He is unable to, but He does not commonly go against the rule of authority that He has established. He is not distant, but neither does He micro-manage His creation. He expects the authority He has delegated to be used well.

PARENTS AND CHILDREN

Scripture is clear that children are to honour their parents. The apostle Paul reminds the Christians in Ephesus that this is not only a command from God but also the first commandment with a promise (Ephesians 6:1–3). In addition, God has clearly given parents authority over their children, and again this authority is to be used to "build up," not to tear down.

Jesus reminds us of how dependent children are on their parents by using children as an example of how we must be if we are going to come to our heavenly Father (Matthew 18:1–6). In this passage, the emphasis is not, as some might say, on the innocence or belief of children but rather on the reality that they are totally dependent on their parents. Consequently, children are not in a place where they can protect, provide, or in any other way parent themselves. It is the responsibility of their parents and other adult authority figures to protect them, provide for them, and in other ways parent them.

In two places Paul provides some general direction for parents in dealing with their children:

And, fathers [parents], do not provoke your children to anger, but bring them up in the discipline and instruction of the Lord (Ephesians 6:4).

Fathers [parents], do not provoke your children, or they may lose heart (Colossians 3:21).

There are two keys in this passage for understanding the role of fathering and of parenting in general. First, in Roman society at the time when this was written, fathers were the absolute authority in the household. They ruled over their wives, children, and slaves with unconditional, and often demanding, harsh authority.

If you grew up in a home where the only acceptable way to complete tasks was perfectly, you will understand what it means to be "provoked," or exasperated. Elizabeth told me of her experience with perfectionism as a twelve-year-old child. She had struggled the previous year in school, but this year she had worked hard and received all A's in her report card, except for one subject where her grade was B plus. She was so excited, she ran all the way home. Her mother was in the kitchen preparing supper. Elizabeth flung open the door. Breathless, she said to her mother, "Mom, I got my report card today. Do you want to see how I did?"

Her mother replied, "Yes, dear, just leave it there on the table and I'll get around to looking at it."

Elizabeth was disappointed. She had wanted to share her excitement with her mother, but Mom was obviously too busy for her. So she went out to the garage, where her dad was busy fixing something.

"Dad, look at my report card. I got all As and one B!"

Her father put down his tools, wiped his hands on a greasy rag, and took the report card from her extended hand. His emotionless response was, "Hmm, so what happened in that one class? You'll have to work harder next time."

She could hardly believe her ears. But in her innocence she thought her dad must be right, and she'd just have to work harder.

Throughout junior and senior high Elizabeth was one of the top students. Unfortunately, her parents seem to miss most school award ceremonies and said little at home about her exceptional marks. She kept working hard, missing out on most social activities so she could study. As the years went by, her heart grew angry and cold. Her desire to please her parents, coupled with their inattention and lack of approval, provoked her to perfectionism. Perfectionism became a pattern that would carry on in her adult life.

There are other ways that fathers and mothers can set up their children to be angry. As discussed in chapter 8, "Family Foundations," any deficiency in providing basic physical, emotional, and spiritual needs can do this. There are no perfect parents, but the damage can be minimized by parents who own their deficiencies and ask their child's forgiveness. Godly authority is not afraid to operate in humility.

Scripture is fairly clear regarding the responsibility of parents to their children. Operating under godly authority, parents are to provide the following basic needs for their children:

❑ Food and other basic physical requirements: "*Is there anyone among you who, if your child asks for bread, will give a stone? Or if the child asks for a fish, will give a snake? If you then, who are evil, know how to give good gifts to your children, how much more will your Father in heaven give good things to those who ask him!*" (Matthew 7:9–11).

❑ Spiritual direction and other life skills: The book of Proverbs is written to instruct in wisdom and is directed toward a son. "*Hear, my child, your father's instruction, and do not reject your mother's teaching; for they are a fair garland for your head, and pendants for your neck*" (Proverbs 1:8–9).

❑ Provision for the future: This is indicated in Scripture by the father's role of blessing and providing a spiritual, material, and emotional inheritance for his children (Luke 15:11–31; Genesis 49, and others)

WIVES AND HUSBANDS

It is unfortunate that in the Church it seems that more attention has been paid to wives' responsibility to their husbands than husbands' responsibility to their wives. While wives are told to submit to and respect their husbands (Ephesians 5:22;33; Colossians 3:18) husbands are given the great challenge of loving and giving their lives for their wives (Ephesians 5:25–33; Colossians 3:19). This is a picture of mutual submission, a willingness on the part of both husband and wife to lay down their God-given authority for the sake of the other. When there is an unbalanced authority from either marriage partner, sin is allowed into the relationship.

MASTER AND SLAVE OR EMPLOYER AND EMPLOYEE

Again it seems clear that in these relationships Paul encourages the Ephesian and Colossian church to treat each other with mutual respect (Ephesians 6:5–9; Colossians 3:22–4:1). A more detailed understanding of this relationship is outlined in Philemon. This little epistle is really a guide for dealing with job difficulties, especially for employers.

CHURCH AUTHORITY

Authority in the early Church was not based on position, but rather on the group confirmation of a calling on an individual's life. Deacons were the first group of people set apart for ministry after the apostles (Acts 6). Having said that, job titles did not seem to be important in the early church; nor were the designations of leaders in the church as clear-cut as we would like them or as we have tried to make them.

Predominantly, it seemed that the early church recognized apostles, prophets, evangelists, pastors, and teachers as key leaders in the Body of Christ (Ephesians 4:11). These were clearly servant leadership roles, with their main function to help the Church be the Church and accomplish all that Christ had called it to be.

Locally deacons were set aside to carry out the mercy ministry of the church (Acts 6), while elders seemed to function more in the area of oversight. Keep in mind that the early church did not seem to have the strictly defined concept of "local church" that we do today. Elders seemed to be over a city or geographical area (Titus 1:5).

Whatever the name given to someone in authority in a local church, Paul's words about authority should be heeded. Authority is intended to build up, not tear down (2 Corinthians 13:10). Evil happens because we have failed, as Christian leaders, to use our authority biblically.

OUR ROLE AS "SALT" AND "LIGHT"

"You are the salt of the earth; but if salt has lost its taste, how can its saltiness be restored? It is no longer good for anything, but is thrown out and trampled under foot. You

are the light of the world. A city built on a hill cannot be hid. No one after lighting a lamp puts it under the bushel basket, but on the lampstand, and it gives light to all in the house. In the same way, let your light shine before others, so that they may see your good works and give glory to your Father in heaven" (Matthew 5:13–16).

Clearly, as Christians we are to make a difference in the world. The Christian life was never meant to be about cloistering as a subculture. We are to go into our culture and make a difference.

In Biblical times salt was used, among other things, to preserve food. If it was no longer salty, it was of no use. As followers of Jesus, we are to be a preserving factor in the world; in a way, we are here to keep humanity from getting rotten! Salt does no good if it is not sprinkled on what it is mean to preserve. If we remove ourselves from our culture, we cannot keep the world from rotting away.

Unfortunately, we have not effectively penetrated the systems of this world—commercial, political, social, and educational—to make a difference. If we see evil happening around us, we are partly to blame.

Christians were instrumental in abolishing slavery. They moved into the world, faced it head-on despite opposition, and things changed. As salt, they were able to take a giant step toward ridding the world of the evil of slavery. While slavery still occurs in many nations, most cultures today look upon it with abhorrence.

Likewise, as light, we are to do good works that people will see and then be drawn to our heavenly Father. Again, it is unfortunate that most people see our buildings, not our good works. Is there a problem with homelessness and poverty partly because the Body of Christ has failed to do good?

Evil exists, not only as isolated acts but also as part of a system. When we fail as Christians to be part of change within these existing systems, we have by our inaction contributed to the presence of evil on this earth.

Recently I was talking with a friend about the issue of divorce within the church. Our talk had come out of some research I had been doing for this book and the statistics I had uncovered about the growth in blended and common-law families. At one point in the discussion my friend said, "I know divorce is not God's plan, and it can destroy people's lives. However, I have heard many sermons over the years about family breakdown but not one sermon about the devastation caused by sexual abuse. Some of the people would have been better off if their parents had divorced when they were kids because their father was sexually abusing them. Other people I know are divorced because they could no longer tolerate the abuse, nor allow their children to live under it. Why does the church not talk about this evil?"

I had to agree with her. Sexual abuse, which includes incest and pornography, continues in our society. While in recent months I have seen some Christian organizations step up to challenge current lax child pornography laws, I still fail to see the church take an active role in exposing the evil of sexual abuse and bringing healing to its victims. We are failing to be salt and light in our world, and, in doing that, we are silent partners to evil.

A WORD ABOUT THE DEVIL

Yes, there is a devil, or Satan, the accuser, or the evil one— whatever name you wish to call him. He does influence our world to sin and to do evil. However, no one can say "the devil made me do it." As we have the free choice to respond to God's love and mercy, we have the free choice to resist the devil. In relationship, he merely influences, or magnifies, the evil that is in our own hearts.

Putting God in the Picture

Many people, myself included, have had life-changing experiences in guided prayer for the healing for memories. Basically this type of guided prayer is fairly straightforward. Ask the Holy Spirit to take you (or the person you are working with) back to a memory of the time when the wound first occurred. (Sometimes this happens right away; sometimes a memory will come later in the session as you dialogue.) Next, ask the Holy Spirit to show you what was really going on when that wound happened. Ask Him to show you the lie the enemy planted at that time, the truth that God wants you to know, and even where Jesus was in this encounter.

My first experience with this type of prayer was when I was in the process of writing a seminary paper. I had taken the book *Healing of Memories* out of the library for research material for a term paper. As I read the book, I thought, *Maybe I should try this method of prayer,* so I did. And God showed up.

He took me back to a time when I was walking home from school. I was in grade two or so, and some older boys were taunting me about my weight. Then it seemed I would be rescued. My dad pulled up in his car to give me a ride home. When I got into the car, relieved but shaken, trying desperately to hold back tears, I asked my dad, "Why do the boys do that?" He didn't reply, just turned and drove us home.

Among the lies I began to believe at that time was that even God could not protect me and that surely I was a mistake in His eyes too. So, in this process of remembrance I asked the Holy Spirit to show me where Jesus was.

In the memory I saw Jesus in the back seat, crying. Tears were streaming down His face. I don't remember if He said these words or I simply felt them, but I knew that He was heartbroken for me. He did not want this to happen. He wanted my dad to protect me and affirm me, but my dad had his own choices to make, which Jesus would not interfere with.

OVERCOMING EVIL

One day, evil will be no more. But today we must live in a world where evil sometimes seems more powerful that God's goodness. We should not be afraid of evil; neither should we minimize its effects of its victims. However, until we address the ways evil rules in our world, we will continue to live under its power.

First, evil exists because of each individual's sinful nature. We must guard our hearts and actions and exhort others to do the same.

Evil also exists because God-given authority has been misused. We must learn to use the authority God has given us to build up and not tear down.

And evil exists because, as the Body of Christ, we have not been salt and light in the world.

When we sit with a victim of incest, we cannot offer them platitudes that discount the destructiveness of evil on a human soul. Nor can we simply offer them academic answers. Understanding that evil exists because of individual sin, ungodly authority, and failing Christians is helpful, but these answers in themselves will not bring healing.

When we sit with victims of some type of emotional or physical trauma, childhood sexual abuse, or other relational pain, we are there as representatives of the fallen human race. We cannot simply offer them words; we must offer them our repentant hearts, for as descendants of Adam and Eve we are part of the problem. By letting their stories break our hearts, we open up the possibility that we can be part of the solution.

Chapter Five

THE HEALING PROCESS

✳   ✳   ✳

How do we heal the emotional wounds we carry? If we are like most Christians, we stumble about, go in circles, backtrack, and go through all kinds of contortions to find a way to alleviate pain. Since our goal is primarily to stop the pain, we are able to find short-term solutions to the perceived problem. However, we fail to recognize that emotional healing is not about stopping the pain; it is a process of spiritual growth that results in long-term gain, even though we may experience short-term pain. If we can learn about and recognized the process, perhaps it won't take so long to find healing.

My own story is an example. My family of origin was emotionally detached and shame-based. It left an aching void in my heart, one that I tried to fill in various ways on my Christian journey. I was trying to find healing, but, not having a road map of the process, it would take a long time.

Sunday evenings were a favourite time of mine as a child. We'd eat supper early so that we could huddle in front of our black-and-white television and watch "The

Wonderful World of Disney," "The Ed Sullivan Show," and "Bonanza." These nights were the few times, other than suppers, when my mom, dad, sister, and I sat together. However, while I was physically sitting in our suburban bungalow living room, I was in another world.

The Disney cartoons and movies sent me into a world of fantasy far removed from the daily shame I faced both in home and in school. I was extremely overweight as a child, and older boys always seemed to think it was their duty to point out the obvious. When I returned home, my father was unable to counteract these shaming comments. With his own deep pain, he did not know how to reach into mine.

And so Sunday nights were heaven. For a few short hours I could escape the dull aching in my heart and fantasize about being a princess in a land where everything turned out happily ever after, usually with little effort on the part of the princess. Those who adored her, including the ever-present handsome prince, ensured a pleasant outcome to her dilemma and danger.

When I became a Christian at the end of grade eleven, it seemed like life would now, finally, turn out happily ever after. My first few months as a follower of Jesus were a mix of euphoria and intellectual doubts. I soon discovered that the intellectual questions I had were common to mankind. Others had asked them, and others had written down the answers, so my theological doubts were dealt with fairly easily.

Unfortunately, my emotional health, as well as my need for improved life skills, proved harder to address. I loved Jesus, and I knew He loved me. Soon, however, the gleam of my new life in Christ faded, and I was left to face the remaining reality of an emotionally-detached, shamed-based family and the empty ache in my own heart. At the time, I could not have put this struggle into words. Somewhere along the line I had come to understand that I was a new creation in Christ, and, while I still had to struggle with sin, I was just fine, really I was fine! I tried to heal the wounds by denying that I had any.

I became a part of a little Pentecostal church in suburban Winnipeg. For a while I was the youth group, and, to be honest, I liked it that way. Adults doted on me, undoubtedly encouraged by my great faith! There were no peers to relate to, so my inferiority buttons were not pushed and I could continue in my little fantasy world. Without other peers to relate to, it was easy to pretend that I was okay. But fantasy is just another form of denial. It was as ineffective a method of dealing with life as outright denial had been.

The reality was that I did not know any other way to relate to life. I transposed my Disney-fied world view onto my walk with Christ and believed that things would turn out happily ever after with little effort on my part. Being a new creation in Christ meant that Jesus, my Prince Charming, would take care of all the hurts in my life. While that is true in some respects, neither I nor those I had come to know as Christians seemed to be able to give me practical ways to apply this to my life. So, I kept reading my Bible, praying, participating in Bible studies, and going to church twice on Sundays. I desperately hoped that these good works would bring healing to my emotional hurts and pain.

Upon reflection, I realize that these activities were life-savers. They kept me afloat. However, as with shipwreck survivors clinging to a life raft, at some point someone has to pull you out of the dangerous waters or you will drown.

Bible study, prayer, and fellowship are good things on their own, but I could not translate the Gospels, Epistles, or Levitical law into a way out of the cold, deep, and dark emotional waters of my soul.

One day—I was now in my early twenties—I was lying in bed looking at a poster on my wall. Its black background was covered with biblical phrases describing Jesus: Prince of Peace; Lord of lords; the way, the truth and the life—and then it jumped out at me—*Wonderful Counsellor.* There it was—I'd found the answer! Jesus was a wonderful counsellor. I had begun to see that I was an emotional mess and that maybe I needed to get some professional help. I really didn't want to go there, so I took that poster as a sign from God: I was safe. Jesus would take care of me.

The next Sunday I stood up in church to testify that, though my life had been hard, I didn't need to bother to go to a counsellor, because Jesus would take care of me! I didn't go as far as a friend of mine who tried to avoid counselling by insisting that all counsellors, Christian counsellors included, were demonic, but I was close. I didn't realize that Jesus brings healing through others and in relationship. And I couldn't even begin to understand that my fear of relationship kept me from meeting with a counsellor.

In hindsight, I realize that my pastor should have taken me aside and encouraged me to see a Christian counsellor. But he didn't, and, while there was some healing in my life, I continued to struggle emotionally and spiritually for another decade before I finally broke and truly let God change my heart. A Christian at seventeen, I lived for fourteen more years in the emotional and spiritual wasteland of denial, fantasy, good works, and self-sufficiency. I failed to understand that growing as a Christian was an intentional process requiring effort and honesty on my part.

As I've recounted in previous chapters, I moved to a new city and a new job, and outwardly my life looked successful. But when I chose to reflect about my internal world, it felt like I was just a hollow bubble. If anyone pierced the surface, not only would I explode but also they'd find nothing there.

Then came that day in church when I heard the youth pastor's message about the issues teenagers need to deal with emotionally in order to become healthy, godly adults. As he went through the list I realized that, at thirty-one, I had not dealt with any of those issues. The veil of denial was broken, and finally I saw the truth. I needed help.

I didn't know enough about what I was feeling inside to know what to do about it, and neither did my close friends or the pastors at my church. It took the Holy Spirit a year to strip away enough of my faulty theology and my human pride for me to make an appointment with a Christian counsellor.

Looking back over my journal from that period I see glimpses, for the first time, of an understanding that somehow what had happened to me as a child was affecting who I was as an adult. Equally important—maybe even more important—I was beginning to grapple with the reality that, despite all my good works for God, I still responded to life sinfully. Yes, I was following Jesus; I loved Jesus; in the midst of all this inner turmoil He was the only anchoring point of my life. However, I began—and it was really only a beginning—to understand that my good acts were nothing but shallow, pharisaical doings and I somehow needed to change.

EMOTIONAL HEALING IS PART OF THE PROCESS
OF SANCTIFICATION

In those crucial days, I was coming to see that my walk as a Christian truly was a process of sanctification. *Sanctification* is a theological word that basically means the process of becoming more like Christ. I had been deceiving myself. It was sanctification of my emotions—the intents of my heart—that was necessary to really be a follower of Jesus. Up until that moment I could talk the talk and walk the walk for the most part. Regrettably, my inner emotional world had remained largely unaffected by the externals of my life. While I cried often during worship and seemed to operate at an emotional level, my wounded soul was locked deep inside my pretense.

Romans 6:22 says, *"But now that you have been set free from sin and have become slaves to God, the benefit you reap leads to holiness, and the result is eternal life"* (NIV). Notice that the benefit of salvation is that it *"leads"* us, or draws us along, to the place of holiness. The great gift of our salvation is that we have been given the power to change!

It should go without saying that the Christian life is one of process and change. We talk about "growing in Christ." *Growing* is a word that connotes change and development. Paul writes to his friends in Philippi, *"Continue to work out your salvation with fear and trembling"* (Philippians 2:12 NIV). The Bible abounds in examples of growth and change. Jesus' disciples, beneficiaries of His direct teachings, were not exempt from the need to grow and change. Even after the exhilarating experience of Pentecost (Acts 2), Peter found out he still needed to deal with attitudes in his heart. It took a vision for Peter to understand that the ingrained prejudice in his heart just didn't work in this new kingdom (Acts 10).

Looking back, I have come to see that somewhere along the line I missed the teaching that growth as a Christian is a heart, or emotional, process. Up until that time, now over a decade ago, I believed that if I could discipline my thoughts and do the right things, everything would work out fine. For an emotionally detached person this was easy to do, but it was largely ineffective in making me more like Jesus.

The reality is that as Christ's disciples we are to love Him with our complete being. When an expert in the law asked Jesus what he needed to do to make sure he was in the kingdom, Jesus challenged him to remember what the Jewish religious law said. The man said to Jesus, "'*Love the Lord your God with all your heart and with all your soul and with all your strength and with all your mind'; and, 'Love your neighbor as yourself'*" (Luke 10:27 NIVI).

We do not need to dissect the first part of this verse to understand that we are to love God with all our being—heart, soul, strength, and mind. Unfortunately, though my emotions (heart) were often stirred in worship, I was so disconnected from them that I could not see the sin that was there. Loving God with my strength (my physical actions) was only a quarter of the equation. Denial blinded me to the ways I failed to love God with my emotions, will, and intellect.

I had somehow missed a process of discipling my heart and soul. I place no fault on the dear people who took me into their lives as a young Christian. In those early years they kept me alive.

Discipling our heart, soul, and intellect is not something we often discuss in Christian circles. This is unfortunate, because it is central to the process of sanctification.

We cannot truly bear good fruit from a diseased tree. Many followers of Jesus stumble and fall morally after years of what appeared to be a faithful walk with God, because while the fruit of their lives looked good, the tree bearing it was not (Matthew 7:17–19).

Ultimately, when we choose to become disciples of Jesus, we enter into the process of sanctification. That process is about making us lovers of God in our heart, soul, strength, and mind. Some people refer to this as "inner healing," others as "discipleship counselling" or simply "Christian counselling."

The process of healing is a long journey out of denial into the truth. What follows is a model of this process of healing, change, and growth that has been valuable in helping me understand what has happened in my life over the last decade. This is not solely my model; it has been adapted from work done by others much more perceptive than I am. These include material presented by Dr. Dan Allender in his book *The Wounded Heart*,[18] as well as the Wounded Heart Seminar, and unpublished material presented in Wholeness Through Christ Seminars[4]. (Please see "Suggested Reading" for further information.) It is presented here to provide a framework for helping leaders to understand the process we all must undergo to become sanctified followers of Jesus.

Healing Our Soul, Body and Spirit

I doubt that, in the early stages of my Christian life, any of those more experienced Christians around me had any detailed understanding of the internal heart process of discipleship. In fact, in the present day most of us who call ourselves followers of Jesus look at discipleship as a "spiritual" discipline, dealing with issues of our spirits, not our souls. We may acknowledge that character is important but often deal only with what we would call the "spirit" rather than our emotional and intellectual life, even though that is what the soul is made of.

Dr. Grant Mullen, in his book *Emotionally Free,* makes a useful distinction between body, soul, and spirit. In looking at the process of emotional healing, he says that there are three components. *Body* refers to our physical body, and, as such, it is important to consider medical components to personal struggles like depression. In other words, if someone is suffering from a down, discouraged mood, is that primarily caused by current factors, such as the end of a marriage, death of a loved one, loss of job, etc., or is it caused by medical factors such as an imbalance of serotonin or dopamine? Mullen would say that discouragement could be primarily a sickness of the *soul*—the past or present emotional wounds that a person may not be dealing with in a healthy way. Further, he says that discouragement can be caused by demonic attack. This is depression more connected to the *spirit* part of a person.[19]

Part of my frustration in finding healing for my wounded heart was that I was trying to heal emotional wounds but was using only spiritual treatments, such as prayer and worship. Because the wound was primarily in my soul, or heart, the treatment helped a bit, but was mostly ineffective.

This does not mean we negate "spirit" issues. The reality is that soul and spirit are intricately connected. The writer of Hebrews says as much when he says that the word of God is a sharp sword, able to divide things that are so intricately connected that they are normally indivisible—joints and bone marrow, spirit and soul (Hebrews 4:12). Consequently, to be free in our spirits, we must be free in our souls, and vice versa. The woundedness in our souls is usually the first thing to rear its head. Paul's admonishment to the Corinthian church to get rid of things of "the flesh," or "carnal" nature, was another way of saying that their wounded soul was getting in the way of their "walking in the Spirit." It would be nice if we could simply ignore our wounded souls, but our sinful responses to our woundedness are a constant roadblock to our ability to walk in the freedom Christ has given us.

Obviously we are a whole—body, soul, and spirit. When Jesus commands us to love God with our heart, soul, mind, and strength, He is really saying that we are to love God with all of who we are. If a part of that whole is wounded, it is impossible to love God completely. The process begins by recognizing that we are reactors.

1. Recognize That We Are Reactors

Think of a situation in the last week where something happened that "pushed your buttons"—perhaps an encounter you had with an individual at work where his or her actions made you angry or afraid or ashamed. Those feelings probably led you to act, or react, in a certain way. Perhaps you replied with equally maddening, frightening, or shaming words (or at least thought them). Maybe, in your anger, you left the room, saying the words "I'll show you." Throughout the remainder of the day the anger simmered in your heart toward the colleague who had harshly judged your work. You worked extra hard for the rest of that week to prove yourself competent in the eyes of your associate. You were reacting to the emotional wounding you experienced, rather than making a moral choice based on the situation.

We all do this, in a variety of ways, in a variety of situations. We are *reactors* responding to the situation based on our emotional trigger points. Because we are created in God's image, and because God has emotions, we too have them. However, as Jesus shows us, we should not respond to people or situations as a reflex emotional response.

Jesus never responded to situations as an emotional reflex. He made clear, volitional responses to situations. In John chapter 13 Jesus washes the disciples' feet. It was an act of true humility, and he was able to do this because... *Jesus knew that the Father had put all things under his power, and that he had come from God, and was returning to God...* (John 13:3). Most of us do not have such a clear understanding of our destiny and identity. Rather, our path in life is directed by a desire to put salve on our wounded hearts, egos and emotions.

Through counselling, when I examined my life, I realized that I was often operating on a reactive emotional level when I was faced with decisions. I enrolled in an environmental science program far away from home when I was eighteen. It was, for the most part, a great time in my life. I was studying things I loved, and I was away from my challenging family dynamics. I discovered in college that if I worked really hard I could be in the top of the class. On the surface, there was nothing wrong with the choices I made back then. However, the underlying motivation for these life choices was largely a reaction against how my life had been. I didn't even consider enrolling in studies in my hometown. What I really wanted was to get away from a home environment that left me feeling inadequate and unworthy. My high grades boosted my shame-filled ego and left me with hope that maybe my father, this time, would be satisfied. I was reacting to the past and to the ongoing wounds I experienced in my family.

In my denial, I masked my hard work and choice of college with spiritual platitudes about God's direction and provision. This was partly true—undoubtedly God allowed me to wander down this path to provide some healing in my life. I lived with a great Christian family at the time. They were a cup of refreshing spring water to my dusty soul. Unfortunately, because I reacted to the emotional woundedness in my life, I continued to function for years afterward in the same way: *Work hard, work really hard, so someone will affirm me and I don't have to feel so miserable. And maybe, if I'm successful enough, my father will notice.* Somewhere along the line I had reacted so often in this way that I transferred this conditional love to my beliefs about my heavenly Father. I could not see that I was reacting to life rather than making responsible choices. I was buried deep in the riverbed of denial, with the silt covering me more every day.

The following figure outlines the steps found in the healing process. Keep in mind that, while each step does seem to follow each other, it is not always a straight path. Life seldom is. Also bear in mind that we proceed through these stages for each significant area of woundedness that needs to be addressed.

For example, let's say that an individual has significant wounds of abandonment and betrayal. He will go through the process as he brings both areas of woundedness to Jesus for healing. This will make more sense when you look at each of the specific wounds. However, the first stage, the beginning part of the entire healing process, is to face the truth about the things that happened to us and step out of denial.

The Healing Process

Reactor

Begin to move out of denial by thinking that, perhaps, painful life events may have affected us.

As a victim we begin to tell our story. Life circumstances are God's tool to shift our perspective. We begin to understand that we have been emotionally wounded and we have not always responded to the wounding in a godly way.

Victim

We are now able to admit our woundedness and take responsibility for our sinful reactions. We now make a choice to receive God's healing and repent of our self-protective sinful responses to emotional pain.

Responsible Agent

2. Identify Denial

"Denial" is not "de" river in Egypt. We are in denial when we fail to see the truth about ourselves. Denial is a consequence of Adam and Eve's choices in the Garden of Eden. In order to find a way out of God's discipline, they projected the blame onto someone else and failed to see their individual responsibility in their rejection of the Father's love. Adam blamed Eve, and Eve blamed the serpent (Genesis 3:11–13). We continue to operate in the same sinful pattern to this day. We consistently fail to see that life is not something done to us; it is something we participate in. Each of our attitudes and actions has some impact on the lives of others and on our own souls.

One of the best pictures of denial comes from a friend of mine. Edith grew up so poor that often there was no heat in their home. This was a pretty big problem, because she grew up in northern Alberta. She recalls that her mother would gather her and her five siblings around the wood stove in the kitchen. Then her mother would pull out her guitar and lead her children in song, trying to keep their minds off the cold.

Edith learned through that and similar other childhood experiences that you should never look at the circumstances around you. Rather, you just push through and ignore the real problem. It led to a lifetime of struggle, first relationally and later with drugs and alcohol. Denial caused her to marry a man who she knew had physically abused other women, because, as she said, "He loves me, so I know he won't hurt me."

Denial, denying the truth about what has happened in our lives and how it has affected us, keeps us in bondage. In reality, when we choose to live in denial, we are living a lie.

When we live lies we put ourselves under the influence of the father of lies, Satan. Jesus reminds us that Satan is the father of lies, and when he speaks a lie he speaks his native language (John 8:44). We are all too well versed in the language of lies.

For years I lived a lie. On the outside I was a compliant Christian, eager and willing to follow those placed in leadership over me. On the outside I looked like a submissive, obedient, and godly young woman. However, the outside picture was far from the truth of my heart. I was so desperate to be loved that I willingly followed, hoping to please those in authority over me. The reality was that my good deeds were a manipulation to earn the love of others. Unfortunately, because I was deep in denial, I could not see the lying manipulation in my heart. The only clue that something was wrong was the rage that would erupt when those whom I wanted to love me did not respond the way I wanted them to.

You would think it would be enough to confess my sin of anger and move on from there. But it never was. The reality is that anger is not necessarily sinful. Immediately after Paul reminds the Ephesians to "put off falsehood," he reminds them to not sin when they are angry (Ephesians 4:25–27 NIV). Notice that he doesn't tell them not to be angry. He then adds that they should not let the day end before they have dealt with their anger.

The problem with anger comes when we handle it wrong by hurting someone else or ourselves. For example, we lash out at someone whom we feel has harmed us with abusive words or language. Alternatively, many people fearful of expressing anger turn it on themselves. Often anger turned inward leads to depression. In any case, anger that is not dealt with in an appropriate way gives the devil "*a foothold*" (Ephesians 4:27 NIV), or an entry point into our lives. Our feeling of anger may be an emotionally legitimate response to our personal boundaries being violated or a deep wound being aggravated or an injustice being done.

Now here's the problem. I had been quietly angry about many things my whole life. In my childhood I was not allowed to be angry, and so I did not receive any tools to deal with my anger other than stuffing it all inside. When I became a Christian I continued to receive the message that anger was not something to be shown or acknowledged. That didn't stop me from being angry. The rage that erupted in me from time to time was simply the root of deep anger in my soul. The deep anger began when I was a young child and was added on to, day by day, year by year, as I grew.

Created in the image of God, we have an intuitive understanding of how things are supposed to be, even as children. We know that we are to be loved. We know that emotional, physical, and sexual abuse are wrong, though we could never put it into words. We know that many things that happen to us over the course of our lives are not what we were created for. Our parents neglect or abuse us; schoolmates tease or bully us; our parents get divorced; people we love die when we still need them. Inwardly, we groan (2 Corinthians 5:1–5), because we know that we were created for paradise, not for the daily grind of this sinful world.

As children we do not have the emotional and spiritual life skills to make sense of the discrepancy between our world experience and what our hearts know. Earthly life and paradise simply do not mesh in our hearts. And, unfortunately, we come to conclusions about the world that leave us in oppression. Our first intuitive understanding is generally correct—this isn't how it's supposed to be. On the other hand, the way we deal with our observation, like Adam and Eve did, casts the blame on someone else and fails to direct us to the condition of our own hearts.

As children, more often than not, we learn that it is easier to deaden the groaning in our hearts. Our own sinful hearts find it easier to either deny the reality of the pain we feel or blame someone else for it. As human beings we are masters of reacting in sinful ways to the sin someone else commits against us. If you don't agree, just think about how you respond to the driver who cuts you off!

3. From Reactor to Victim

The first step out of denial and into healing and freedom is to acknowledge that something bad happened to us and that it has affected us. This helps us to understand that we are victims. Being a victim isn't a bad thing unless we get stuck there. Identifying ourselves as victims simply means that we have acknowledged that we have been emotionally, physically, sexually, or spiritually wounded and that it has affected us. Without doing this we are unable to step out of the role of reactor. I've have never met anyone who has moved into true healing and freedom without first acknowledging what had really happened to them. This is not about blaming someone else; it is about moving out of living a lie to living in the truth. It is about moving out from under the authority of the father of lies into the kingdom of truth. Jesus is truth (John 14:6).

For example anyone who has been sexually abused cannot move into freedom without first acknowledging that he or she has been sexually abused and that this has had devastating effects on his or her life. The truth is that sexual abuse is evil. When evil enters our lives, it is not benign; it will affect us. The greater the evil, the greater the damage to our souls and even, at times, to our spirits. Any form of sexual abuse is the greatest type of evil perpetrated against a soul. Above any other trauma it seems to do the greatest damage to our hearts, shutting us down from loving God and others the way we were intended to. Undealt with, its effects span generations.

The Old Testament account of David and Bathsheba (2 Samuel 11–12) paints a clear picture of the devastation to a family caused by sexual sin. Even though David was a man after God's own heart (1 Samuel 13:14), sexual sin affected his life and the lives of his family for generations. While he confessed his sin to God (2 Samuel 12:13), he failed to acknowledge the way his sin had affected his relationship with others. In 2 Samuel 13:1–21 we read the account of incest between David's son Amnon and David's daughter Tamar.

Amnon *"fell in love"* with his half-sister Tamar (v. 1). Really, it wasn't love; it was lust. Feigning sickness, he asked that Tamar be sent to him to make special bread for him, which she did. Then Amnon commanded everyone in the room to leave except Tamar. He grabbed her, demanding that she go to bed with him. She very loudly and insistently said no, so Amnon raped his sister Tamar.

After the rape, the Scriptures say Amnon *"hated"* her (v. 15 NIV). He sent her away, barring her from his presence. In her anger, grief, and torment, Tamar ripped the orna-mented robe worn by all virgin daughters of the king and wept. Her brother Absalom knew something was wrong but didn't do anything about it until two years later. King David *"was furious"* (v. 21 NIV), but Scripture gives no account of him disciplining Amnon or even acknowledging Amnon's sin. Though David repented of his own sinful choices with Bathsheba, a few chapters later we see David unable to take a stand against his son's sexual sin.

Tamar was disgraced, and she lived in her brother Absalom's house, a desolate woman. Absalom and David never had a great relationship after that. In fact, Absalom tried to take away the crown from David. Had David's denial of the truth, and subsequent inaction, destroyed any respect he might have had from his son?

The chapters that follow deal in greater detail with the effects of all types of trauma on the human heart and the process of healing. In all cases, there can be no true healing until we step out from under the authority of lies and into the kingdom of the truth.

4. Circumstances: God's Wake-Up Call

Ultimately, change only begins to happen when a set of circumstances causes us to question the reality of the lie we have been living. One day we realize that our problems are not about everyone else; they're about us—our pain, our choices, our life. For example, King David could have used Amnon's rape of Tamar as an opportunity to take a clear stand against sexual sin in his own life and in his kingdom. Unfortunately, he chose not to.

Carmen was having a problem with relationships. They started well, but friends kept drifting. One day, it happened again: a friend didn't invite her to a party that everyone else was going to. After another lonely weekend she began to ask God what was wrong with these people. "Why can't people keep up their end of the friendship?" she wondered. After all, she was always calling people and asking them to go to a movie or some other activity, but they weren't reciprocating. It forced her to confront the issue. Carmen realized that the cool disdain that seeped out of her heart was, perhaps, partly responsible for her difficulty in keeping friendships.

Slowly she began to catch a small glimpse of the truth. Maybe, just maybe, she was part of the problem. While she was social, chatty, and fun to be with, she shied away from any serious conversation. She deflected any perceived pain or difficulty with humour. Finally, the pattern of disappointing relationships had forced her to look at what was really wrong.

Circumstances in our life are God's wake-up call to reality. When something challenging happens to us, it is an opportunity to allow the Holy Spirit to probe the depths of our heart.

5. Telling Our Stories

When we begin to break free of denial, it is essential to begin to tell our stories. The more we tell our stories, the more we begin to see the truth about our lives. Writing in a journal is helpful, but sharing our stories verbally with someone is essential.

Carmen timidly began seeing a counsellor, trying to fix this problem she had with relationships. As she talked with the counsellor, she began to see the truth of her story. As a child, her home vacillated between chaos and quiet anger. Her parents were often fighting about something, and, while the arguments never became physical, the tension in the house was often unbearable. She began to see how she had used humour and activity as a distraction from the turmoil and fear of her home.

At school her teachers found her a willing and diligent

student. She was often picked as the leader of groups because of her ability to avoid getting bogged down with problems or challenges of a given project. As a child and teen, Carmen's humour, stick-to-it-ness and social skills were rewarded. As she left university and entered the work force full-time, she found herself quickly promoted, often beyond her abilities, but Carmen didn't worry about that for too long.

By listening to Carmen's story, her counsellor was able to help her see how her humour and sociability was an asset in the work world but a drawback in personal relationships.

Telling our story helps us make sense of things, helping us to see ourselves in relation to the big picture, as well as giving us a place to express our disappointment, pain and anger. It can help us understand how we had hoped things would have been for us, so that we can understand why we can't let go of the past. Telling our story, even in an informal way, helps us understand that things have happened to us, some good, some bad, and some downright ugly. As well, telling our story helps us begin to see how we have responded in good and bad ways to the events and people in our lives.

A wounded person cannot move on unless someone listens to his or her story. That process may start with a pastor or Christian counsellor, and it must include someone outside of a designated leadership position. Why? It's important to tell our stories to a "real person." There's a certain sense of safety in talking to a "professional." We expect them to be accepting, caring, somewhat detached, and we don't have to have contact with them outside of a one-hour session. A pastor may or may not fit into the category of being a detached professional. It depends on a variety of factors: if you are the listener, what is your relationship to the storyteller, how do you present yourself, and how does the storyteller view your authority in his or her life? Regardless, to be a person, professional or otherwise, to whom a wounded heart can tell his or her story, you must be able to listen without judgment or without telling them what to do with the information they've discovered. When we listen to someone, we are saying that their life, their story, has value.

Because the telling of stories is so important to healing, we will go into this step in some detail.

Telling the Story: How to Be a Good Listener

Being a good listener is an acquired skill. It is actively entering into someone else's world. Consequently, listening is as much a function of our head and heart as it is of our ears!

When Jesus spoke to the churches in the book of Revelation, He said, "*If you have ears, then listen to what the Spirit says to the churches!*" (Revelation 2:7 GNT). In saying this, He meant so much more than merely hearing words. It is clear that this phrase is spoken with the intent that the churches would have the courage not only to listen but also to respond appropriately to what the Spirit says. Jesus is urging the churches to have the courage and will to respond.

It is critical that we listen as actively to each other as we do to the Spirit. If we listen very carefully to the people who come to us with wounded hearts, we will hear, really hear, what they are saying. That kind of listening, the listening that is done with the heart, will also help us to respond appropriately to what they are saying.

Think about it: when someone listens to you they value you. Listening is a free gift we can give to each other.

Here are some tips on being a good listener:

1. Be a safe listener. As we discussed earlier, it is critical that we be safe people to those walking through emotional and spiritual healing. Listen in confidence, not repeating a word someone shares with you.

2. Listen actively. Respond to what your friend is sharing with you. Look at the person, nod your head, say "uh huh," do something to let them know you are with them.

3. Listen with curiosity. Ask them to clarify what they said if you don't quite understand what they are trying to tell you. "Are you saying that being betrayed by your best friend in high school is one of the reasons you find it difficult to trust me?" Or simply say, "I don't understand how this betrayal affected you. Can you tell me more?"

4. Listen with sincerity. If you don't have time or you need to attend to something else, be honest. Let them know that you can't talk with them now, but you can meet with them at 7 p.m.—and make sure that you are there! Also, it is difficult (if not impossible) to listen with sincerity to someone's concerns when you are making supper, channel surfing, or planting the garden. Honour them by giving them your undivided attention.

5. Listen with honesty. Do you really care about your friend (or spouse or child)? Or are you merely waiting for them to finish talking so you can tell them how to fix their problem or tell them *your* story? In a healthy relationship you can allow for

equal time, but when you are dealing with a hurting person, building a healing relationship takes time.

If you want more information about the skills of active listening, you might consider taking a course—it's that important! Also, you'll find additional resources listed in the "Suggested Reading" list at the back of the book.

Helping Someone Tell Their Story

People who are living in denial have great skills for burying the truth and few tools for facing the truth. Hopefully, someone—perhaps you?—will give them the great gift of actively listening to their story. They may still be at a place, however, where they need to think about their story—they're not quite sure what it is. You can help someone arrive at the truth of their story.

Following are some questions that may help in the process.

❑ Where were you born? How many are in your family? Are you the oldest, youngest, or middle sibling?

❑ What was the worst thing that happened to you as a child? If this happened to someone else, how would you respond to him or her?

❑ What is the best thing that happened to you as a child? This is often harder to answer than telling about the worst thing. If your storyteller can't answer the question, or if he struggles to come up with an answer, he probably had a difficult and painful childhood. Generally, having few childhood memories is an indication that the storyteller has tried to forget childhood altogether.

❑ What emotions, if any, were expressed in your family? Who expressed them?

❑ What type of physical touch was used in your family? As an adult, how do you feel when someone gives you a hug?

❑ How did your family deal with conflict? If there was never conflict in your family, why?

❑ How did your mom and dad relate to each other? Was it obvious that they loved each other, or did you wonder why they ever got married?

❑ Were you allowed to be a kid, or did you have adult responsibilities at an early age?

❑ What was it like for you at school? Did you have friends? Did your friends come to your house or did you go to theirs?

❑ What do you think about God? Be honest.

❑ What are the highlights of your walk with Jesus?

It is important to understand what happened to us so that we can begin to take responsibility for the way we have responded to life. As adults, by and large, life is what we make of it, but if we are in bondage to childish ways of responding to pain and disappointment, we will continue in that pattern. Life will continue to be painful, disappointing, frustrating, and empty.

People need to tell their stories often. Each time, the Holy Spirit brings new insight. It can take a long time. It can be frustrating listening to someone's story, but it is an essential part of the healing process. Remember, this is part of the journey, not the final destination.

6. Being a Victim and Moving On

Jason slumped in my office chair and began to recount the last two weeks of his life. His wife—his second wife, no less—had dumped him. He came to me to try to understand what had happened. "Women!" he moaned. "They are just out to take advantage of me, use me for whatever they can get, and then move on to the next sucker." He was a whirl of emotions—disappointment, rage, rejection, and apathy.

Jason spewed out these emotions for about twenty minutes. Then I asked him, "What was your role in this breakup?"

"My role?" he replied, clenching his fists and jaw. I could almost hear his teeth grind. "My role? That woman took me for everything I had! I provided for her and her kids. I tried to be a leader spiritually, but after we were married she never had time to pray together...let alone anything else! I did everything I could to please her."

And then he said the clincher: "She ended up being just like my last wife...cold."

"So Jason," I responded, "this seems to be a pattern in your life. Let me ask you again, what was your role in the breakdown of this marriage?"

He thought for awhile, noticeably uncomfortable. Then he replied, "Well, I don't know; maybe I'm just attracted to women that need to be taken care of. But what's wrong with that? My dad took care of Mom and us kids because Mom was sick with multiple sclerosis. She didn't leave him."

I responded, challenging him to look for a pattern. "Jason, it seems to me that you pick women who are emotionally detached and needy. A husband is supposed to love his wife like Christ loved the church, but it's a two-way street. A wife, a woman, needs to respect her husband. Could it be that you make yourself such a doormat that women quickly take advantage of you and lose respect for you? When you feel that respect fading, you counterattack by doing more and more, which just makes the problem worse. Your wife may have felt trapped by your kindness."

He sat there for a while, thinking. It seemed to be the first time that he realized that maybe, just maybe, he had some sinful patterns in his life. What happened to him wasn't just about what women did to him; it was about how he tried to manipulate and control women through his apparent kindness.

At some point in our healing journey, circumstances and the Holy Spirit conspire to cause us to look at our own sinful patterns of relating. We begin to see that we have to take responsibility for our own actions. Life isn't just something that happens to us; as adults it is something in which we actively participate.

7. Being Responsible for Our Own Lives

Jason had talked to me often about his childhood home. There had been good times, but mostly his childhood was a struggle. His mother developed MS when he was nine years old. Three years older than his brother, he had done what he could to help his mom around the house. When the disease flared up and she became bedridden, he helped his dad try to keep the house clean, food on the table, and some semblance of order.

Eventually his mother had to be moved into a nursing home. His dad withdrew even more emotionally. Jason became the emotional centre for the household, listening to both his dad's and his brother's outbursts of either tears or anger. He remained calm and stable through it all.

After his first divorce, a friend had suggested he take a divorce recovery program through a local church. Through that course he became a Christian. Within three years he had met and married a single mother he met through some mutual friends.

It took his second divorce to help him see how he used his good deeds to manipulate people, especially women, and keep his heart at a safe distance. That day the Holy Spirit helped him make a significant shift in his attitude and behaviour. He asked forgiveness for his manipulative behaviours and began a journey of responsibility for his own actions.

It hasn't been easy, but he has continued to grow spiritually and emotionally. He is now honest about his own need to be loved and cared for. He no longer does everything for everybody.

When we are emotionally wounded, our human tendency is to react in a sinful way through some sort of blame or self-protection. This pattern begins with our first childhood wounds. If the sinful reaction seems to help us numb the pain and cope, we will continue responding to the same type of wounding in a similar way. Over the years, this sinful pattern becomes bondage. Healing comes when we ask the Holy Spirit to heal the initial wound, ask forgiveness for our sinful response, and allow God to break the bondage.

8. The Long Journey Home

Like Jason, most of us fail to see our own sinful behaviours, because we have lived lives of pretense and deception. Unable to admit the truth about the pain in our lives, denial keeps us blind to the pain we have caused others. We must admit the truth about our lives in order to truly see our sinful behaviour.

This is a significant step in the healing journey, and it's very important that wounded persons make this discovery and admit the truth about their pain themselves. Unfortunately, despite how well we can see the sin in others, telling them about their sinful behaviour does little good. Often church leaders think it's their responsibility to proclaim the truth or to identify errors. That may be okay for certain situations (like Jesus did with the Pharisees), but generally it won't work. It's the revelation that the Holy Spirit brings to their hearts that brings true changes. If people do not have this inner revelation, they will respond to our words of correction in the same old ways that do not result in change. If, like Jason, they have covered up their pain with good works, they may repent just to make you happy. Or, if they have covered the pain in their heart with a thick impenetrable wall, they may respond with an icy rage. In either case, the person has not truly repented.

The only way we can help someone move from being a victim to being responsible for her life is to let her tell her story, then challenge her a bit and pray that God will line up circumstances in her life so that she can see the truth.

Leading people to repentance is God's job, not ours. Our task is to journey beside them, encouraging and setting boundaries where appropriate. The Bible gives us a good picture of the process in the following story. Like the young son, people usually need to find out for themselves that it is the father's home that is the place of celebration and belonging.

> *"There was once a man who had two sons. The younger said to his father, 'Father, I want right now what's coming to me.' So the father divided the property between*

them. It wasn't long before the younger son packed his bags and left for a distant country. There, undisciplined and dissipated, he wasted everything he had. After he had gone through all his money, there was a bad famine all through that country and he began to hurt. He signed on with a citizen there who assigned him to his fields to slop the pigs. He was so hungry he would have eaten the corncobs in the pig slop, but no one would give him any.

"That brought him to his senses. He said, 'All those farmhands working for my father sit down to three meals a day, and here I am starving to death. I'm going back to my father. I'll say to him, Father, I've sinned against God, I've sinned before you; I don't deserve to be called your son. Take me on as a hired hand.' He got right up and went home to his father.

"When he was still a long way off, his father saw him. His heart pounding, he ran out, embraced him, and kissed him. The son started his speech: 'Father, I've sinned against God, I've sinned before you; I don't deserve to be called your son ever again.'

"But the father wasn't listening. He was calling to the servants, 'Quick. Bring a clean set of clothes and dress him. Put the family ring on his finger and sandals on his feet. Then get a grain-fed heifer and roast it. We're going to feast! We're going to have a wonderful time! My son is here—given up for dead and now alive! Given up for lost and now found!' And they began to have a wonderful time" (Luke 15:11–24 The Message).

The healing process is a long journey out of denial into the truth. It was a journey of rebellion, self-discovery, and repentance for the youngest son. Unfortunately, there are no shortcuts. God continually puts us in places that cause us to come to our senses. The uncomfortable spots are not fun spots to be in. They cause us pain and cause pain to those who love us. At one time or another in life, we are both the wandering son and the loving father. May God give us grace for each other in the process.

Chapter Six

Walls and Boundaries

Emotionally, we are constructed like icebergs!

With an iceberg, it's easy to see what's on the surface, but the destructive parts are what lurk below. People are not all that different. What we see are addictions, compulsions, fears, and unhealthy styles of relating—the usual things that lead people to seek out individual counselling or a recovery group. People cannot keep a job, their marriage is in shambles, they don't like themselves, and they are beginning to see that their use of alcohol, drugs, work, or food is having negative affects on their lives. All their attempts to change their behaviour have failed.

In reality, the stuff below the surface (shame, abandonment, experiences of powerlessness or betrayal, and wounded sexuality) is what produces addictions, compulsions, and unhealthy relating styles. These issues are directly connected, and it is impossible to address one without addressing the others.

Counselling often fails because we focus on the symptoms or behaviour without looking at the roots of the problem. Other counselling methods fall short when they focus on healing the inner wounds without challenging people to let go of their sinful ways of dealing with their pain. And ultimately any Christian counselling must address the reality that we were created to enjoy fellowship not only with God but also with each other.

Those who say, "I love God," and hate their brothers or sisters, are liars; for those who do not love a brother or sister whom they have seen, cannot love God whom they have not seen (1 John 4:20).

So, How's Your Love Life?

Often, after speaking at a Christian gathering, I will be approached by an individual who says something like this: "I was sexually abused by my father as a child, but I've prayed and forgiven him and God's healed me of that [*I never really know what the "that" is*] and I'm fine now!" It all sounds wonderful: the healing power of forgiveness and God's miraculous touch on a person's life. I do not want to minimize or mock those experiences at all. I believe in the healing power of forgiveness, and I know that only God can heal a broken heart. However, inevitably, as the conversation continues I discover that the person's relational life is a wreck. The truth is that they say they love God, but their relationships—how they love their brothers and sisters—prove otherwise.

Gwen approached me after I shared at her church. She said she had been sexually abused but God had healed her. However, she was having problems with her husband. We set up an appointment later that week to talk about her situation. When we met, she began to talk about the difficulties in her marriage. Her husband, who had at first seemed to be a calm, thoughtful person, had begun to become distant. No matter what Gwen did to involve him in family life, he remained passive and disinterested. Eventually, Gwen told me that this was her second marriage; her first husband had been verbally and physically abusive, and that marriage had ended after seven years. She had struggled in her past with an alcohol addiction and eventually admitted to using food as a comfort in her current relationship. Often, purging herself with the use of laxatives or vomiting followed the binging.

She was, for all practical reasons, estranged from her family of origin. Occasionally she would talk with her mother, who lived in the same city she did, but she had contact with her father only a few times a year (and then only by telephone, as they lived on opposite ends of the country).

While she and her current husband attended church on Sunday mornings and volunteered for special projects, neither were part of a small group. Friendships (the few that Gwen had) seemed to be more functional than emotionally supportive.

As well, Gwen appeared to have a latent anger, which surfaced when I asked her to talk further about her father. At first she was detached, couching her conversation in spiritual-sounding words, but eventually the anger surfaced in pleasant but barbed words. "Well, you know what men are like."

She did love God but clearly had difficulty loving other people!

STYLES OF RELATING: WINDOWS TO OUR SOULS

At one time or another, most of us have done a test that is supposed to tell us about our personality type. These tests,

137

ranging from the formal Myers-Briggs format to more whimsical tests that describe our personality as a type of animal, can be helpful. However, most of them fail to look at the motivation behind how we relate to people.

I was having coffee with a friend one day and complained about a difficult relationship. My friend simply replied, "Why don't you let God protect your heart?" His words terrified me. It was that terror that caused me to see how much I had been trying to protect myself rather than allowing God to be my protector.

His statement scared me because of my understanding of what it meant to trust God. Somehow, I had come to the conclusion early in my Christian life that trusting God meant naively assuming that He would work things out in any relationship or situation. I had incorrectly expected God to take responsibility for areas of life where He had given me primary stewardship. Consequently, in my relationships, I generally failed to see ungodly behaviours in the other person that should have warned me that this person was not emotionally safe. Eventually, I would get hurt and then wonder why God had let that happen. I would blame God for not protecting me, when in reality He had allowed red flags to be raised that I had chosen to ignore.

What's My Responsibility?

When I look out my back window at home, it's easy to define my responsibilities, or my boundaries. A dark brown fence clearly defines my property. I must maintain everything that falls within the fence line. I don't have to concern myself with my neighbour's lawn, garden, or patio—

that's her job! Often I have a more difficult time defining personal boundaries.

A personal boundary is everything (emotionally, spiritually, and physically) for which I am responsible. To some extent we naturally develop boundaries as children; we realize that if we try to walk through a table it doesn't work! However, many times we are not taught healthy personal boundaries by our parents or other adults, simply because they did not have healthy boundaries themselves. Consequently, we struggle with relationships throughout our lives, hurting ourselves and other people because we do not know the boundaries God has laid for us.

Here's a summary of things that we, others, and God are responsible for.

My Responsibilities

I am responsible for *my own emotions.* No one can make me sad, angry, or happy. These are choices I make, albeit often unconsciously, in responding to a situation.

I am responsible for *my own healing.* When I realize I have been wounded, it is my job to seek healing. While only God can heal a wounded heart, I need to posture myself to receive that healing.

I am responsible for *my sin.* No wounds of life, no matter how traumatic, give me the right to blame someone else for my sinful responses.

I am responsible for *my own thoughts and attitudes.* I am expected to think about the world around me and, with God's guidance, to come to some conclusions. I may disagree with how someone else views the world, but it is not my responsibility to change his or her mind. I am responsible to submit my thoughts and attitudes to God and to ask Him to conform them to His mind. A note of caution here: some people erroneously think that they should never believe anything too strongly, because maybe they might be wrong! Unfortunately, these people either don't believe anything or are easily swayed to believe the most convincing voice around them. Know what, and why, you believe what you do.

I am responsible for *my own behaviour.* No one can make me do anything I don't want to do. If I find myself doing things I don't want to do, the problem may be that I don't know what I think is right or wrong. Consequently, I need to know what I believe.

Others' Responsibilities

Other people are responsible for *their own emotions, healing, sin, thoughts, attitudes, and behaviour!*

God's Responsibilities

God is responsible for providing us *a way back* to Him through Christ. The reality is that without God giving Jesus to die for our sin and rising again, we would have no power to truly change and take responsibility for our own lives. Only He can forgive us when we sin, and only He can break the power of that sin in our lives. Our will power will not do it. Our good intentions will come up short. Only God can heal our hearts.

*God is **not** responsible for either the effects of our bad choices or the effects of other people's bad choices on our lives.* For example, if I eat a constant diet of French fries, hamburgers, and chocolate and wonder why I don't have any energy, or can't think through things, or am gaining weight, all the prayers in the world will not change the effects of my bad choices on my body or mind. Likewise, if I am struggling with lustful thoughts but keep putting myself in a position of temptation, it is not God's responsibility to deliver me. Rather, it is my responsibility to get out of there!

Sometimes God will intervene in a bad situation where another's bad choices will affect us, but often that is not the case. In our present world, God does not take the blame for other people's sinful choices. He did that once, on the cross. People who sin against us have the power of the cross at their disposal to stop their sinful behaviour. God provided the way out; it is up to them to make the choice to take it. When God intervenes in these situations we rightly call them "miracles" because they are not the norm for our daily lives.

Once, someone asked me if I believed in our free will or God's predestination. I replied, "Yes"—to both. God's plan is unfolding for this world and for my life. There are things that God has ordained for me to be and do; it is my choice to be a part of it.

Often we struggle in our lives because we expect God to do things for us that are clearly not His responsibility. The "Serenity Prayer" becomes more real to me every day. It is a prayer about boundaries!

> God grant me the serenity
> to accept the things I cannot change;
> courage to change the things I can;
> and wisdom to know the difference.[20]

Evaluating Your Boundary Health

If you find yourself constantly anxious in relationships and situations, you may be struggling with a lack of boundaries, fearful of what will happen to you. Likewise, if you realize that you are controlling and overly direct with people, you are taking responsibility for things that fall inside *their* boundary lines, not yours. If you find you're mad at God, you may be blaming Him for something that was never His responsibility in the first place! And if your life feels out of control, stop blaming everyone else and start taking responsibility for the things you are responsible for. Don't be afraid; God will help you rebuild your boundary lines.

Oh, and one more thing. Yes, God is responsible for walking us through this process. He's chosen to be responsible. He is the one who nudges us in the direction of healing, because He wants us to have an abundant life. He wants us to be free. Things that may seem painful, unfair, or just unexpected are the life circumstances He allows to cause us to look deeper.

My Life as a House

Whenever we are in relationship with someone, we can do one of two things: we can offer our heart to the other person or we can withhold our heart. To put it another way, we can open the door and let the person come in, or we can close the door and bolt it tight.

Imagine that you are sitting at home enjoying a quiet evening and you hear a knock on the door. Looking through the peephole, you see it is an acquaintance from church. You open the door, say hello, and then have a choice to make. You ask yourself, *Do I invite this person into my house, or do I tell them I'm busy and send them away?*

This individual has seemed friendly and interesting enough, so you invite them in for a cup of tea. As you sit talking at the kitchen table, your new friend gets up and proceeds to walk into your living room and look around. *Okay,* you think, *the rooms are attached, so this is no big deal.* Then she proceeds up the stairs, entering each bedroom and opening closet doors. Not wanting to appear rude, you let this behaviour continue for a while, but after she rifles through your underwear drawer, you are appalled and ask her to stop—which, thankfully, she does. However, you feel the visit has gone long enough and ask her to leave—which she does.

Think of emotional relationships in the same way. Someone knocks at the door of your heart. You have the choice, after a preliminary assessment of the person's character, to let her in or not. If you choose to let her in you have another choice: how much do you allow her access to your life? Clearly, you would think it strange to have a new visitor walking into rooms where she has not been invited and peeking into places she is not allowed. Most of us would rightly end the visit. (If you thought otherwise, you need to take a hard look at your own lack of personal boundaries!)

You can ask this individual to leave your house, because you have authority over your own physical space, just like you have authority over your own emotional space. This authority is God-given; all the way from Genesis to Revelation, Scripture is clear that we are responsible for our own actions and attitudes.

At the other extreme, imagine that one of your best friends has knocked on the door. You invite him in for a cup of tea and eventually retire to the comfort of the living room to chat. This friend has been into your home often, always showing respect to you and your property. In a previous conversation, you had mentioned that you were doing renovations in one of the bedrooms. At that time your good friend, with whom you had spent many hours conversing, asked to see the renovations. You replied, "Things are still a real mess; give me a couple of weeks to put things in order." Your friend agreed, and the conversation continued.

It's now two months later, and you have still not invited your friend into the newly renovated room, even though you have invited him to your home many times. Again, on this visit, your friend's gentle curiosity and excitement about your new room is rebuffed. However, this time your friend replies, "I'm offended by your reluctance to invite me into all the rooms of your house. It's not like I'm planning on moving in; I simply would like to share that part of your life experience. Why won't you let me in?"

Your friend politely listens to your explanation about the mess of the renovated room, finishes his tea, and leaves. A week passes, and your friend has not knocked on the door. Two weeks, a month passes, and no one visits. You see your friend at church and things are pleasant enough, but you miss the intimate conversations you had enjoyed. When asked, your friend replies, "Well, it seemed like you really didn't trust me or want to get to know me any better."

Maybe you should have taken the risk of letting him see that other room.

Fig Leaves or Animal Skins

Often, because of our fear of being hurt, we choose to protect ourselves rather than to allow God to protect us.

In the beginning, there was no need to protect ourselves from the gaze of another. Adam and Eve lived a life without shame or fear of what each other might think or even what God might think of them. The first consequence of the fall was that Adam and Eve saw each other's nakedness, realized their own vulnerability, and tried to cover up with fig leaves (Genesis 3:7). Fig leaves represent our human desire to cover our shame and vulnerability through our own means. But fig leaves do not last long or provide effective coverage!

After God "found" the couple and laid out the consequences of their disobedience, the first thing He did was to provide them with garments made of animal skin (Genesis 3:21). God's method of providing protection from exposure was infinitely better than man and woman's choice.

Identifying our Fig Leaves

If we do not have healthy boundaries in relationships, we will relate to people in one of three ways:

1. We control the encounter.
2. We post a "No Entry" sign.
3. We keep them guessing.[21]

People of varying "personalities" will use one or another of these relational styles to try and protect themselves from being wounded in relationship. They may relate differently to different people. For example, they may relate differently to men than to women, or differently to peers than to those they view as authorities.

None of these styles of relating is godly, because all three are ways of sinfully protecting ourselves rather than letting God protect us.

Style of Relating #1: Controlling the Encounter, or "I hope they'll like me!"

Dr. Dan Allender refers to this style of relating as a "Good Girl" or "Nice Boy." People who use this style are masters at doing what they think needs to be done to ensure that everyone will think they are nice people and like them. They are the people who volunteer for everything, endlessly doing good works even if the good works have a negative effect on their own health or on their significant relationships. Because of their willingness to do good and be nice, they often feel others take advantage of them, when in reality they have put themselves in that situation.

Marion was a classic good girl. If a volunteer was needed for something, she was eager to participate. Busy with community and church groups, she had contact with many people but in her few quiet moments felt an internal aching emptiness. She noticed that this pain would subside the busier she became so felt that this was God's way of encouraging her to keep going with all her good work.

While she knew many people, few people really knew Marion. No one knew about her life before she moved to this city. No one knew her hopes and dreams. Even Marion had lost them somewhere in her busyness.

Especially in evangelical and charismatic Christian circles, being "good," and doing "good things" is often given such honour that it almost seems like a way of salvation. Saying "No, I can't help you with that today" is not well received, so many continue to work, work, work.

In a men's group Frank said, "You know the saying, 'Nice guys finish last'? Well, it's true, especially in my life. I try not to complain when my boss expects me to work on a day off or to put in some unpaid overtime. I mean, I'm a Christian, after all. But then, another guy in the office got a promotion ahead of me. I never saw him putting in the extra hours!"

"So Frank," I asked, "why do you keeping doing nice things if it seems like you're just getting stepped on?"

Frank thought for a minute, then sighed. "I guess I think if I say no, or say what I feel, I'll be rejected. And besides, I cannot stand conflict. If my dad would have just done what my mom asked him to, I wonder if they would have stayed together. As Christians, aren't we suppose to be nice?"

Nice men and women are constantly stepped on or taken advantage of. Sometimes it is because they fail to see the warning signs of abusive people, but other times it is simply because they insist on being underfoot!

Good works, no matter how well intentioned, are simply that—good works. Scripture makes it clear that they do not provide an "in" with God. Remember that Eve and Adam chose to eat of the tree that led to the knowledge of *good* and evil. "Good" no more leads to life than evil does. Choosing to do a good thing does not mean that you are choosing life. God evaluates our hearts on our choice to choose *Him,* not our choice to choose good.

If you live your life always doing what you think people want, hoping that they'll like you, it's time to stop. Choose *life* instead of choosing good. When we continue to offer only our hands in good deeds, we fail to give others the excellent gifts that have become buried deep in our souls. The fruit of the Spirit is *"love, joy, peace, patience, kindness, goodness, faithfulness, gentleness and self-control"* (Galatians 5:22–23 NIV). Developing these godly character traits is our most important task.

In my own journey, when I began to say no to many "good" things I could do, it became evident that my heart was not truly full of goodness or kindness. Soon I noticed that all the good things I had done for others, for the church, for God, were really so that I could feel liked and appreciated. And, by doing good works, I never had to run the risk of letting someone see my heart and reject the core of who I was.

"Am I now seeking human approval, or God's approval? Or am I trying to please people? If I were still pleasing people, I would not be a servant of Christ" (Galatians 1:10). The only way out of people-pleasing is to learn to say the word "No." Like most addictive behaviours, people-pleasing is difficult to give up unless we also heal heart wounds. Bring Jesus your fear of rejection and fear of being shamed or exposed. Ask Him to show you godly ways to protect your heart. Learn to allow others to say no to you, too.

Style of Relating #2: No Entry!

This was the sixth recovery group I had facilitated for adult survivors of sexual abuse. The six women sat in the room, unresponsive. My question hung in the air, but no one said a word. At this point, we had been together for five weeks, a time when group participants generally have learned to trust each other and open up. Somehow the Holy Spirit had directed six "Tough Girls" to be participants in this group. The "No Entry" sign was clearly posted over their hearts. Neither I nor anyone else was getting in!

Like these women, we can choose to protect ourselves by raising a thick, impenetrable wall around our hearts. Emotions are not to be trusted—no joy or laughter, no sorrow or tears, no love or tenderness. And, certainly, other people are not to be trusted.

Men and women with "No Entry" signs posted are often self-sufficient and competent at anything they do. If challenged, they will defend their actions to the end, believing in their hearts that you are wrong. It's never them!

I thought she'd be an interesting person to talk with, and she was. Rachel had travelled extensively both with her job and on her own. She had great stories to tell, and our coffee time flew by. But when we met a few weeks later I noticed that she deflected any queries about her hopes and dreams or previous disappointments in life. She was glad her marriage had ended. Though, she stated matter-of-factly, she knew that it was probably not what God would have wanted. "But," she continued, "you just have to go on with life, don't you, and try to do the best you can." It was the first and only time she came close to exposing her heart.

The women in the recovery group I mentioned earlier finally began to open their hearts, but it took weeks of patient, loving prodding, and personal vulnerability on my part, for them to get there.

Paul wrote to the Corinthians:

We have spoken freely to you, Corinthians, and opened wide our hearts to you. We are not withholding our affection from you, but you are withholding yours from us. As a fair exchange—I speak as to my children—open

149

wide your hearts also...Make room for us in your hearts
(2 Corinthians 6:11–13;7:2 NIV).

Clearly, many of the Christians in Corinth chose to post a "No Entry" sign over their hearts despite Paul's statements of the personal sacrifices he had made for them and, more importantly, the love he and his ministry group felt for them. Paul and the Corinthian Christians had been through a lot together. There were many good things, and some times of rebuke and correction. It seems that their response to the correction was to now close their hearts and distance themselves from Paul.

If you have a "No Entry" sign posted over the door to your heart, it is important that you ask God to direct you to trustworthy people with whom you can begin to be honest. In this process, again, you will need to learn godly ways of protecting your heart from shame. As you do this, you will be able to open your heart to safe people and remove the wall.

Style of Relating #3: Keep Them Guessing!

I had a good friend. We'd talk for hours, sharing our hearts—our hopes and dreams, our God-encounters, relational successes and struggles. I grew to rely on her friendship. And then, one day, she just wasn't there. She hadn't left the city or moved, but she was just gone. When I finally tracked her down and asked her if I'd done something to offend her, she replied that she had been busy. So we simply picked up where we had left off.

Then it happened again. The same pattern. We'd share at a heart level, and then after a while she was gone. After many similar episodes of a "hello–goodbye" relationship, I finally realized she was what Dr. Dan Allender calls a "Party Girl."

No, she wasn't out hitting the bars or being promiscuous or anything like that. But she had a way of drawing people—in this case, me—into a relationship and then pushing them away when things got too close.

People who use this fig leaf to protect themselves are adept at seducing others into relationship and then pulling away, or sabotaging the relationship when things become too intimate. A relationship with someone like this is always like a guessing game; you're never really sure where you stand. And it goes without saying that guys can be "Party Girls" too!

The ways of sabotaging relationships are legion. Some people simply become busy with work or activities so that they're physically unavailable. Others shut down their hearts and back away emotionally. The open, intimate, caring individual you had known has somehow changed into a detached ice maiden or ice man.

In dating relationships, "Party Girl" individuals will find themselves becoming attracted to someone else. I've seen men bounce from relationship to relationship. Any of the women they dated would have made excellent marriage partners, but somehow they always managed to find something wrong. Women do this too!

It's possible to stay in the guessing game for a time, but eventually most people tire of the sport. Often the one keeping you guessing is hurt and confused when you end the relationship. Their fig leaf—keep them guessing—has failed to provide their heart with a godly covering, and they are left wounded and determined not to let it happen again. And so the pattern continues with the next friend. Many people who use this fig leave bounce from relationship to relationship, church to church, wounded and wondering why they cannot seem to maintain relationships.

It's difficult to break this style of relating. "Party Girls" need friends who care enough about them to hold them accountable for the destructive pattern of allowing others to get close and then pushing them away. If you are one of these people, you need to do the very difficult act of keeping yourself in one place for long enough to develop long-term relationships—not just a relationship of weeks, or even months, but years. As God heals your heart and shows you better emotional boundaries, allow people to speak into your life, and hear them.

RELATIONAL HEALTH

In the last few years I have been reading my Bible with the purpose of finding out more about relationships instead of looking only for doctrinal statements. I am amazed at what I have discovered.

Did you know that Paul passed up an excellent ministry opportunity because he was concerned about his friend Titus? *"When I came to Troas to proclaim the good news of Christ, a door was opened for me in the Lord; but my mind could not rest because I did not find my brother Titus there. So I said farewell to them and went on to Macedonia"* (2 Corinthians 2:12–13).

Or, did you know that Paul's friendship with Priscilla and Aquila was so deep that they risked their lives for him? *"Greet Prisca [or Priscilla] and Aquila, who work with me in Christ Jesus, and who risked their necks for my life, to whom not only I give thanks, but also all the churches of the Gentiles"* (Romans 16:3–4).

Did you catch the depth of relationship between Paul and the runaway slave Onesimus and between Paul and the slave owner Philemon?

For this reason, though I am bold enough in Christ to command you to do your duty, yet I would rather appeal to you on the basis of love—and I, Paul, do this as an old man, and now also as a prisoner of Christ Jesus. I am appealing to you for my child, Onesimus, whose father I have become during my imprisonment. Formerly he was useless to you, but now he is indeed useful both to you and to me. I am sending him, that is, my own heart, back to you. I wanted to keep him with me, so that he might be of service to me in your place during my imprisonment for the gospel; but I preferred to do nothing without your consent, in order that your good deed might be voluntary and not something forced. Perhaps this is the reason he was separated from you for a while, so that you might have him back forever, no longer as a slave but more than a slave, a beloved brother—especially to me but how much more to you, both in the flesh and in the Lord. So if you consider me your partner, welcome him as you would welcome me. If he has wronged you in any way, or owes you anything, charge that to my account (Philemon 1:8–18).

If you did a survey of a thousand people, the vast majority of them would say that they desire better relationships. If you doubt that, look at the relationship section of any bookstore. We are desperately trying to find the way to healthy, fulfilling relationships. We want to know that there's someone in the world who truly would die for us. We desire relationships that call for sacrifice—both theirs and ours. Unfortunately, our human attempts at reaching such lofty goals always fall short. All these "self-help relationship improvement" books, tapes, and TV shows simply touch the surface of our relationship angst. They are, after all, merely fig leaves.

Paul and his friends related in such a way that they could risk loving others intensely, because they knew that God would protect their hearts. You can't lay your life on the line for someone, give up a great career move, or go against the prevailing culture if you are protecting your heart with a fig leaf.

In summary, in order to help others heal, and in order to have healthy relationships in our own lives, we must acknowledge where we are. All too often we try to cover our shame and vulnerability through our own means, like Adam and Eve did with fig leaves. God's protection of our hearts, like an animal skin, is so much better. Faulty styles of relating are like fig leaves—ineffective ways of covering our emotional scars. In order to be an effective soul surgeon, friend, parent, or spouse, we must take responsibility for our own boundary health. We cannot shove the blame on to others or on to God.

Chapter Seven

CONFESSION AND FORGIVENESS

❋ ❋ ❋

Summers for me consist of time off and a road trip through most of western Canada, visiting with family and friends. Often God uses this time to help me understand a few things. This year was no exception. Somewhere in the middle of the expanse of the prairies of Saskatchewan, the light bulb in my head lit up!

Earlier in the summer I had attended a Christian conference. I must confess that my attendance was motivated by two very unspiritual factors. The first was that my home church sponsored the conference, and the second was that I could walk to the meeting place.

I tried to come to terms with my reluctance to attend. I finally concluded that I didn't want to be part of another spiritual experience that didn't result in any long-term change. "Well," I sensed the Holy Spirit say to me, "that's a good thing! You desire to see the true power of God, and there's nothing wrong with that." So I went on to the meeting and am pleased to report that the conference was a good, genuine encounter with God.

However, my questions about what experiencing God meant in my Christian faith tradition continued to cause mild discomfort in the back of my mind for the next month. I've talked with many others who struggle, no matter what their expression of faith, to live with the tension of sincere encounters with God that only change us for a short time.

In my own Pentecostal background, those experiences included such things as speaking in tongues and participating, often skeptically, in whatever else the Holy Spirit seemed to be about. I remember on a couple of occasions falling down on the floor and wondering how I got there. I remember lying there for a long time. But when I look back, it's hard for me to see that the experience resulted in any significant change in my character or sustained healing in my damaged emotions.

People from other faith traditions recall similar memorable spiritual experiences—insights revealed during meditation, inspired worship services that united their fellowship in praise, prayer meetings that resulted in common causes, teachings that changed the direction of their vocations, experiences of service in foreign lands that opened their eyes to political realities. Yet they also admit that, in the long run, the experiences did not result in any significant change in their basic character or bring sustained healing to their damaged emotions.

That day, under the open prairie sky, bored with my tapes and unable to pick up a radio station, I asked God again to help me understand why the spiritual experiences I'd had did not change my character or heal my emotions. As I continued to ponder all this, I realized that the problem wasn't with the spiritual experiences I'd had. Rather, it was with the lack of spiritual experience in all areas of my life, specifically with the

Christian discipline of confession. As I've walked with people from all parts of the Christian community, I've come to see this as a common situation. We simply do not understand the power of confession and forgiveness both for ourselves and for those we minister to. If we wish to experience change in our basic character and find healing for our damaged emotions, we must begin with confession and forgiveness.

CONFESSION: AGREEING WITH GOD

Confession, I have come to understand, is simply agreeing with God about the true nature of my soul. It's that simple. We agree with God about sin on all levels—our attitudes, our behaviours, and our thoughts. Without the gift of confession we are forever bound and tormented, as the psalmist David writes:

> *Blessed are those whose transgressions are forgiven, whose sins are covered. Blessed are those whose sin the Lord does not count against them and in whose spirit there is no deceit.*
>
> *When I kept silent, My bones wasted away through my groaning all day long. For day and night your hand was heavy on me; My strength was sapped as in the heat of summer.*
>
> *Then I acknowledged my sin to you and did not cover up my iniquity. I said, "I will confess my transgressions to the Lord"—And you forgave the guilt of my sin* (Psalm 32:1–5 NIVI).

Unfortunately, I must have missed the Sunday school lessons on confession, because, despite the tears I had shed over my perceived shortcomings, I continued to be racked with guilt. I struggled to read my Bible and spend time with God, since I was sure that He'd find some other despicable thing to "convict" me about. When I did talk to God about the things that I felt were wrong with me, I seldom felt the relief David alludes to: God's hand still felt heavy on me.

Furthermore, I didn't really understand what the true nature of the sin was that I was supposed to confess. I cried out to God often about feeling lonely but did not understand that it was the sin in my heart that kept me from entering into relationship with others. The various ways I had chosen to protect myself made it difficult, if not impossible, for me to enter into relationships at a heart level. I could not confess my sin to God, because my understanding of sin was limited to a list of do's and don'ts. I did not understand that my ways of protecting myself—erecting barriers against relationships, perfectionism, people-pleasing, and a host of other protective mechanisms—were also sins. They separated me from God and from others.

As you proceed through this book, I hope your heart will be challenged to look differently at the sin we all struggle with. Often as leaders we can get all the externals right but miss the sin of our heart—sin that is a reaction to protect us from further wounding. This understanding is a vital key when we are helping people heal from the wounds that have imprisoned them.

CONFESSION FIRST, THEN REPENTANCE

Part of my problem was that I had missed an understanding of confession and jumped right ahead to repentance. Repentance (Greek *metanoeo*) can be defined as deciding to think differently afterwards. In other words, we realize after we have done something wrong that it wasn't the best thing to do, and we decide we should try something different next time. Confession (Greek *exomologeo*), on the other hand, simply means to acknowledge or agree fully.

As Christians, we often move to repentance without first going through the crucial stage of confession. We realize we need to do something differently; however, we do not fully agree with God that what we have done (or thought, or left undone) is sin. Put another way, we can identify the outcome of our sin, and desire to change—that is, we repent of our sin—but we fail to see the reality of our heart sin.

This may seem legalistic or petty to some, but it is not. If we try to change our behaviour without taking the power of the cross to break sin in our life, our behaviour change will be largely ineffective. Without the practice of confession we become mere behaviouralists, dealing with the external reality but never dealing with the heart of the matter—our sin. Indeed we can have an appearance of wisdom in promoting self-imposed piety, humility, and severe treatment of the body but fail to really make any lasting change in our motivation (see Colossians 2:23). Without the first step of confession, we may not truly see the depth of our hearts. Instead, we'll simply respond by changing our behaviour.

For example, I often cried to God about my failure to share the Good News of the gospel with others. I would determine to do better in the future, telling God, "I repent of my failure to tell others about You." This went on for years without any real apparent breakthrough.

Then one day a great realization came to my heart and mind. There was a reason I didn't share my faith in Christ with friends and family: I was afraid they would reject me. I then confessed this to God and asked Him to forgive me for my fear of rejection and the sinful way I chose to protect myself. Soon I noticed a change in my heart and in my behaviour. When my sin of being afraid of rejection (and therefore not trusting in God to be there for me) was brought before God, the full power of the cross came into contact with that sinful part of me and broke the hold this fear had on my life. The change didn't happen overnight, and I did need to continue to confess my fear of rejection to the Lord, but the change did happen.

Likewise, I often repented of my lack of commitment to God. But that repentance had turned my eyes away from the reality that my heart had become cold to God. I couldn't have a different level of commitment to God until I saw the true nature of my heart. I had a cold heart toward God because I didn't think He really cared for me. I had false assumptions about where God was in the bad times of my life. I asked God's forgiveness for my sin and asked Him to turn my heart of stone into a heart of flesh. As my memories were healed, and after I asked God's forgiveness for my true sin, I began to find freedom to really love God.

By jumping to repentance without a clear confession of our sin, we miss the opportunity for that area of our life to be cleansed from unrighteousness. John wrote to the early Church, "If we claim to be without sin, we deceive ourselves and the truth is not in us. If we confess our sins, he is faithful and just and will forgive us our sins and purify us from all unrighteousness" (1 John 1:8–9 NIV). For years I quoted that verse, clutching on to the reality of Christ's forgiveness. (After all, it is a vital truth to embrace!) But I had failed to understand that what the confession of my sin did was give Jesus permission to purify or cleanse that part of my heart. It is confession that opens the door for the Holy Spirit to change us at the deepest level, the level where we devise sinful protective strategies to mask our emotional wounds. Now, whenever I say this verse either to myself or in a counselling session, I emphasis the truth that as sin is confessed, the Holy Spirit takes out the heavy-duty cleaner and begins to cleanse that area of my heart.

THE FREEDOM OF CONVICTION

Our incomplete understanding of confession leads to a great confusion over the difference between conviction and condemnation. Even Christians who know and can recite Romans 8:1—*"Therefore, there is now no condemnation for those who are in Christ Jesus"*—struggle continually with condemnation.

Condemnation is really false shame that the Enemy of our souls uses to intimidate us. We feel ashamed of what we have done and also of who we are. Then, knowing that as Christians we shouldn't feel condemned, we proceed to condemn ourselves for feeling condemned! We continue running on that treadmill, certain that God cannot possibly forgive us for what we have done or not done.

Many people who struggle with condemnation are actually struggling with shame. As we will discuss later,, shame is the feeling that we are somehow defective. Shame says that we have not simply made a mistake but that we are a mistake. For those struggling with condemnation, it is important to have them answer the question "Do I feel bad about what I did or about who I am?" If they answer that they feel bad about who they are, they are struggling with shame.

(Refer to chapter 10, "Freedom from Shame," for a deeper understanding of that issue and ways to deal with it.)

Conviction, on the other hand, never leaves us with a sense of things being unfinished. When we are truly convicted by the Holy Spirit, we understand that we can confess our sin, ask forgiveness, and know that through Christ we have been forgiven of that particular sin. It is finished!

Imagine that you have just finished listening to an amazing sermon on reaching out to the lost and you realize that your heart has grown cold. It's been a long time since you spoke of Jesus' love with someone, and you know that is wrong. There are two ways to respond to that message. The first is to say "Oh God, I am such a wretch. How can I be like that? I need to change and do things differently." You leave the service feeling guilty. All week, though you have many encounters with seekers, your guilt and shame get in the way, and you keep your mouth closed.

The second response to the sermon is simply to say "Lord, I have sinned by not telling others about you. Thank you for your forgiveness and for changing my heart. Give me opportunities this week, and help me to take advantage of them." You leave the service feeling excited about what God is going to do over the next week. And you do have opportunities to share your faith with others. You are able to tell a work associate that you will pray for him and his wife, and then, right there, you have the courage to say a short prayer with him. Other opportunities come your way as well, and though you know you may not handle each situation perfectly, you keep trying to walk through the open doors God has put before you.

The first response is condemnation, the second is conviction. Which would you rather choose?

RECEIVING FORGIVENESS

A few years ago someone challenged me, saying that I was proud. Since I had gone around most of my life feeling sorry for myself, I was taken aback by his words. Of all people, I was certainly not proud! I knew how horrible I was, and I was well aware of the horrible things that had happened to me. I constantly wallowed around in self-pity, so wasn't that proof I wasn't proud?

A few days later I was hit between my haughty eyes with the truth. My self-pity was a shallow cover for a false humility that said I was so bad, and what happened to me was so bad, that God was obviously unable to change me or redeem my life. Somehow I had taken on the belief that my sins and my pain were too grievous for the power of the cross to overcome. While God could forgive others and bring healing in their lives, certainly what I had done and what I had suffered was more than He could handle.

Talk about pride! In effect, I was telling God that my sin and pain were so hopeless that even Jesus' suffering, dying, and rising from the dead were not enough for me! I had finally seen my pride. More importantly, I was able to truly understand what it meant to be forgiven. I could not truly understand forgiveness until I saw the significance of the sin—namely, pride—I had been committing. I had been a good Pharisee for most of my Christian life, but on that day things changed and I began to truly experience the joy of being forgiven.

Recently, in a leadership training session with ministry leaders, I asked them the simple question "Over the last few years, who has had to forgive you?" I think they were expecting the question "Whom have you had to forgive?"—a question which, for most of us, is much easier to answer. Suppose one of our leaders had said, "Well, I've done everything perfectly for the last year. No one needs to forgive me." Without a doubt others in the room could name a few "faux pas" worthy of forgiveness! If we cannot believe that we may have done something to wound someone over the last few years, then it's time for some serious self-examination.

OFFERING FORGIVENESS

It is impossible to forgive someone if you don't know what it is like to be forgiven! And don't take my word for it. Jesus gave a picture of this truth.

"For this reason the kingdom of heaven may be compared to a king who wished to settle accounts with his slaves. When he began the reckoning, one who owed him ten thousand talents or about [3 billion dollars][22] *was brought to him; and, as he could not pay, his lord ordered him to be sold, together with his wife and children and all his possessions, and payment to be made. So the slave fell on his knees before him, saying, 'Have patience with me, and I will pay you everything.' And out of pity for him, the lord of that slave released him and forgave him the debt. But that same slave, as he went out, came upon one of his fellow slaves who owed him a hundred denarii;*[or about 8 thousand dollars][23] *and seizing him by the throat, he said, 'Pay what you owe.' Then his fellow slave fell down and pleaded with him, "Have patience with me, and I will pay you." But he refused; then he went and threw him into prison until he would pay the debt.*

When his fellow slaves saw what had happened, they were greatly distressed, and they went and reported to their lord all that had taken place. Then his lord summoned him and said to him, 'You wicked slave! I forgave you all that debt because you pleaded with me. Should you not have had mercy on your fellow slave, as I had mercy on you?' And in anger his lord handed him over to be tortured until he would pay his entire debt. So my heavenly Father will also do to every one of you, if you do not forgive your brother or sister from your heart" (Matthew 18:23–35).

We can be well aware that we are to forgive others in the same way that God through Christ has forgiven us. However, if we have not realized how much grace God has given to us, we will not be able to extend grace to others.

God's grace is an incredible gift to us. He gives it without any expectation of performance or payback on our part. There was no way the first slave could have possibly paid back the 3 billion dollars he owed. How would a slave even have got himself in such a financial mess? His master, of course, represents God. Out of pity, compassion, mercy he graciously forgives the debt.

Early on in my healing journey, God gave me the incredible gift of a friend who was willing to listen to me and validate my story. Somehow, by the mere act of listening, he extended God's grace into my life. He knew I was deeply wounded, and still he listened to me. He knew I was extremely sinful, and he challenged me to change, all the while extending grace. Over the next few months and years, this gift of grace received gave me grace to forgive others.

I could not have truly forgiven anyone else until I came to a true understanding of my sinfulness. God's grace, extended through my friend, helped me to see the truth and receive God's grace. Remember that he did not begin by telling me how sinful I was but by listening to me, accepting me, and, by doing that, tangibly extending God's grace to me.

At one point I remember complaining to this friend about a colleague who was continually undermining my ministry and me. I had tried to talk with her about her actions, but to no avail. She pretended that she didn't know what I was talking about. My life began to revolve around trying to fix her and vindicate myself. I had talked with a counsellor, who asked a very appropriate question: "Why have you given this woman so much power over you?" It was a question I needed to look at, but these words didn't change my situation in the least.

Over coffee, my gracious friend challenged me. "You can't confront her again unless you are willing to die for her." What a stupid statement! Of course I didn't want to die for her, though in my very ungodly rage I would have been quite happy if she died, or left, or something. All that week those words continued to bounce around in my head: "Are you willing to die for her?"

I knew theologically what my friend was talking about. Forgiveness is, after all, being willing to carry the consequences of someone's sin against us. That is how God forgave us. His Son died on the cross, the consequence of our sin.

It was not easy, and the forgiveness I offered to her was not offered with any great sense of release. I knew very well that her words and actions continued to undermine my life and ministry, but I chose to forgive her. While I was able to establish some healthy boundaries, her behaviour continued to affect me negatively and there was little I could do about it.

There were times when this forgiveness had to be extended any time I saw her or thought about my situation.

I'd like to tell you that eventually things changed, but the situation didn't improve. It continued to bring sorrow and confusion in my life. But somehow I knew I had to let go and let God deal with her. This letting go is key in the process of forgiveness. It was up to God to change her; it wasn't my job.

When a wounded heart comes to us for help, the first step in the healing process is to offer them grace. This unconditional acceptance is the key to building a relationship of trust and is part of being the safe person discussed in chapter 3. In this atmosphere of grace we hear their stories, bring God's healing to their wounds, and then, only then, help them see their own sinful ways of relating.

I've been facilitating groups for adult victims of childhood sexual abuse for over ten years. In that time I have come to realize that as these women and men begin a four-month group they enter into the journey of forgiveness. When someone is deeply wounded, saying "I forgive the person who hurt me" is only the beginning. They tell their stories, they are received and validated as they are, and they are encouraged to change themselves and leave the abuser in God's hands.

THE JOURNEY OF FORGIVENESS

My dad, who was actually my stepdad, died in March 1997, at the age of eighty-six. At that point, the rest of my family were not believers, so there was a simple memorial service held around the grave. The officiating minister said a few words that no one could hear over the wind, and the crowd dispersed. I stood in front of the resting place of my father's remains. Cancer had moved through his body quickly, and it was now my time to say goodbye.

Shortly after becoming a Christian, someone had told me that I needed to forgive my dad. Anxious to do the right thing, I had repeated the words "I forgive my father" and went on with my life. Nothing much seemed to change, and I admit that I began to doubt that forgiveness really changed anything. He was still emotionally abusive and detached. I still tried hard to win his approval or attention.

What I did not understand was that those few words had simply been the starting point on the journey of forgiveness. Over the next twenty years I faced the deep wounds in my life; some, but not all, of the wounds were the result of my father's own woundedness. One by one I had forgiven him for not teaching me how to relate to men, not cherishing me as a daughter, not encouraging me, for exasperating me, verbally abusing me, emotionally neglecting me...and the list goes on.

Forgiving others, it turns out, is very much like how God forgives us. He forgave us all once, through the cross, and it is our choice to receive this forgiveness. He forgives us every time we sin after that. That is what I did with my dad. I made a choice to forgive him once—for everything, and that forgiveness was acted out in all the ways I specifically forgave him.

Dad and I never had a big talk about how he had hurt me. By the time I had forgiven him and understood what it meant to be forgiven, he was in his early eighties. It seemed more appropriate and honouring to set healthy boundaries in our present relationship than to confront him over things he wouldn't even remember.

Somewhere along this bumpy road, as I knew I was forgiven I was able to forgive my father. I finally got to the point where I could say, along with author Anne Lamott, "Who is it who said forgiveness is giving up all hope of having a different past?"[24]

So far we have looked at the foundational aspects of helping a wounded heart find healing. We have acknowledged that we live in a messed-up world, where people are hurt and wounded in a variety of ways. To find the healing that people really need, they do need the church—the Body of Christ. We offer the only hope a wounded man, woman, or child can ever have. Others may offer behaviour change, but we can offer a new heart.

Having said that, we have acknowledged the painful reality that much of the Body of Christ is unable to help people in this heart surgery, because it lacks understanding of the healing process. Its members are sometimes wounded themselves and need to experience healing before they can offer it to others.

We also now understand the need to have a sound theological understanding of the reality of evil, and of God's place in the world. As well, we need to be able to hear people's stories without judgment, offering grace as we help them walk through the process of confession and forgiveness.

In the following chapters we will look more closely at the root wounds we all experience by being part of the human race.

THE MESSY CROSS

In the process of walking with others, you will surely get a little messed up yourself. I trust that through reading this book you have discovered the strange mix of pain and pleasure in realizing that the Creator of the universe loves you enough to tip over your jar and create a big mess.

Last night at our worship service we shared communion. In our tradition we use nicely arranged one-shot cups of grape juice and a piece of bread or cracker. It's all very organized and put together.

Every time I participate or officiate at a communion service I am reminded of how different our tidy ceremony is from the real thing. Jesus' crucifixion was a mess. He was bruised, beaten, and bloody. Mixed in with the physical mess were the jeers and wailings of the onlookers. It was not a pretty sight. I've often thought that we would remember Jesus death better if we simply dumped the grape juice over our heads! The mess would make our remembrance more realistic.

As I've walked my own healing path, and as I journey with others, I've realized that it is only in the mess of life that we truly see the redeeming power of Jesus. May you experience that grace in your own life and walk alongside others as they experience it, too.

Chapter Eight

FAMILY FOUNDATIONS

❋　❋　❋

Remember the jar of stones analogy from chapter 3? If you don't put the foundation stones in first, you won't get them in when the jar is full of other stuff! Once again, the large stones are the foundations that must be laid early in our lives. Much of what we do in pastoral care and counselling is restoring those foundation stones.

When I landed in my current home church, I was in the middle of an intense healing process in my own life. One of the key issues God was helping me face was how my relationship with my dad had affected my relationships—or lack thereof—with men. I had had a couple of dating relationships in my twenties that ended painfully despite my unhealthy attempts to do everything I could to keep these men around.

I seemed to be able to have relatively healthy female friendships, but overall I had never been able to develop any healthy male relationships. I had numerous work-centred male relationships. With men, it seemed that as long as I could keep the relationship in a box—work—things were okay. Outside of the box of "function-oriented relationship," I was lost.

My dad was an emotionally distant man. We never talked about anything outside of the weather. He never showed physical affection, not to me or to my mother. They never kissed, held hands, or hugged in front of us kids. Mom and Dad never fought in front of us, but I remember painfully long periods of stony silence when it was obvious Dad was upset about something.

As a result, I was missing a vital foundation stone in my life—relating to men. I clearly remember the intense grief I experienced when I began to understand that the struggles in my own life were connected to an unemotional, noncommunicative relationship with Dad. My counsellor encouraged me to try to build relationships with men that were not task-oriented. He might as well have told me to teach myself how to speak Chinese. I lacked the basic male-female relational skills to even know where to start.

My home church was a new church plant. I was on the advisory council. I liked our pastor. He was not much older than I was, happily married with four kids. And he seemed to be relatively emotionally healthy. We'd connect to discuss ministry related stuff often. He and his wife would invite me to their home.

Then, horror of horrors! One day he starting talking with me about stuff you'd talk about with a friend! I remember the terror that came over me. Anxiety rose up inside of me. What do I say now? What do I do? Is it time to leave the church?

He was surprised to learn how overwhelming his overture of friendship had been to me. But he persisted, and through friendship with him and his wife, God helped me to gather some foundation stones for male-female relationships.

God has given us families and other adult caregivers to lay these types of foundations. If they are not put into place, we grow into adulthood missing some key foundational principles for our lives. These principles are to be primarily planted through what psychologists call our "family of origin."

FAMILY OF ORIGIN CHART (BOB SMITH)

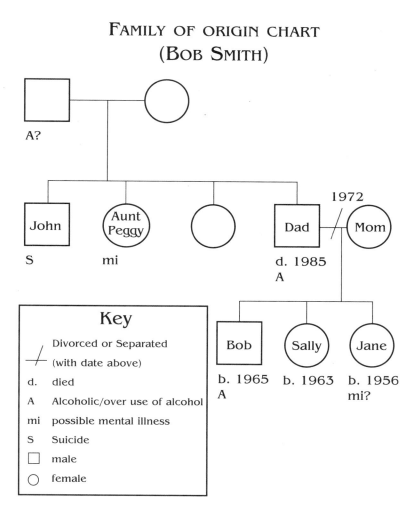

There is ongoing discussion about what has a stronger effect on our character and personality. Is it how we are nurtured that determines what kind of person we become? Or is our character simply determined by our genetic encoding? (That is, do genetics determine everything; no matter how we are raised, will we become what we were genetically programmed to be?) This debate is often called "nature versus nurture" in the psychological world.

The truth appears to be somewhere in the middle. Any parent will tell you that each of their children had a distinct personality from the time he or she came into the world. However, it is also clear that events which happen to us can, in many cases, affect the person we become. For example, upon reflection, parents of sexual abuse victims will recall that there was a distinct change in their child's behaviour when the abuse began. A child who was once outgoing and interested in everyone became withdrawn and seemed to be fearful around certain individuals. Both nature (our genetic code) and nurture (what happens to us) have a hand in our development.

We are, of course, genetically children of God whether we have acknowledged it or not. The truth is that we are all created in the image of God (Genesis 1:27). We are a reflection of the character of God, but we are also marred by the fall. Still, if we look long enough into the reflection in the cracked mirror, we can see something of our Father's face. Isaiah affirms this with these words: *"Yet, O Lord, you are our Father; we are the clay, and you are our potter; we are all the work of your hand"* (Isaiah 64:8) Our heavenly Father wants to restore us to be who He created us to be, not merely what genetics or experience would dictate. While we must acknowledge how our family and life experiences have shaped us, we must also be aware that the potter wants to remake us, removing the cracks and flaws and replacing them with His character.

HOW DO WE LOOK AT SOMEONE'S FAMILY OF ORIGIN?

First, we need to define the members of a person's family of origin. Try this with your own family. Make a list of all the people who had a significant input into your early childhood and childhood development.

Our family of origin consists of birth parents (even if you did not have any contact with them), siblings, adoptive and foster parents, and any other primary caregivers you may have had at an early age. For example, if you were born to a single mother who left you with your grandparents five days a week while she went to work, your grandparents could be considered a part of your family of origin. However, if you lived five hundred miles away from your grandparents and only saw them twice a year, they may not have had as significant an impact on your early childhood development. (But remember, your grandparents had a significant impact on your parents!)

If you were adopted or spent a significant amount of time in foster care, you should consider these parents as part of your family of origin as well. You should also include any step siblings or foster siblings as part of your family of origin.

Once you have made this list, draw a chart similar to the one following entitled "Family of Origin." In pastoral counselling, this is a helpful tool for recognizing family patterns. In addition to placing boxes for males and circles for females, record other information on this chart such as addictive patterns (alcoholism), illnesses, or other items of interest. This chart can be a useful reference point when we begin listening to people's stories and helping them to deal with their emotional wounds. A picture can sometimes show patterns that would take more than a thousand words to describe.

SOME KEY AREAS OF CHILDHOOD DEVELOPMENT-BONDING

Now let us look at a few key areas in childhood development to be considered when looking at our family foundations. The idea of being rooted, planted, or solidly founded can be found in Paul's writing to the Christians in Ephesus.

> *For this reason I kneel before the Father, from whom his whole family in heaven and on earth derives its name. I pray that out of his glorious riches he may strengthen you with power through his Spirit in your inner being, so that Christ may dwell in your hearts through faith. And I pray that you, being rooted and established in love, may have power, together with all the saints, to grasp how wide and long and high and deep is the love of Christ, and to know this love that surpasses knowledge—that you may be filled to the measure of all the fullness of God* (Ephesians 3:14–19 NIV).

Many people are now aware that the early years of a child's life are crucial. Child development experts have identified many stages children go through in their emotional growth and development. If you need more information on the developmental stages of a child's life, refer to the book list in "Suggested Reading" for more resources. It's good to understand the importance of these stages.

However, nothing is more significant than the need to be *"rooted and established in love."* Even in Paul's prayer for the Christians in Ephesus, being established in love was a prerequisite for exercising power, being able to interact with others (i.e., *"together with all the saints"*), and grasping the magnificence of God's love.

In the book *The Mum Factor,* authors Henry Cloud and John Townsend share a helpful analogy to explain what happens when critical points in child emotional development are missed.

> We are talking here about the development of a child's relational equipment. We can relate this process to the manufacturing of a car. The car will only run in 1996 if all the cylinders were installed in the engine in 1960. It does not matter that the car was built so long ago. What matters is whether or not all the parts were installed. This is how early development affects later life: It leaves us with or without ability.[25]

The first emotional stage in our life is bonding with our parents as babies. When you think about it, God has so created babies that everything they do draws a parent to them. When babies cry, we rock them, cuddle them, try to find out what's wrong. All these activities help the bonding process by helping babies learn that they are safe and, in fact welcome in the world. A baby must first bond with a parent (often the mother, but this can be the father or other primary caregiver) in order to be able, later in life, to bond with the world.

This consistent, constant care from a parent builds within a child a sense of stability and security. All of these interactions are designed to let the child know that the mother is always there, and always will be. Over time, the child gains a sense of safety and security. "Whenever I cry, Mom responds," the child unconsciously reasons, "so I know that even if it's taking a little longer this time, Mom will still be there."

I have worked with many adults who have missed this bonding and development of security. As adults they live in a constant turmoil because they cannot remember, from one time to another, that God really does love them and will respond to their cry.

Shauna (mentioned in chapter 3) struggled to remember from one moment to the next that God loved her and provided for her. In our first meetings it was a constant source of frustration for me. I thought she was just choosing not to remember or had memory problems. As I learned more about personality development, I realized that Shauna had never developed something that is often referred to as "object constancy."

Shauna's parents were abusive and neglecting. In addition to the abuse Shauna suffered, she did not have a mother who responded to her cries. As a young baby she did not experientially learn that if she cries someone will respond. As an adult, and now a follower of Christ, she did not know either experientially or intellectually that caregivers respond to a baby's cry. This translated into her Christian life. She had no place in her soul to hold on to God's consistent care. If I talked with her about this, her internal experience was similar to my struggle to build male friendships—I might as well have been asking her to learn Chinese. She neither understood what I was saying nor knew where to begin in the healing process.

Here's a visual of this childhood development process. Imagine that you rolled a ball behind your couch. You would know that the ball is still there even though you can't see it; a baby wouldn't understand that the ball was still there. If its not visible its gone. On an emotional level, an adult who has not bonded and has not developed a sense of security will panic, thinking their friend or God has disappeared, never to return. Child development experts call this developing "emotional object constancy."

This lack of emotional object constancy is more common that you might think. Imagine a baby under the care of a mom with postpartum depression, or any other illness. Mom, at home while Dad works, may not be abusive but may not have the emotional strength or physical ability to respond to her baby's needs.

To help develop emotional object constancy with God, I often encourage people involved in our ministry to keep a "Book of Remembrance," a place where they can record all the times God "came through" for them. The reason is simple. People who have not developed the security or stability of knowing that their mom would respond to their cries do not have the internal emotional mechanism to know that their heavenly Father will respond to their cries. God is like the ball that rolls behind the couch and ceases to exist. When He doesn't seem to be there, in their minds He really isn't. It's not that these individuals are forgetful, or unthankful, or can't trust God; it is simply that the life skill needed to hold on to the reality of God's constant care was not developed in their lives. Having them keep a Book of Remembrance and gently reminding them of all the times God has been there for them are tools that we can use to help them develop the gift of emotional object constancy.

A Book of Remembrance is, in its simplest form, a notebook where an individual records all of the times God has been there for them. In their own words they record what the struggle was and how God worked things out. This might be something for the counsellor to do with them at the end of counselling session, as by the time they leave the office they might have forgotten.

For example, in Shauna's case developing healthy new friendships and a social life to help fill her intense loneliness was a frequent prayer request. When God started to bring these people into her life, she had to be constantly reminded how things had been in the past and how they now were. Then she was able to record how God had blessed her with new friendships.

Developing Identity

Infants also need to develop a sense of who they are. This happens in two ways. First, they have experiences that let them know they are different from their mother. Next, they have experiences that let them know who they are. You cannot have the second without the first. The uncooperative "no" of early childhood is essential to this development. Allowing them to have their "no" experience teaches them that they are different from the person who has always said "yes" or "no" for them. When they say no, and live with the consequences, they will learn whether or not they like the choice they made.

In many respects children go through this stage again in their teenage years. Often what is viewed as rebellion is simply trying to find out who they were created to be.

We cannot talk about the importance of family of origin without also mentioning the impact of abuse and neglect.

What Is Abuse?

There are two main ways children are wounded in their family of origin. One is overt abuse: a child is beaten and bruised by a parent or told to go without food for a day as punishment for his misbehaviour. The other form of abuse is covert, or undercover—not as outwardly noticeable as the first. An example of covert abuse is a parent who leaves a child unattended for a long period of time at an early age. The parent may have had to run an errand or attend a job interview and could not find a babysitter. However, their absence from their child may have left the child with feelings of abandonment and may have also endangered his or her life.

These acts, whether overt or covert, are abusive because they are a misuse of authority that has been delegated by God. All authority is to be used to build up, rather than tear down (2 Corinthians 13:10). While the acts of discipline mentioned above as "overt abuse" may be intended for the child's benefit, the effect is to wound the child's soul. Discipline is key to helping a child grow, but it is never to be so harsh as to promote anger or exasperate the child (Ephesians 6:4; Colossians 3:21).

There are certain things that parents are to provide for their children. These are:

1. Food
2. Clothing
3. Shelter
4. Medical and dental care
5. Physical nurturing

6. Emotional nurturing

7. Spiritual direction

8. Financial guidance

9. Sexual guidance

10. Access to education and life skills

When any of these is not provided—whether intentionally or unintentionally—the child will be wounded. If they are withheld knowingly, that is abuse. If they are withheld unintentionally, that is neglect.

Meredith grew up in a home where food was always on the table; she had good clothes, access to schooling, and medical and dental care. But she never received nor saw any warmth or affection expressed in her household. As a result, she grew up needy for love and affirmation. Somewhat overprotected by her parents, she did not have the emotional life skills to discern safe people from unsafe people. Desperate for affection, she started dating any man who showed any interest in her. Despite her Christian upbringing and her own Christian morals, she could not resist the strong physical attraction that seemed to fill the love gap in her heart so began having sex with her boyfriend. Feeling guilty about her behaviour, she chose not to use any form of birth control, thinking that she should be strong enough to resist the temptation next time. But she was not, and she soon became pregnant. While Meredith and her boyfriend eventually married, her married life has been riddled with overwhelming feelings of guilt and self-contempt.

She had a hard time seeing how her upbringing had set her up for the choice she made. Although she had not

experienced any overt abuse in her home, the lack of physical affection and the overprotection on the part of her
mother still affected her. While she has received forgiveness
for her choices, she has also been able to acknowledge her
need for true love and extend that to herself. She is now
actively seeking God's healing in this area of her life by,
very simply, allowing others to love her and learning to
receive that love.

In looking at family of origin issues, there are two things
to consider. First, what abuse or neglect has the person
experienced? Second, what was her response to that abuse
or neglect? As discussed in a previous chapter describing
the process of healing, our wounds from abuse or neglect
need to be healed, and we each need to hold ourselves
responsible for the way we have reacted sinfully to the
wounding experience.

Authors Henry Cloud and John Townsend say this well.

Sometimes people in recovery and psychological
movements encourage "parent bashing"; every negative thing is the fault of one or both parents. Mothers
do fail in being all that they need to be. Some fail in
being almost anything that they needed to be. Still
others do a pretty good job and just leave a few things
undone or in need of fixing. But children have defen-
sive and inappropriate responses as well, and as adults
they often continue in inappropriate patterns.[26]

Our goal in looking at our family of origin is not to
blame our parents for their lack. Rather, it is to help us see
what might have caused us to relate to others and God in
unhealthy and sinful ways. Our response in the present,

which is no doubt a self-protective way of responding to a
past wound, is what ultimately needs to change. If we identify the past wound but do not change our response to it, we
are not free. Freedom comes as God heals the wounds and
as we, with His help, change our sinful reactive patterns.

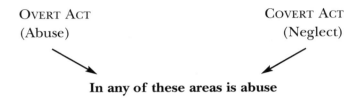

OVERT ACT   COVERT ACT
(Abuse)   (Neglect)

In any of these areas is abuse

Food	*Clothing*
Shelter	*Medical/Dental Care*
Physical Nurturing	*Emotional Nurturing*
Financial Guidance	*Spiritual Direction*
Sexual Guidance	*Access to Education*

All abuse is an intentional or unintentional misuse of
divinely delegated authority in relationship.

A WORD TO ALL PARENTS

The danger in looking at family-of-origin issues is that,
eventually, all parents realize that they are far from perfect.
Welcome to the human race! I heard someone say that we
all come from dysfunctional families, but the family name
is not Smith, or Lee, or Kowalski, or Blackbear, or Shea.
The family name is Adam. We are part of a fallen family of
sinners, and there is no way around it.

The good news is that whatever our shortcomings may be,
we have a perfect parent who offers forgiveness. If, in reading

this chapter, you realize an area where you have failed as a parent, give that failure to Jesus and ask His forgiveness.

You may need to ask your child's forgiveness as well. I have seen amazing healing in families when parents have been able to own their failures, humble themselves enough to ask forgiveness from those they have wounded, and do what they need to do to change.

If you are a parent who is still parenting children or teenagers, there is another step you can take. You can equip yourself for the task by reading and learning all you can about your job. Ask God for wisdom, and take advantage of all the help you can get. Remember, we tend to parent the way we were parented ourselves, copying the mistakes we grew up with. Unless we add to our life skills, we tend to simply pass on what we learned growing up.

HOW DO WE RE-PARENT PEOPLE?

All of the chapters in this part of the book deal with deep developmental issues that can be either Father or Mother wounds. Father wounds are wounds that resulted to our soul and spirit as a result of abuse or neglect from our father. Mother wounds are wounds to our soul or spirit as a result of abuse or neglect from our mother. They require God's healing touch, and they require the healing relationship of an earthly mother or father.

A few years ago, I realized that a ministry that had started as a recovery group had become a place where people came to be re-parented. Most of the time we do not talk about "re-parenting," or even Father or Mother wounds, but what we do is come alongside people and walk with them through the rebuilding process. We take the place of their fathers or mothers by becoming emotional and spiritual parents to them.

As an example, let's go back to the jar analogy. When the Holy Spirit tips over someone's life in order to rebuild the foundations, it is a messy, confusing and often frightening time. If he does not have someone to walk with him through this time, one of two things will happen. He will either leave the mess and continue on in a life that is shattered and confused, or he will try to put the foundation stones back himself. If he tries to rebuild the foundation on his own, he will simply put the stones back the way they were, because no one has shown him a better way.

Our role is to walk with people as they discover a better way spiritually and emotionally. To do that effectively, we need to develop core heart characteristics, some of which we have already discussed.

1. Confidentiality and respect

2. Safety

3. Consistency: this includes setting healthy boundaries

4. A spirit of teamwork: don't expect that you can do this on your own

The foundations of my life have been rebuilt as I worked with a team that included the Holy Spirit, my pastor, my counsellor, and other friends. We must be there for others when God tips over the jar and, like a loving parent, help them in the process of cleaning up the mess.

Part Three

UNDERSTANDING WOUNDS

✳ ✳ ✳

O ver the years I have seen that while the situations in which people are wounded may vary, the heart wounds have certain similarities.

In the early days of my ministry I facilitated groups for women who had been sexually abused as children. These victims exhibited the same core wounds: a deep sense of personal shame, feeling abandoned by those who were supposed to protect them, and confusion about their sexuality and identity. Their accounts of childhood sexual abuse were always different, but the wounds these victims experienced and the path to healing they walked was always similar.

When I began meeting to counsel with people from seemingly "normal" households, I was surprised to find that they had experienced similar areas of wounding. Time after time I have seen that, no matter what the instrument of wounding was, the resulting wound is the same. As you search these chapters for help for others, you will no doubt recognize similar experiences of wounding in yourself and in people you know.

For example, many have experienced shame through bullying at school or through living in a shame-based family. We may experience abandonment when a parent leaves or is unable to emotionally bond with a child. Rejection comes in a variety of forms, whether it's being picked last for the school baseball team or being told that a B-plus is just not good enough. In our childhood and adolescence, we begin to realize that we are powerless over many aspects of life. What do we do with that revelation? People break our trust in small and big ways on a daily basis. And, as if those wounds weren't enough already, we live in a world that is constantly giving us ungodly messages about our sexuality and what it means to be male or female.

As you will see in part 3, "Understanding Wounds," the following emotional wounds are common to the human race:

1. Shame: I'm a mistake.

2. Abandonment and rejection: People always leave.

3. Powerlessness: No matter what I do, nothing changes.

4. Betrayal: No one can be trusted.

5. Sexuality and identity: Who am I?

The process for treatment begins with stepping out of the darkness of denial. Let's use a medical analogy that may seem somewhat absurd. Imagine that you are in an accident and break your leg. But you have places to go and people to see, so you say to yourself, "It's not that bad. I can manage." Off you go with a broken leg. You can tough out the pain with the help of some strong painkillers. After a few months, your broken bone has mended itself—true, it's somewhat crooked and you can't really walk properly, but the pain is gone!

We do this all the time with emotional wounds. Rather than identify the problem, we pretend we can continue on unaffected. But we can't. The pain relievers we all use are the coping mechanisms we have been taught. These are only bandages; they do not heal the wound.

Once an individual has come out of denial, the wound can be identified and the healing process can begin. As discussed in previous chapters, safety and relationship are key parts of this process.

All emotional healing takes time, but it is not true that time heals all wounds. Left unattended, emotional wounds, like physical ones, become further contaminated. Be patient with those under your care. Emotional healing takes time. As the apostle Paul was with those under his care, we, too, should be *"gentle among [them], like a mother caring for her...children"* (1 Thessalonians 2:7 NIV).

A final word: you need to be aware of two important issues if you are to be a competent soul surgeon.

Mental illnesses such as clinical depression or anxiety and schizophrenia are not uncommon in society. Worldwide, over 120 million people suffer from depression.[27] It is important to consider that some of the spiritual and emotional struggles a person is facing may be compounded by an untreated mental illness.

Mental illnesses are medical conditions. They are biological dysfunctions in our bodies. Unfortunately, while most of us do not have a problem wearing glasses to correct the physical problems of far- or nearsightedness, we often balk at medication for mental illness.

Proper treatment of mental illness can be a determining factor in a person's spiritual and emotional well-being. Checklists, such as those from *Emotionally Free,* by Dr.

Grant Mullen, help determine if someone is struggling with a mental illness. These symptom checklists are reproduced with permission at the back of this book. Please use them, and do not hesitate to refer someone for medical attention if necessary.

It is equally important to acknowledge that some medical conditions—thyroid imbalance, anemia, and others—can present symptoms that look like depression. Before I meet with someone for individual counselling, and even as part of our intake process for groups, we recommend a physical checkup.

The next issue to consider, in conjunction with emotional woundedness, is the reality of living in a spiritual world. We don't simply wrestle with flesh and blood (Ephesians 6:12). Demonic activity can be involved and often is involved when people have been severely wounded. Dr. Neil T. Anderson's material, among others, is a good starting place to address demonization. Make yourself familiar with it, and search out people who have specialized training in deliverance if you are uncomfortable or unskilled in this area.

Chapter Nine

Overcoming the Fear of Abandonment and Rejection

In the motion picture *Cast Away,* Tom Hanks plays a man who becomes stranded on a deserted tropical island after a plane crash. Before leaving on the ill-fated business trip, he had finally proposed to the woman he loved. He had a life full of loving friends and family.

Then his life changed. Washed ashore on the uninhabited island, he lived for years without human contact. He was utterly alone, abandoned, forsaken. *Cast away:* the term connotes absolute desolation and rejection.

To be emotionally abandoned as a child is to be "cast away." As Tom Hanks's character struggled to stay alive by his own devices, so do children who have been physically or, more commonly, emotionally abandoned strive to live using their own resources. Like the *Cast Away* character discovered, sometimes life hardly seems worth living when you are abandoned. Hanks was able to survive the years of abandonment because of the skills he had developed earlier in his life. His logic helped him figure out how to survive and ultimately how to escape his island prison. But young children usually haven't had the opportunity to develop those skills.

From time to time the media reports stories about babies found dead in garbage dumpsters. We are rightly appalled at the disregard for life shown by the baby's parents. What goes unnoticed by most of us are the untold thousands of children who are cast away emotionally every day. Just as much as babies in dumpsters are, these little ones have been abandoned; they are left to somehow survive emotionally and spiritually by depending on their own limited skills.

Children are emotionally abandoned in a variety of ways every day. Perhaps the adults in their lives are too concerned about their own survival to pay attention. Perhaps their parents don't give them the support they need when a crisis occurs. Perhaps the adults responsible for their safety turn a blind eye to obvious instances of abuse. Perhaps a parent leaves the family picture, sometimes by choice, sometimes through death. These and more are acts of abandonment that leave deep scars in a child's soul. Without healing, people carry this childhood fear of abandonment into adulthood. Though things may appear fine on the outside, internally they constantly feel cast away.

Gary was the oldest child. His father, looking for new job opportunities, had moved their family to a rural community. For the first winter the family lived in a tent, hardly sufficient protection from a harsh prairie winter. While we might have expected this of homesteaders in the late 1800s, this was the 1950s.

The relocation became one long string of frustrations as his father drank away any income he earned in the logging camp. Gary's father was seldom around, and his mother had to keep the household running, so she had little time for anyone. All six children were left to fend for themselves. While they had some physical protection from the elements and food on the table, emotionally they were abandoned and left on their own.

As a result Gary always felt that the world was a very tentative place: it seemed to him that you never knew what was going to happen next. He believed life worked against you and you never knew if your needs would be met. So even as a young child he began to take care of himself. As he grew physically into a young man, he worked hard at school to prove that he was more than his father. Anything less than perfection was not enough. As an adult, his perfectionism led to a successful career and a marriage that looked good on the outside but was emotionally dead.

Gary, like all children of alcoholic families, experienced abandonment, since one or both parents were unable to provide the consistent emotional and physical nurture that God intends children to have.

A young woman came to talk with me one day about the anguish she was feeling over the change in a friendship. Her friend, who had been a good neighbour for almost a decade, was moving to another part of the city to benefit her career. The young woman was afraid that the change in career for the other woman would spell the end of a friendship that was important to her.

The woman who brought her problem to me was competent, successful, and had many other good friendships. When she told me her story I learned that, when she was eighteen, her father and mother had separated after a year-long affair on the part of the father. From time to time both of her parents had drunk alcohol excessively, but she didn't consider them alcoholics. She had met with

Christian counsellors and prayer ministry teams over her fifteen years as a Christian and received healing for many areas in her life. She had dealt with instances of rejection in the past. She had forgiven, and walked out this forgiveness, with both of her parents. Still, she struggled with deep soul loneliness. She hated to be by herself and did everything she could to ensure that she was either always busy or always had people around her. Now she was confused about these new feelings.

As we prayed and I began to explain to her what abandonment is, the Holy Spirit began to bring healing to her wounded heart. The counselling and prayer restored her at a deeper level.

Abandonment happens when a parent emotionally deserts a child. It is the role of godly parents to establish their children in a place of loving security. When children are emotionally abandoned, their hearts become filled with self-doubt, rejection, insecurity, and fear.

What Abandonment Looks Like

Over the last few years I have taken great pleasure in planting and developing a garden in my backyard. When I moved into my house, the backyard was a barren landscape of lawn and a sidewalk. So I began planting. While cultivating garden plants has been relatively easy, nurturing sapling trees is a completely different venture, and so far not a successful one.

When I purchased a young tree, I received instructions from the tree nursery on its care. Besides the obvious need for water and soil came instructions to stake the tree. I was told that no matter how straight the tree looked, it needed to be staked in order to grow properly. I was even instructed on what materials should be used.

I had seen trees that had been improperly staked or staked with the wrong materials. If improperly staked or if the supports are removed too early in the tree's life, there is a possibility that the tree's trunk will become crooked and in the long run may not support the tree adequately. Or, if the tree is staked with incorrect materials and the staking is not adjusted with the tree's growth, the materials—such as wire—will cut into the tree, damaging the ability of the tree to grow properly.

This is an illustration of how abandonment can affect us. God's intent for young children is that they be supported by the love, godly discipline, and encouragement of parents and other adults. If this support is not provided, there is a good chance that they will not grow properly.

Likewise, if the wrong materials are used to give support to our developing souls, we may become damaged and not reach our full potential as adults. Abandonment occurs when the supports, or stakes around the tree, are removed and we are left to fend for ourselves. Abandonment also occurs when we are not supported with the right materials. For example, when excessive or inconsistent discipline is used with a child, that child is in effect abandoned because he has not been supported correctly.

For people to become all that God has intended them to be, they need to be properly supported and nurtured as children. Parents must be present and provide healthy emotional, spiritual, and physical support to a child. If they neglect this God-given responsibility, the child will suffer whether or not the neglect is intentional.

Sometimes I explain the effects of this loss by using a

large jar. I've used this illustration in the first chapters of this book, but it bears repeating. First I fill the jar with large stones and ask the group, "Is the jar full?" Most people quickly understand that it is not. So, I continue by filling the jar with sand, gravel, and water. By the time the jar is full of water, it is truly full. The air pockets between the large rocks have been filled with gravel and sand; the air pockets in the gravel and sand have been filled with water.

I explain that if we didn't put the large rocks in at the beginning it would be a mess to do it now. The big rocks are the foundation stones of our lives, and one of the most important of these foundation stones is that we are rooted and grounded in love (see Ephesians 3:17). If this essential foundation is missing, the only way to insert that foundation stone is to tip over the jar, empty it of its contents, make a big mess, and start all over again.

This is why the process of rebuilding our souls takes time and is a messy business. Our loving heavenly Father, in His mercy, comes along and tips over our jars so that He can put in the foundation stones that have been missing.

It is important to understand that it is truly only our heavenly Father who can restructure our souls. He is the only one who can put in the foundation stones missing from our youth. The most important foundation stone in this process is, of course, a living relationship with Jesus Christ (2 Peter 2:4–6). Time and time again I have watched as people who are not yet followers of Jesus struggle to come to any degree of emotional wholeness. Once they come to a place of submitting their lives to the Lordship of Jesus, the process becomes quicker and, while not painless, certainly has a hope that was not evident in their pre-Christian lives.

WAYS IN WHICH CHILDREN ARE ABANDONED

Parents abandon children in a variety of ways. This list is by no means exhaustive but provides some understanding of the scope of emotional abandonment experienced by children. Please keep in mind that helping people receive healing for abandonment issues is not a cut-and-dried issue. Everyone's story is unique.

Types of Abandonment

1. **Physical Abandonment**
   - Parent dying
   - Parents divorcing or separating
   - Parents never marrying

2. **Addictions**
   - Drugs
   - Alcohol
   - Gambling
   - Work

3. **Abuse**
   - Physical
   - Sexual
   - Emotional
   - Spiritual

4. **Emotionally Detached Parent**

ABANDONMENT VERSUS REJECTION

Often people confuse the issue of rejection with the more foundational issue of abandonment. For clarification, let's go back to our illustration of the young tree. Abandonment is having the necessary supporting structures removed; rejection is having someone come along and cut into the outer bark with a knife. While the cut may affect the healthy development of the tree, it will not affect it in the same way as the absence of support structures will. A deep cut in the bark may allow insects and disease to enter, but most trees, even young saplings, seem to be able to ward off these attacks. The cut in the bark may continue to be apparent as the tree grows; however, the overall structure and integrity of the tree is not affected. On the other hand, removing the support structures from the young tree will cause the tree to grow up physically deformed, perhaps leaning to one side or overall crooked.

Rejection issues can usually be traced back to a specific incident. Abandonment issues are more systemic. In other words, abandonment has to do with the family system and the overall way the child was related to or not related to, cared for or not cared for by the parents.

For example, a rejection issue may centre on a child's academic ability. In grade 5, the child has returned home from school with a failing report card. A drunken father tells the child he is stupid, and then his attention wanders back to the football game and his beer. This is a rejection wound to the child. The enemy of our souls is very adept at irritating these wounds, making them fester, contaminating our souls and our relationships with God and others. As this boy becomes a young man and grows into adulthood, he continues to believe the lie that he is stupid. The reality is that he has slightly above average IQ and, given a little encouragement, he could have excelled in school. The rejection issue is that he feels he is stupid and inferior to most of his peers. His self-worth is based upon, and proved by, the marks on his grade 5 report card.

Abandonment issues look different from the above scenario. When this boy was in grade 2, his dad was demoted at his job. Because his father did not have skills to deal with the emotional trauma of this event, he turned to the only thing he knew that seemed to ease the desperate pain in his soul—alcohol. His father was not emotionally available for his son because he was an alcoholic and was not capable of dealing with his own disappointments in life.

The rejection the boy experienced over his report card was only one incident in the more pervasive pattern of emotional abandonment that left him without support, love, or encouragement.

HOW ABANDONMENT AFFECTS US AS ADULTS

Abandonment is something that we all experience. In the Garden of Eden, Adam and Eve were created to have a completely vulnerable, supportive, and ever-present relationship with God. As a result of their sin, that relationship with Father God was broken. That broken bond is now reconciled only through the death and resurrection of His Son, Jesus.

The intimate relationship Adam and Eve enjoyed was destroyed, too. We experience the violent echoes of this break in all of our interpersonal relationships. In essence, Adam and Eve abandoned each other when they chose to follow their own desires rather than obey God. They both willingly chose the knowledge of good and evil rather than life. In all the scenarios in this chapter a parent chooses what he or she feels is good, rather than choosing life. As a result they abandon their God-given authority to protect and nurture their children. Now the children are faced with trying to find their own way through life. Ultimately, this is the tragedy of abandonment. Children are forced to make adult decisions and take on adult responsibilities for which they have neither the emotional nor the intellectual abilities.

As children, none of us is able to cope with the horror of abandonment. When a child is abandoned in any form by a parent, it is a taste of the self-imposed abandonment Adam and Eve experienced. As children we are simply not able to cope with the pain. We have not learned healthy, godly life skills needed to bring our sinful natures under submission. Consequently, we make bad choices that put us in bondage, sometimes for decades. While our parents are responsible for the initial abandonment, as adults we are responsible for addressing how we have coped with the experience of abandonment. These coping mechanisms are sinful—they separate us from a healthy relationship with God and with each other.

A common experience for me as a child was to be taunted by other children. I was extremely overweight. While I had friends in my homeroom class, outside of the schoolroom (particularly when walking home from school) I daily faced ridicule and taunting.

One day, when I was in second grade, I was walking home by myself. I had stayed after class for some reason and my friends had gone ahead. Two older boys walked behind me, taunting me all the way. My mother had taught me the phrase "Sticks and stones may break my bones, but names will never hurt me." I began to recite it like a mantra in my little-girl mind. But it wasn't working, and I was on the verge of tears.

Finally, I saw my dad's car coming down the street. He pulled up to the curb and I hopped into the car, relieved to finally find a safe place. I looked at him and said, "Dad, why do the boys do that?" There was silence. He looked at me, turned back to the steering wheel, and drove home.

I was devastated. I had experienced abandonment. Somehow I knew that my dad should have done or said something. He could have told me that I was his beautiful little girl, he could have said something to the boys, he could have got their names and called their parents. But he did nothing. I took his silence as agreement with them.

As an eight-year-old child, unable to cope with both the shame from the boys and the emotional abandonment by Dad, I came to a conclusion about the world. I concluded that the boys were right and, even worse, that I could not depend on Dad (or any man) to take care of me. I would have to take care of myself.

This judgment drove me to extreme lengths of perfectionism and workaholism. I developed a love-hate relationship with men. I wanted their love, attention, and approval, but when I received it I was so afraid of losing them that I pushed them away. It was a cycle rooted in a fear of being abandoned again. These were the sinful coping mechanisms I used to keep the pain at bay. It was a cycle that was not broken until Jesus revealed it to my heart and brought people full of His grace to help soften my tough heart. Abandonment is such a deep wound and my response was so ingrained that it took years of persistent love from God, flowing through others, to set me free. Ultimately, Jesus died and rose again not only to reconcile us to the Father; He experienced abandonment on the cross so that we would not have to experience it in its complete power ever again.

Fear of Abandonment

So far we have discussed how children and adolescents can be emotionally, physically, and spiritually abandoned by their parents. As adults what we experience is a fear of abandonment. Fear of abandonment is, very simply, fear of being left alone or deserted. This is such a deep soul fear that adults go to extreme lengths to try and ensure that they are never deserted or cast away again. When we are ministering to adults, it is not the actual abandonment issue that manifests itself; it is the fear of abandonment.

Think of it as an iceberg. What we see on the surface is just that: only the surface. The actual abandonment issue is buried beneath a myriad of behaviours, all aimed at trying to ensure that the abandonment they experienced is never experienced again. Some of these behaviours can be addictions to alcohol, drugs, work, or almost anything else. I have known women who were addicted to cleaning or fantasy novels, and men who were addicted to television sports broadcasts or their work. Depression, eating disorders, suicidal thoughts or actions, and relationship addictions are other behaviours that indicate there is a real problem buried beneath.

For a Christian, fear is the exact opposite of faith. The admonition "Do not be afraid" is repeated over sixty times in the Bible (NIV). The New Testament strongly conveys a similar message in a variety of ways. Jesus talks about not being afraid, as our basic needs will be met (Matthew 6:25–34). Timothy reminds the early Church that the spirit that comes from God is not fear, but power and love and a sound mind, or clear thinking (2 Timothy 1:7). For the Christian, fear of anything, including the unresolved fears of childhood abandonment, is clearly not what God intends for us. He has died to deliver us from the biggest fear of all, fear of death (Hebrews 2:14–15), and consequently wants to set us free from all fear.

Remember that, though we may now physically be adults, we experience the fear of abandonment not as an adult but as a frightened child. When trauma happens in our lives, it is like we get emotionally stuck at that age level. If a ten-year-old child responded to his mother's continuing alcoholism by saying "I'll just have to take care of myself," then he will continue to do that into his adult life. While he may have grown to be competent in business, his internal world and relational life will continue to be held in bondage to the fear of abandonment. Every day he will make decisions that appear intellectually adult but are emotionally childish.

John was a successful local businessman. An engineer by trade, he had formed a company that continued to secure significant international work in the petroleum industry. He was married and had two children, now in their young teens. John and his family were faithful members of their church, tithing and actively participating in church life. On the outside things looked good.

What John's facade of thriving had been able to hide was the reality that he and his wife had not really communicated in years. His relationship with his children was equally distant. John expressed his care for his family only through winter holidays and summer excursions to their cottage on the west coast.

No one knew about John's childhood. Once, an icebreaker question at their home group had provided an opportunity to disclose some of his childhood pain. The group leader asked, "What was the best thing that happened to you when you were in elementary school?" John managed to avoid the question with a quip about that being too long ago to remember. Really, he hadn't forgotten a thing about that painful time, but he couldn't remember anything good happening at all. John lived in the constant fear of being abandoned again.

When he was six years old, his father had lost his job. The depression that set in did not resolve, and John's father was too proud to ask for help. Over the months, the job search grew more and more frustrating. Within a year, John's father had developed the pattern of looking for a job during the week and drinking with his buddies on the weekend. John's mother seemed to be powerless to do anything to change his father's behaviour. When John's father drank, he was loud, obnoxious, and could be physically violent. Often all his mother seemed to be able to do was to create a physical distance between John and his father.

The situation continued to deteriorate. One day John made a promise to himself that he would do everything he could to keep his dad happy and that he would not be a further financial burden for the struggling family.

He took a paper route, keeping some of the money for school expenses and turning the rest over to his mother. When he reached high school, he continued to work twenty hours a week to help support the family. By this time his father and mother had divorced. John wanted a career that would provide well for him in his adult life, so, on top of his part-time employment, he studied hard and graduated with honours. After high school, he attended university and graduated with a degree in engineering. Shortly after university he met his wife, and they were married within a year.

Even though John had a profession with reasonable job security and excellent pay, he continued to work long hours. He was quickly promoted. Eventually John left the company to start his own consulting engineering firm.

There is nothing wrong with being successful. But John's success was driven, not by a desire to use the gifts God had given him, but to ensure he was never abandoned again. Somehow John had felt that his mother had left his father because he was not able to provide financially for his family. While John's addiction to work had been well established before he entered university, his marriage meant that he must work even more diligently to make sure his wife didn't ever leave him.

Unfortunately, the long hours at the office and the extended work trips continued to cut the emotional ties between John and his wife. He was drifting from his children as well; his extended absences had meant that he had missed most significant events in their lives. Now, as young teens, they were beginning to resent their father's attempts to buy their affection with expensive gifts and holidays.

John had turned into his father. While not an alcoholic—in fact he never drank—he was as emotionally absent and abusive as his father had been.

John was held in bondage by a deep-seated fear of abandonment. Despite his intellect and abilities, the wounded boy inside of him was still trying to protect himself from being abandoned ever again by the people who loved him.

In John's case the tip of the iceberg was workaholism. Workaholism covered his inability to express his emotions and the deep detachment he felt from those closest to him. While it appeared that relationships were of no importance to him, the reality was that they were, and in fact John was trying desperately to ensure that he was never abandoned again.

John's deliverance from the fear of abandonment began the day his wife said she wanted a divorce. In response, John agreed to go for counselling. He began to see that the "good" he felt he was doing was driving his family away. Slowly he began to turn more responsibility over to his business partners so he could limit the time he was away from home. He began spending time with his wife and children and started to show his affection in more appropriate ways than expensive gifts. It took a few years, but through the loving persistence of his wife and friends, prayer, and a wise Christian counsellor, he was able to be free from the fear that had held him in bondage since his childhood.

ROOTS OF PHYSICAL ABANDONMENT

I had never known my birth father. He left before I was born. My mom married my "dad" when I was three and a half.

When I first talked to a Christian counsellor, I mentioned at the end of the session that the man I referred to as my "dad" was not my biological father. My counsellor asked me if this bothered me, and I said, "Of course not!"

Over the years the Holy Spirit healed many abandonment issues in my life. Then, after a powerful prayer counselling session, I felt it was time to locate my birth father. Over the years I had gleaned some information from my mother, including a picture, and through a series of events I was able to mail a letter to him. Unfortunately, the response to that letter was a reply from his employer saying that he had died eighteen months before.

I was devastated. For three days I couldn't even get out

of my house. Most of the time, I sat numbly in front of my fireplace. Sleep was another good anaesthetic.

Like most of my friends, I was baffled over the intense grief I was experiencing. One friend said, "I don't see why you're so upset. You never even knew the man!" The grief I felt was more intense than the grief I had experience with the death of my "dad." Though I had never met my birth father, there seemed to be some deep emotional connection that I had previously denied.

There is increasing evidence that abandonment, or other trauma, can affect a child while still unborn. In her book *The Cloister Walk,* author Kathleen Norris describes the situation surrounding a poem written by an elementary school boy as part of an in-class workshop she taught.

My Very First Dad

> I remember him
> Like God in my heart
> Like the clouds overhead,
> And like strawberry ice cream and bananas
> When I was a little kid.
> But the most I remember
> Is his love
> As big as Texas
> When I was born.

The boy said, rather proudly, that he had been born in Texas, but otherwise told me nothing of his story. It was his stunned teacher who filled me in. She said things that did not surprise me, given my previous experience as an artist-in-residence—"He's not a good student; he tries, but he's never done anything like this before"—

but then she told me that the boy had never known his father; he'd skipped town on the day he was born.[28]

This boy had a big space in his heart for a father who had left even before birth. When abandonment happens this early in a child's life, it seems to become the platform on which all of life's experience is measured. It becomes the platform to receive and hold any other instance that looks remotely like abandonment.

In the case of a child being physically abandoned by one or both parents, fear of abandonment can be evident in ways similar to John's response to his father's alcoholism. But, what seems to be characteristic of this type of abandonment is a deep-seated loneliness.

Loneliness, beyond the day-to-day reality of living in a fallen world, is perhaps one of the most significant indicators that an individual has experienced abandonment early in life. The heart-deep pang of loneliness can drive individuals to extreme measures to try and fill the hole that ultimately only the love of God and the godly love of others can fill.

This was the case in my own life. I constantly needed to be at the centre of things and the centre of attention. In school I volunteered for every job possible, especially if it put me within the sphere of attention of an adult, especially a male adult. As a young woman I gravitated to careers that were traditionally male-dominated—partly because of interest in these occupations, partly because of my need to be affirmed by men.

Physical abandonment of a child early in life, by one or both birth parents, is a form of trauma that leaves wounds. In *Adoptee Trauma: A Counselling Guide for Adoptees,*[29] author Heather Carlini lists the following signs as the indicators of early childhood abandonment.

Core Issues of Adoption for Adoptees

- ❑ Fear of rejection
- ❑ Impaired trust
- ❑ Control madness [extreme need to be in control]
- ❑ Being out of touch with their feelings
- ❑ Feelings of guilt and shame
- ❑ Difficulty with intimacy
- ❑ Tendency to bond with objects rather than people
- ❑ Lack of self-esteem
- ❑ Perfectionism
- ❑ Aggressive feelings
- ❑ Codependency
- ❑ Loneliness
- ❑ Restlessness
- ❑ Dislike of special occasions
- ❑ Feeling like two different identities
- ❑ Identity diffusion [difficulty making a commitment to a specific identity][30]
- ❑ Difficulty giving and receiving love

While these issues may be evident in people for a variety of reasons, extreme loneliness and dislike of special occasions seem to be unique to those physically abandoned at or shortly after birth.

HELPING PEOPLE RECOVER FROM ABANDONMENT
OR REJECTION WOUNDS

In my experience, fear of abandonment is at the root of most relational issues we struggle with. A fruit of the fall is that, as individuals, we are never able to give to another the emotional and spiritual support they need. In spite of our best intentions, we abandon each other, sometimes in our times of greatest need. As we have seen in this chapter, children are abandoned in many ways by their parents.

It takes the inner working of the Holy Spirit, forgiveness, and committed relationships to heal from the devastating effects of abandonment. In reality, most people struggle at some level with this fear. It can be a deep, long struggle to break all the bondages it has created. There is healing and a way out, but it takes time and it takes a community. This is a summary of the process. Keep in mind that recovering from a fear of abandonment is an experiential and relational issue. And remember the illustration of the tree. The tree did not develop properly, and re-staking it so that it will grow straight will be a process.

1. Scripture and Prayer

As a leader, you have the wonderful job of proclaiming God's good news to an abandoned heart and leading him to the Father whose love is eternal. The beginning of a wounded heart's healing journey is hearing the good news that our heavenly Father never leaves us or abandons us. Jesus warned His disciples that there would be a time of physical separation, but the Father would send the Holy Spirit to fill this gap (John 14:26). Jesus' last words to His disciples were a promise that He would be with them always (Matthew 28:20).

Later, the Holy Spirit gave the apostle Paul this understanding of a basic human need: to know that we are loved and will not be abandoned. He writes the following words to his spiritual children in Rome:

> *For I am convinced that neither death nor life, neither angels nor demons, neither the present nor the future, nor any powers, neither height nor depth, nor anything else in all creation, will be able to separate us from the love of God that is in Christ Jesus our Lord* (Romans 8:38–39 NIV).

To the church in Ephesus he sent this prayer:

> *And I pray that you, being rooted and established in love, may have the power, together with all the saints, to grasp how wide and long and high and deep is the love of Christ, and to know this love that surpasses knowledge—that you may be filled to the measure of all the fullness of God* (Ephesians 3:17–19 NIV).

The need to belong, and to be rooted and grounded in love, is central to our identity as children of God. Ultimately, the only one who will never abandon us is our heavenly Father. This is a beginning place for healing. It is important to experience the unconditional love of the Father. Reading Scriptures like those mentioned above and a prayer like the following are helpful tools in the healing process. Individuals can pray this themselves or you can pray it for them. Keep in mind that this is not a one-time prayer. It is merely the beginning of a healing journey. As a starting point, encourage the individual you are working with to pray this prayer daily, meditate on the previous

Scriptures, and commit to the healing journey, seeking other help as necessary.

Prayer for Healing from Abandonment

Heavenly Father, I thank you that You have promised never to leave me. Thank You that nothing can stop You from loving me and that Your love is beyond what I can imagine. Forgive me for doubting Your love for me. As I confess this to You I ask that You will heal the wound of abandonment in my heart. Specifically, I ask You to heal the wound that happened when [name the incident].

I ask Your forgiveness for all the ways I have chosen to protect myself from the possibility of being abandoned by others, specifically [name the coping mechanisms used here]. *Thank You for beginning this healing process. Help me to remember that I am loved by You always and forever. Help me to receive the love others share with me, too.*

Prayer for Healing from Rejection

Heavenly Father, I acknowledge to you that when [name the incident] *I felt rejected and now believe that I am "rejectable." Forgive me for all the ways I have tried to protect myself from being rejected by others, specifically* [name them]. *Help me to understand how much you love me. Help me to walk in that truth and not be afraid of rejection.*

2. Acknowledge Emotions

Next, people who struggle with abandonment wounds need to begin to acknowledge their emotions—good, bad and some that may be downright ugly. Even if people seem "emotional"—often crying or acting angry, for example—it doesn't mean that they necessarily know what they are feeling or why they are feeling it. They need help to identify their emotions. I have a chart I sometimes use in this exercise, listing over fifty words describing emotions.

If we are not taught how to handle emotions we grow up with a undeveloped EQ (Emotional Quotient)! What that means is that we do not have the skills needed to properly manage our emotions. As a result, they become a detriment rather than an asset. It is for this very reason that many people submerge, bury or repress their emotions. Repressed emotions are like an old jack-in-the-box. Keep turning the crank and out they pop—often giving us quite a start!

Depending on the type of abandonment or rejection people have experienced and how they have responded to it, they may have years of pent-up sorrow and rage that need to be brought to the surface so the issues can be addressed.

An individual needs to be able to say "When you cancelled that appointment, I felt abandoned, all alone. I felt like I always did as a kid." It's at that point, with help from the Holy Spirit, that you are able to pray with that person for healing of that wound. Ask the Holy Spirit to take you back to the particular time of wounding and to heal the wound.

3. Entering into Forgiveness

It is so very important that the individual enter into the process of forgiveness as outlined earlier in this book. Like sanctification, forgiveness is both a one-time event and an ongoing process. Read chapter 7, "Confession and Forgiveness," for more information on this process.

A Prayer of Forgiveness

> *Heavenly Father, I choose to forgive* [name the person] *for emotionally/physically abandoning/rejecting me when they* [name the situation]. *I forgive them and release them into your hands.*
>
> *Now, I ask Your forgiveness for the way I protected myself from the fear of being abandoned/rejected again, specifically* [name the self-protective behaviour pattern].
>
> *Thank you that I am forgiven. Cleanse me of my unrighteous relating patterns (1 John 1:9), and, as I have confessed this sin, come and heal this wound of abandonment (James 5:10).*

4. Be Present and Consistent

People need you to walk with them through the entire process. A key component in the process of recovery is for wounded people to know that there are people who will do their best to be there for them, people who will, with healthy boundaries, show them consistent love, care and friendship. It does not mean you are available 24/7. But it does involve making commitments you can honour.

Part of a leader's responsibility in this process is coming to understand the limits of their role. People in recovery do need care, but the crisis in their life happened many years ago. At Mars Hill Centre we specifically make it known that we are not a crisis-counselling centre. We tell people that the incident that is causing the current pain in their lives is rooted to things that happened in their past. As a result, it will take time to heal the wounds. We let them know that we will be there for the long haul. I let them know that they may have some bad moments and they need to have access to crisis support. (Most urban centres have at least one twenty-four-hour crisis phone line.) "However," I tell them, "I am not that person. You can call me, and I will get back to you as soon as I can. What I will give you is consistent support in our weekly meetings." And I make sure I follow through on that.

Walking with people through the healing process is a serious commitment. They have been abandoned before and are quite sure you will abandon them too. In a sense, God heals us as adults through other adults who come alongside us as spiritual parents. I desperately needed a godly man to be a spiritual father to me. I needed a father who was there physically, emotionally, and spiritually. By God's grace, I found such people. Through those relationships the Holy Spirit brought healing to my heart. Equally important, I acquired emotional and spiritual life skills that I had missed in my youth.

Those who are dealing with abandonment issues in their lives need to know that you are there for them, not simply for a few meetings but for the long haul. Ultimately, the fear of abandonment can only be broken by the power of the Spirit and the love of God the Father working through real people.

Chapter Ten

FREEDOM FROM SHAME

❊　❊　❊

At age thirteen, I was a severely overweight teen. I'd been on the large side all my life; as a child and teen, schoolmates had ridiculed me as I walked home from school. These days they would call it bullying, but in 1972 it was just something that happened. Mom, doing her best, taught me the little ditty "Sticks and stones may break my bones, but names will never hurt me." Needless to say, I struggled with more than the normal adolescent angst about body image.

I had worn my prettiest dress to school that day. My friends and even a number of teachers commented on how good I looked. My ego was soaring. My turquoise blue dress was slimming and had all the trendy accents of the time. There was only one problem. The zipper didn't hold very well at the top. Consequently, I would reach behind my neck to pull it up. On one such occasion I couldn't seem to reach the zipper pull tag and quietly asked my friend to pull the zipper up for me while the teacher continued to talk. She replied, rather flatly, "I can't." I asked, somewhat angrily, "Why not?" She replied, "Your zipper's broken."

I was horrified. This was not a mere six-inch zipper. It extended from my neck to the base of the spine. I slumped in my chair, horror flooding my soul. Meekly I raised my hand to ask my teacher if I could go to the washroom. I don't remember how this happened, but before I could leave the class I had to tell him why I needed to leave the room—my zipper had broken and my dress was falling off!

Somehow I managed to get out of the room with some of my fragile soul intact. The next step was to get to my locker to put on my coat. I hoped my coat would do two things: keep my dress from falling off and cover the body shame that had flooded over me. Next I had to go to the principal's office and ask for permission to leave the school. The vice principal, thinking that I was just another student with a creative way to skip class, asked to see what the problem was. Fortunately, the secretary saved me from further shame by intervening on my behalf. Finally, I made it home, changed, and eventually returned to school. But I didn't wear that dress again (or any other dress, for that matter) for a long time.

We all have these stories of utter embarrassment. But, as horrific as they may sound, they are but a taste of the anguish of shame.

OUR IDENTITY DNA

As human beings we are the amazing masterpieces of a wonderful Creator. We are—male and female—created in His image. This means that woven into the DNA of our identity is the image of God, our Creator, Lord of the

Universe! But that identity has been defaced by the fall. Prior to Adam and Eve's choice to find life apart from God, they never knew insecurity, embarrassment, or shame. Their choice of disobedience introduced shame into our human identity.

They hid from each other, and from God (Genesis 3:8). They covered their exposure with plant leaves (Genesis 3:7). And each shifted the shame they felt onto the other. Once the DNA of our identity was affected by sin and shame, we have never been the same. All of us carry with us a sense of not being quite good enough. It is, in fact, something we are all born with. Ultimately, it is what causes us to realize our need for a Saviour.

SHAME AND GUILT

For the purposes of this book we will look at two related but different experiences that we commonly refer to as "shame," namely, shame and guilt.

Guilt is realizing that we have done something wrong or feeling that we should have done something different. Guilt is about an act or attitude that is, or is perceived to be, sinful. When we are convicted by the Holy Spirit about a sinful action, thought, or attitude, we know that we can take it to Jesus, ask forgiveness, and we will be forgiven (1 John 1:7–9). As Christians, we have the power of forgiveness and confession to break the power of sin in our lives (James 5:16).

Regrettably, in other situations we can sometimes feel guilty because we have an overwhelming sense of being responsible for everyone and everything. Consequently, we do not have clear boundary lines between what we are responsible for, what others are responsible for, and what

God is responsible for. In an effort to please everyone, keep the peace, be liked, be the centre of attention, or be in control, we can feel guilty for not doing things that really are not our responsibility at all. Ultimately, all any one person is responsible for is her own emotions, attitudes, and actions. This "guilt" is never really addressed through repentance or change, because although we may feel we have done something wrong, we really haven't. If you feel guilty or responsible for everything and everyone all the time, you need to ask God to tighten the circle of your soul and show you what you are truly accountable for.

TRUE GUILT

Alicia's insides felt like they were ready to explode. The butterflies in her stomach felt like elephants. Moments earlier she had been called to her boss's office. She was feeling sick because the project that she had recently completed and placed on her boss's desk was less than complete. In her rush to complete the project, she had neglected to include some key market information that had been provided to her the day before. Including the information would have meant working later than she wanted to last night, and so she had decided to leave it out. She was sure that her mistake had been made known and that she risked reprimand or possibly dismissal. She knew she had made an unwise choice, and she would work through the weekend if that's what it took to make things right. Alicia was feeling guilty about her decision.

In this scenario, Alicia had made an unwise choice. Whether she could change things now or not, she had learned from her mistake and would not do it again.

True guilt is always about a behaviour, action, or attitude that we can take to Jesus, ask forgiveness for, and change. In Christian terms, this is repentance. We can confess our sins to God (and preferably another person as well—see James 5:16), receive forgiveness, and ask God to change that pattern in our life. While habitual sins do not usually change overnight, we do not need to feel guilt, provided we continue to confess to God and another each time we slip up. Shame is another story.

I Must Be Wrong!

Shame is not the feeling of making a mistake; it is feeling like I am a mistake.

Shame is *not* about our behaviour; it is about our identity and how we feel about ourselves. It is not that we have done something wrong but that we, at the core of our being, believe we are wrong, a mistake, a failure.

While Alicia continued to wait outside her boss's office, the old familiar lines continued to repeat in her head. "I'm such an idiot! Why did I even think I could ever make something of my life? My mother must have spoken the truth—I'm lazy and can never do anything right."

Shame is always about our identity. We feel self-absorbed, alone, fat, skinny, ugly, stupid, too short, too tall, too smart, not smart enough, and inadequate.

Shame Does Not Happen in a Vacuum

In grade seven, if the zipper had broken on my dress while I was sitting in my room listening to music, I may have been upset but I might not have experienced shame.

Shame came because I was concerned about what others thought about me and, particularly, my body.

I cannot think of a moment in my life when I did not feel ashamed about my body until recently. The shame had taken root in my life at an early age. I have a vague memory of my mother introducing me as a three-year-old to a woman from her hometown. Her response to my mother was, "She's rather big for her age, isn't she!" It's the first time I remember feeling different from everyone else, and the tone in the woman's voice gave the impression that this difference was not something to be proud of. Like it always does, shame entered my life in the context of a relationship. I had been compared to other three-year-olds and found to not measure up.

As residents of a fallen world, we receive shame messages on a daily basis. Women and men struggle to come close to the models portrayed in magazines and movies. Our North American picture of beauty has, increasingly, become something few of us can measure up to without extreme dieting, exercise, and plastic surgery. Advertisers grab us with images of things that they say will make us feel better about ourselves. Whether it's a new car or the right deodorant, our lives are always being compared to an elusive standard of perfection. And we fall for it hook, line, and sinker because most of us have felt some level of shame from an early age.

Our understanding of who we are comes from the messages we receive from the significant people in our lives. Our mothers and fathers, other family members, schoolmates, soccer coaches, and piano teachers all play a hand in shaping our identity. Because they are people we look to for affirmation and direction, we believe that their words must be true.

SHAME MESSAGES

When people whose opinion about us matters say something, we listen. These shame messages fall into a variety of categories. They become the lies we believe about ourselves. They are the strongholds in our thinking that we use to define who we are.

- ❑ **Direct put-downs** are the most obvious shaming messages, such as when Alicia's mom told her she was lazy and could do nothing right.
  "You can't do anything right."
  "You're stupid [or ugly or...]."

- ❑ **Comparisons** are shaming messages too. In an attempt to encourage their children to reach their full potential, many parents say, *"I wish you were more like your cousin Richard."* Or the comparison may be more discreet, merely talking about cousin Richard's accomplishments and never complimenting their child on their own accomplishments.
  "I wish you could be like your sister; she always eats her supper without complaining."
  "Your brother never had problems with math!"
  "My, she's big for her age."
  "When I was your age I loved taking piano lessons."

- ❑ **Devaluing a child's interests, activities, or friends** are shame statements. A friend recently told me of a trip back to his hometown to visit family. Never once in the weeklong visit did his family ask him what he does in his new job, if he likes the new city he is living in, or anything else about his life. He said that it was like he didn't exist for the whole week he was visiting his parents. Usually a good conversationalist, he chose to shut down and detach emotionally because of his family's disinterest. As a child and teen he had done much the same; any sense of worth he felt came from accomplishments outside his family. Though he had excelled in school, sports, and a variety of extra-curricular activities, when his high school basketball team reached the regional finals, neither his mother nor father was in attendance when he was awarded MVP.

❑ **Put-downs of others** can be shaming statements to a child. If a child grows up in a family where every group of people is spoken of in a derogatory way, the child may feel that there must be something wrong with her, too. A friend's father never had anything good to say about anyone. She had heard him say harsh, shaming statements about every politician, world leader, and neighbour. Consequently, she lived in constant fear that one day she too would be disapproved of by her father. For years she carefully walked a tightrope, never expressing opinions, likes, or dislikes in her home.
"I can't understand what you see in those friends of yours. They'll never amount to anything."
"Those academics, they really don't have any practical purpose."
"All (fill in the blank—women, men, pastors, students, politicians...) are idiots!"

❑ **Any form of physical abuse or neglect** is a type of shaming, because it says to the child that he is of no value. Unmet physical, emotional, and spiritual needs give children the clear picture that they are not worth bothering about. A mother who spends her money on alcohol, bingo, or other perceived personal needs, so that there's never enough money for a child's basic needs, says that her addiction is more important to her than her child. Likewise, a father who shuts down his child's emotions with messages like "Big boys don't cry" gives the message that his child's emotions are wrong.

❑ **Any form of sexual abuse** is, obviously, shaming to the victim. Victims are told in no uncertain terms that their body is primarily for the sexual enjoyment of another.

THE FRUIT OF THE SHAME ROOT

Often, we try to fix our behaviour without dealing with the root of the issue. It never works. However, shame is much easier to recognize from its bad fruit than from seeing its deep root in our lives. Jesus talked about identifying a tree as good or bad by the type of fruit it produces.

"No good tree bears bad fruit, nor does a bad tree bear good fruit. Each tree is recognized by its own fruit. People do not pick figs from thornbushes, or grapes from briers. The good man brings good things out of the good stored up in his heart, and the evil man brings evil things out of the evil stored up in his heart. For out of the overflow of his heart his mouth speaks" (Luke 6:43–45 NIV).

While we will spend some time identifying shame fruit, don't stop there. Sadly, most of us try to remove the bad fruit in our lives without destroying the root of shame. If the rotten root of shame is not removed from our lives, we will continue to produce bad fruit. Nevertheless, as a starting place, here are some of the more obvious fruits of shame which we will explore in greater depth:

❑ Perfectionism
❑ Procrastination
❑ Envy
❑ People-pleasing
❑ Feelings of inferiority or inadequacy
❑ Workaholism
❑ Secretiveness or withdrawal
❑ Religion

Perfectionism

As I write this I am sitting in my home office, looking absent-mindedly out into my backyard and the alley beyond. It had been spring here, but in the last two days we received another five centimetres (two inches) of snow! Like me, most of my neighbours seem to be trying to ignore the white stuff, but there's a man down the back alley who has been cleaning out his driveway.

When he finished with his driveway, he began shovelling the alley that is adjacent to his property. After he finished shovelling, he took out a broom and swept off the last remaining vestiges of snow. I suppose he might be bored and have nothing better to do. He might be tired of looking at the white stuff and trying to control its invasion of what was a cleared cement driveway. Or he may be a perfectionist who simply cannot leave something undone. And once a job is started, it must be completed perfectly.

My neighbour reminds me of my dad. In our house the slogan was "If you can't do it right, don't do it at all." Our front lawn was always perfect. I never knew how to run a lawn-mower until I owned my own house—in my childhood home no one cut the grass but Dad! It had to be done perfectly. He would rather do it himself than instruct young imperfection-ists on the art and science of lawn maintenance.

My father, without any exaggeration, was a perfec-tionist. Due to my shame, my response was simply to not try anything unless I could do it perfectly, because I could not endure disappointing my father when the job was not com-pleted to his satisfaction. It was, of course, my father's own shame that drove his perfectionism.

For years I thought I had escaped the shame-based pat-tern of perfectionism, until the day I decided to repaint some floor lamps for my apartment. I laid down some plastic on our balcony, grabbed the lamps, and started painting. It really wasn't as hard as I thought it would be, and I was finished in less than an hour. Not only did I pos-sess the technical skills required for lamp painting, the completed project looked great! I had some other errands to run, so I left the lamps in the sun on the balcony to dry. I felt like I had accomplished a great task. It was the first real "home reno" I'd ever done!

When I returned, I was horrified. The wind had picked up and blown the plastic onto the lamp. It was stuck onto the drying paint! I was out of control. I began a litany of self-recrimination that would have caused anyone over-hearing my words to think I had just ruined a Picasso. It was crazy—I know that now—but at the time all I could feel was the intense emotional response I had always felt to my father's mantra, "If you can't do it right, don't do it at all." Because I had never seemed to be able to do it right, I had generally just not tried to do anything at all, unless I was fairly sure I could do something perfectly. This minor setback with lamp painting brought this shame root to the surface and exposed its fruit in my life—perfectionism.

I thought I had managed to steer clear of my father's perfectionist attitude, but all I had managed to do was steer clear of any activity I knew I couldn't do perfectly the first time. The result was that I didn't really try too many new things outside of my realm of expertise. Those things I did do, I did really well. I was a diligent employee, attentive friend, and never late paying a bill.

Perfectionism is just one of the more obvious fruits of a deep root of shame. It can be manifested by individuals who do everything right and berate themselves when they have less than perfect behaviour. Or, it can be revealed when a person, like me, steers clear of any activities that she may not be able to do perfectly.

Anne Lamont, in *Bird by Bird,* writes: "Perfectionism is the voice of the oppressor, the enemy of the people. It will keep you cramped and insane your whole life."[31] How true!

Procrastination

Procrastination is the comrade of perfectionism. Often procrastinators simply are avoiding doing something because, deep down inside, they are afraid they won't do it the right way. They put off tasks that they don't feel competent to complete. Then, at the last minute, they plunge headlong into the task, hoping to complete it in time and well.

At this point one of two things happens. They may succeed in doing well what they were avoiding so long. In that case their habit of procrastination is, unfortunately, confirmed. Or, they don't do it well. In this case the lie that they are incompetent is deepened. The reality could very well be that they need more time to successfully complete the task or that they simply need to learn some basic skills to succeed at it.

Envy

Envy is a feeling of discontent or resentment that we have when we perceive that someone else is better off than we are. Envy says that if I had what they had, everything in my life would be fine. Envy is a fruit of shame because it says that I am not okay—and cannot be okay—just the way I am. I need something more. If I had what that other person has, I would be doing just fine. Envy looks at external measures of success, not at the condition of my own heart as the source of happiness.

Envy drives our consumer-based society. If I only had that new car, bigger or nicer house, or the latest fashion, I'd feel fine. You know that you are driven by envy if none of these things make you feel satisfied.

People-Pleasing

As Christians, it is easy to fall into the pit of people-pleasing. In some circles, people-pleasing—though not called by that name—can be seen as a virtue. However, living our lives to keep others happy is never a virtue. It is the bad fruit of the root of shame. The apostle Paul wrote: *"Am I now trying to win human approval, or God's approval? Or am I trying to please people? If I were still trying to please people, I would not be a servant of Christ*" (Galatians 1:10 NIVI). It's a pretty clear statement that people-pleasing is in direct opposition to being a follower of Jesus.

Shame drives us to make sure that people will like us, so that they will never see the hideous root we carry inside. Deep down we feel so wrong; we assume no one could possibly love or accept us for who we are.

The writer of Proverbs puts it this way: "*To fear anyone [or to fear man] will prove to be a snare, but whoever trusts in the Lord is kept safe*" (Proverbs 29:25 TNIV). People-pleasing is the exact opposite of trusting God. When we seek to please people, we are using our best efforts to get someone on our side so that we will not be hurt. In essence we are trying to protect and promote ourselves. This is God's responsibility, not ours.

In church circles, people-pleasers are the ones who always do everything asked of them. They are volunteers par excellence; however, this commitment is almost always based on receiving some type of recognition. Cut off the recognition and see what happens! (This is not to say that people shouldn't be recognized for their efforts; but if, as a leader, we feel compelled to always acknowledge certain people, they may be operating out of the fruit of people-pleasing rather than out of a spirit of true service.)

Feelings of Inadequacy or Inferiority

It may seem obvious to some that feelings of inadequacy or inferiority, including low self-esteem, would be the fruit of the root of shame in someone's life. However, it bears repeating because of the ways people usually try to make themselves feel better. Often these recovery methods have nothing to do with removing the shame root in your life.

For example, people may daily recite personal affirmations. These may be Scripture-based or not. Or they may try to do good things for themselves—small personal indulgences they may not usually feel worthy to accept, like a massage, manicure, etc.—in an attempt to convince themselves that they are worth it.

On one level there is nothing wrong with either of these practices. Unfortunately, using self-affirmation to remove shame is the equivalent of trying to move a mound of dirt using tweezers. You could probably, eventually, accomplish the job, but it would take a long time and you would be really frustrated! We cannot talk our way out of shame.

Workaholism

Workaholism is the twin sister of perfectionism, and it is not limited to your place of employment. Working too much, too long, too hard is used to cover shame by stay-at-home moms, businesspeople, and ministers of the gospel. In our society, when we consistently spend more than forty or so hours at our job each week, it is usually for the wrong reasons. Generally speaking, we are workaholics because we do not feel that on our own, with average, healthy limits, we are acceptable. So we work long hours to please our boss, our kids, or even God!

While parents are parents 24/7, they are not solely responsible for their child's character development. Teachers, extended family, neighbours, and other adults also have a part to play in the character development of any child. No parent can possibly assume all these roles; nor can any parent compensate for the downfall of any of these other mentors. When a parent becomes a workaholic in the role of parent, she (or he) is basically trying to cover up a deep sense of shame over her own inadequacy. Her internal logic tells her that if she works hard enough, she can make sure her kids turn out okay. This workaholism does two things: it gets in the way of the child's free choice, and it denies the power of God at work in the child's life.

Secretiveness or Withdrawal

Shame produces in us a deep fear of exposure. Consequently, we may intentionally or unintentionally be secretive about things in our lives, afraid that if someone really knew the truth, we would be rejected or shamed further. I knew of a young woman who never had a different response to "How are you?" than "I'm fine." On those days when the smile was very obviously phoney, any further show of concern would raise a higher wall of secrecy. This young woman struggled with loneliness but was unwilling to take the risk to let anyone into her world.

I've known numerous individuals who seem unable to voluntarily disclose any details about their lives. These people are often pleasant and kind but lack the courage to risk showing the world their hearts.

Religion

Most evangelical Christians would agree that we are saved by faith, not by works (Ephesians 2:8–9). Unfortunately, their actions and their lives would indicate otherwise. They are caught in the trap of religion, carrying out spiritual disciplines as religious duties, hoping to find favour with God. Prayer, Bible reading, worship, gathering with the saints, and fasting are all good spiritual disciplines that can help us connect with God. Unfortunately, these practices can easily become religion.

By religion I mean not a set of beliefs but rather the acts we perform with the hope of currying favour with the Almighty. Religion is good works without relationship.

Many married couples I know have a practice of honouring their relationship by ensuring they have a regular "date time" with each other. If these dates lack affection, openness, and desire and become a mere ritual, they will soon be nothing more than a perfunctory meeting. Likewise, our relationship with God can become a useless, empty act if the shame in us keeps us from receiving His unconditional love.

I was the type of Christian who diligently prayed and read my Bible daily. I couldn't understand why others struggled with doing their devotions. But then it happened to me too! It began to be increasingly difficult to connect in this systematic way with God. I chastised myself for my lack of discipline, but that didn't help. I confessed my laziness, but to no avail. Somewhere along this process, I realized that this change in me was actually initiated by God. Part of the healing of the shame root in my life was through the Holy Spirit breaking the religious patterns in me. My relationship with God had become based on my expectation that if I did the right things, then—and only then—God would love me.

In this time, I struggled to enter into a relationship with my heavenly Father based solely on accepting His unconditional love for me. I had been a Christian for ten years and had lots of "Bible" in me. What God needed to do now was get His love into me. My relationship with God began to become more "of the moment." I encountered God daily, in new ways. I began to read my Bible because I wanted to meet with God—not because I felt I had to read my Bible to prove to God that I loved Him.

My Significant Other

I was trying my hardest to focus on the Lord in a recent worship service, but the thought "You're such an idiot" kept coming back to my mind. I felt so ashamed. I had approached someone with an offer of friendship. I think I said the wrong thing; at least the person's body language indicated that. And then every time I tried to approach this person and start a conversation so that I could clarify things, I seemed to put my foot in my mouth again.

Finally, I grabbed another friend, and we went off and prayed, and I was able to return to the service and focus—more or less. However, for a few days longer this shame feeling kept rumbling around in my soul. I would manage to forget the encounters for a brief time, and then they'd come flooding back. I felt like I had made a fool of myself in front of someone that I had hoped would care about me.

This was the strongest sense of shame I'd experienced in a long time, and I can see clearly what the problem was. The problem wasn't that I felt shame; it wasn't that I did (or think I did) something wrong. The real problem was that I had given this individual the power to judge my worth. Who I am really had not changed at all since these few meetings, but somehow I felt diminished because the person did not seek me out and affirm me.

Years ago, I went to see a Christian counsellor. It was the first time in my life that I was able to muster the courage to face the truth about myself. I don't even remember the counsellor's name or the name of the Christian counselling centre. Over twenty years have passed since my first small steps toward wholeness, and yet I remember everything he said.

We talked mainly about my relationship—or lack of relationship—with my father. I did everything I could to please him and win his affection. At that time I was in my mid-twenties, and I was still driven by the need for my father's approval. He never offered one word of affirmation, despite my excellent university grades and upwardly mobile career. As a result, my self-esteem was continually shattered. As far as I could see, I had to be the most horrible, unattractive, and stupid young woman on the planet!

After I poured that all out, the counsellor paused briefly and then proceeded to draw something on his whiteboard. He explained that God had created us to get our sense of identity from the significant others in our lives. ("Great," I groaned, "and they all think I'm worthless.") As he continued on, he explained that truly the only significant other who has the right to shape our identity is our heavenly Father. He thinks we're all amazing; we're created in His image, after all.

I left that office with a new revelation of who I was and whose opinion really mattered! In fact, the counsellor had done such a great job that I didn't return, because I was feeling so great. Of course, it was only another step in the healing process that God kicked into high gear a few years later.

Shame *always* has to do with a sense of exposure. Someone sees us and gives a bad (or perceived) bad report, and shame enters our eyes.

Most of my life I have dealt with shame by merely building bigger and thicker walls around my heart. I have believed that these walls would keep out the prying eyes that perceived me as a mistake, but the walls never worked.

Ultimately, the only antidote for shame is the Father's

love. And ultimately, it is only God who has the right to judge us and determine the value of our life. When we give that power to anyone else, we risk falling into the chasm of shame.

A WAY OUT

Unfortunately, I have seen many people take this the wrong way. They become super-spiritual, cutting themselves off emotionally from others because only God has the right to judge their worth. They have taken a spiritual truth and made it into a brick to build walls around their hearts. Inside, they are still crying for human affirmation.

The truth is that only God has the right to judge our value. The other part of this truth is that God has created us for relationship with Himself and with others. In the Garden of Eden, Adam and Eve had a shame-free relationship with God and with each other. While all that changed after they sinned, it remains the essence of our redemption. We are to enjoy shame-free relationships with God and with others.

HELPING PEOPLE CUT OUT THE ROOT OF SHAME

Unfortunately, much of the Christian world uses shame as a cheap motivational tool. How many of us have sat through, or preached, sermons where we endeavoured to make people feel so bad about their behaviour that they had no choice but to change. However, if we are honest, we know that those changes are short-lived. They are short-lived because they only deal with superficial guilt, not the deep root of shame we all carry. So here are some shame-free ways to help people be free from shame.

1. Be certain that shame is not a part of your own life.

If we have not been healed of the shame in our own lives, we will pass it on to others. Despite our best efforts, we will try to use shame to motivate and change people. We will preach salvation by works, not by faith.

A friend tells an extreme account of shame-based ministry. While a teenager, he attended family camp. It was an annual tradition and for him a great time to connect with friends. He had given his life to Christ years earlier and was walking out his commitment as best he could.

One night the preacher, wanting to have an altar call, used the following technique.

First the preacher called people to the front who wanted to respond to what God had spoken through his message. A few came forward, but obviously not enough to satisfy the preacher's ego. So he turned the heat up.

"Everyone who loves Jesus, stand!" he commanded. My friend didn't really want to stand. Like many teenagers, he wanted to get out of there and hang out with his friends.

Since not everyone was standing, the preacher added, "Everyone stand and come to the front who wants to serve Jesus. Everyone stay seated who wants to serve Satan."

Well, my friend was caught. He certainly wasn't a Satan-worshipper, so he had no choice but to respond to the altar call.

This preacher used guilt and shame to motivate people to respond. No matter how much you may feel people should respond to a great word delivered by you, *never* manipulate people into responding.

Jesus never hesitated to confront sin, and He never hesitated to deal with the real issues. He never shamed people into responding. The woman caught in the act of adultery had sinned (John 8:3–11), but Jesus was well aware that she was not alone in her choice to find fulfillment in her life apart from God. He challenged her sin and accepted her. Her life mattered to him.

The woman at the well was ostracized by most. Jesus valued her enough to spend time with her and help her find the truth her life was missing (John 4:4–42).

People cannot be healed of shame if they are in a shame-based environment. I hope that as you have read through this chapter you have identified some fruit of shame in your own life. Begin with your own healing first, using the steps that follow. This is crucial in order for you to be able to be used by the Holy Spirit to perform "heart" surgery on someone else

2. Help people confess the sinful ways they have responded to the shame root in their lives.

Individuals must begin to identify and acknowledge the sinful ways they have responded to the root of shame, such as perfectionism, envy, etc. It's important to remember that they have to see these behaviours in their own lives for this step to be effective, and this takes time. You may clearly see certain shame-based behaviours, but if you simply tell the person, and they are still struggling with people-pleasing, they may agree with you simply to please you. Let the Holy Spirit be the one to convince them of their shame-based behaviour.

Here's a helpful prayer model:

Heavenly Father, I confess that I have used [name the fruit of shame] *to protect myself from feeling ashamed. Specifically, I have* [name the specific outworking of, say, perfectionism]. *In doing this I have chosen to pro-tect myself and not trust in You. I ask Your forgiveness for this sinful pattern and receive Your forgiveness today. Help me put down my self-protection so that You can heal the root of shame in my heart.*

3. *Lead them to acknowledge that they have been shamed, and help them forgive those who have shamed them.*

In this step they must first confess that they have given power to other people, rather than to God, to determine their worth. They also need to pray and ask God to remind them of people who have specifically shamed them. At that point they need to forgive those people.

Here's a helpful prayer model:

Heavenly Father, I choose to forgive the people who have shamed me. Specifically I choose to forgive [name] *for shaming me by* [incident]. *I release them into your hands.*

4. *It's helpful to ask God to break the lies they have come to believe about themselves.*

Every time we are wounded, Satan plants a lie in our hearts. The lie cannot be made to go away simply by our saying that we choose not to believe it. The lie is rooted to an actual event, and because of that it is usually impossible to convince someone, at a heart level, that what they came to believe about themselves is not true.

Using guided prayer, ask the Holy Spirit to take them back to the shaming event. After a few moments ask the Holy Spirit to reveal to them what the lie was that they came to believe. Then ask Him to reveal what the truth is. The lie that we are mistakes is the cornerstone of much of our sinful behaviour and dysfunctional relationships. This lie must be replaced with a deep heart understanding of being fearfully and wonderfully created in the image of God. Psalm 139 is a good place to start.

KEEP THIS IN MIND

Healing prayer is important in healing the shame of a wounded heart. Healthy, shame-free relationships are mandatory in the healing process. A shame-free relationship says that the other person is valuable, that her life matters and that she is not a mistake.

While healing prayer is always important, being a shame-free leader is paramount to releasing healing. Every day we do things that communicate the opposite of our desire. Unreturned phone calls and cancelled appointments may seem like small matters to us, but they are not to those who struggle with a deep sense of shame and failure. The phone calls that are left unreturned and the appointments missed say that the person is not really as important to you as your words say. Especially in the early stages of walking with someone through their healing process, it is critical that your actions speak as loud as your words in affirming their worth.

I doubt that I would be the person I am today if a certain individual had not taken a risk to love me as a friend. He was steady and persistent in showing his care for me, even when he didn't know what to say or do to help heal the pain. This man is far from perfect, but God has placed on him a gift of grace that has deeply touched my wounded soul. We've had our share of disagreements and disappointments with each other. But he has continued to be there. I doubt he knows how much that consistent grace has changed me.

Consistent grace is the only antidote for a life full of shame. Consistent grace cannot be bestowed through a sermon or a few short meetings. It can only be poured out in the context of relationship and community. There are no shortcuts or easy fixes. God never intended the journey out of shame to be that way. He intended us to be healed in the very way we originally experience shame—in relationship.

Chapter Eleven

ACKNOWLEDGING OUR POWERLESSNESS

�֍ ✲ ✲

I had intended to take the day as a prayer and planning day. No appointments, no necessity to make a trip into my office. I was going to spend some concerted time asking God for His wisdom about our ministry. Before I started my day, I wanted to catch up on the news and turned on the TV.

It was September 11, 2001, about 8 a.m., Mountain Standard Time. I could not believe what I was seeing. I started channel surfing. Every station showed the same horrific images of a plane flying into a skyscraper in New York City. Like many North Americans, I spent most of the day riveted to my television screen. Part of me did not want to keep watching, but the bigger part of me was focused on the television images, trying to make some sense of the chaos.

My mind churned with grief for those directly involved in the crisis. Fear crouched at the edge of my mind as I wondered, like other North Americans, if something else was about to happen.

When I finally ventured out of my house, most people I encountered that day had a noticeable look of shock, disbelief, and grief written across their faces. We all struggled with an overwhelming sense of powerlessness—unable to change what had happened, unable to ease the pain of those affected, and unable to stem the tide of fear and uncertainty in our own hearts.

POWERLESSNESS ON A SMALL SCALE

Powerlessness is an inevitable part of being human. Every day, in big and small ways, we face the reality of our inability to take control of events in our world. Investors are powerless to control the fluctuations in the stock market or the value of our currency. Parents of rebellious teenagers soon realize that they have little power to change their children's behaviour. When you were handed that lay-off notice, you were powerless to do anything to change the company's decision, and once the job hunt began you were ultimately powerless to make anyone give you a job.

The old joke goes, "How many psychologists and psychiatrists does it take to change a light bulb?" The answer: "Only one, but the light bulb must want to change!"

Everyone who has tried to lose a few pounds, get control of his anger, or to otherwise exert some self-discipline with regard to persistent habits knows the feeling of powerlessness as he tries, by sheer force of will, to change himself. While we may go to extreme measures to try and take control of a world that seems often out of control, facing the truth about our powerlessness is another key step in emotional healing.

The apostle Paul wrote to the Christians in Colossae that trying to do things to make themselves better had no power to truly change them.

Since you died with Christ to the basic principles of this world, why, as though you still belonged to it, do you submit to its rules: "Do not handle! Do not taste! Do not touch!"? These are all destined to perish with use, because they are based on human commands and teachings. Such regulations indeed have an appearance of wisdom, with their self-imposed worship, their false humility and their harsh treatment of the body, but they lack any value in restraining sensual indulgence (Colossians 2:20–23 NIV).

Alcoholics Anonymous (AA) and other "Twelve Step" groups build on this basic understanding that our regulations, our external attempts to change ourselves, do little to change our internal world. "Step One" of a Twelve Step program says: We have come to admit that our lives have become unmanageable and that we are powerless over our separation from God.

WHAT DO I HAVE POWER OVER?

In this life the list of things that we truly do have power over is limited. Before we look at what powerlessness does in our hearts, let's first look at the things that God has intended us to have under our authority.

❑ As adults, we should ensure that in any relationship we have the power to make a choice. This means that, when faced with any given situation, we should have:

1. The permission and freedom to assess all choices or options.
2. The time to reflect on these options.
3. The freedom to talk with others to gain perspective and wisdom on the particular situation.

If, in any relationship, we are not given freedom and time to assess options, gain perspective, and seek advice, we may be in an abusive relationship. We should always have the ability to make a choice.

❏   We have the power to agree with God about the exact nature of our hearts. This is confession, and it is the most powerful gift God has given us for changing our lives. While we often cannot change ourselves, confession gives the Holy Spirit permission to have access to the deep parts of our hearts. *"Therefore confess your sins to each other and pray for each other so that you may be healed"* (James 5:16 NIVI).

❏   "We have power through intercessory prayer to change the world." Well, yes and no. As Christians, we have the power to agree in prayer with God about anything. He wants us to be active participants in His plan. However, it is not our power that actually changes anything. It is always the power of God intervening in a person's heart or in a situation that brings any form of change.

Recently a friend of mine was struggling to come to terms with the end of her son's marriage. As we talked, she expressed regret that she hadn't prayed enough for her children when they were teenagers. She came to the realization that, over the years, she had become disappointed with prayer. She had been taught that prayer changes things, but in her son's situation prayer hadn't changed anything.

The prayer movement over the last decade has been vital to God's plan for our world. We should never stop praying. All of us could learn to pray more effectively and discipline ourselves to pray more often. However, in our zealousness to pray and see God's kingdom come on earth, we need to face the truth. If, every time we prayed, our prayers caused the person we were praying for to do what we desired, that would be manipulation. Prayer clears away the distractions, but ultimately everyone has a choice to make in their response to God's call on their lives.

Someone once asked me, "Do you believe in man and woman's free will or in God's sovereignty and predestination?"

I replied, "Yes." They looked at me quizzically, like I had missed the question. I went on to explain: all throughout history theologians have been trying to understand how God's world works and what part we play in it. I doubt we'll ever comprehend how our free will and God's sovereignty interconnect. Honestly, I think they're two sides of the same coin. The more years I live, the more I hear of people's life stories, the more I realize that this side of heaven we will never clearly see how these two work together. As Paul wrote, here on earth we do see through a mirror dimly (1 Corinthians 13:12).

We do have power, through our prayers, to influence the world! But we need to be careful about the expectations we place on others to respond to our prayers. False expectations lead to disappointment and disillusionment. Allowed to fester, our disappointment can turn into bitterness.

THE POWERLESSNESS OF CHILDHOOD ABUSE OR NEGLECT

My father never laid a hand on me in my entire childhood. It's not that I didn't receive my share of spankings, but that was my mom's job. Still I clearly remember wishing, as a teenager, that my father would hit me. If he did, the pain would at least be something tangible that I could deal with. The emotional neglect and shaming that I experienced was elusive. I could not grasp it or analyze it to help me deal with the pain; nor could I show anyone else how it was killing my soul. At the very least, a bruise was a tangible evidence of pain. The elusiveness of the emotional pain developed in me a deep sense of powerlessness.

Now, many years later, I am thankful that my father was not physically abusive. If he had been, I would have had much more than the emotional bruising of my soul to contend with. Nevertheless, the dynamic in my family of origin left me powerless to do anything to change my family, stop the abuse and neglect, or even bring some relief to the persistent pain in my soul.

It wasn't that I didn't try. I did my best to be a compliant, well-behaved child. While I was the princess of pouting, I never talked back to my parents or other adults. As a teen, I was overly diligent in keeping my curfew and avoiding the high school drinking scene. I was a good kid. I was hoping that my good behaviour would make my dad happy, so that he wasn't so angry all the time. (I now know that he wasn't angry with me. He had his own pain and disappointment and lacked the life skills to deal with his emotions in a healthy way.) I was hoping that my good behaviour would win his approval and I'd hear those words my soul thirsted for, "I love you; I'm so proud of you." But it never happened.

As a child, and later, as a teenager, I tried to lessen the pain of my soul by being nice to everyone, watching too much TV, and eating a lot. My eating was so out of control during childhood that in grade three I weighed 128 pounds. My efforts to ease the emotional pain were ineffective. In my later teens, still trying to find a way out of the chaos of my internal world, I contemplated suicide. I never moved beyond the thoughts, but even the thoughts gave me some illusion of control in my hopeless life.

In normal everyday life, children and teens have little real power in the world. They must often, for their own safety, health, and emotional well-being, submit to the rules of the adults around them. Kids need to go to school to learn to read and write, add and subtract, learn about the world around them past and present, and develop other essential social skills. To be able to live successfully in our society as adults, kids need to learn to eat well, get enough sleep, and be responsible for completing the tasks they are given. In that mix, healthy families give children the ability to learn to make wise choices, and give their children permission to do so. Growing up in a healthy family is an empowering experience.

However, many children grow up in families where their power to make any choices or have any influence on their world is severely limited. They grow up either trying hard to make choices or not trying at all. Either lifestyle leads to the same deep soul frustration, because, whether they try or whether they give up, they cannot change anything— including the deep pain in the core of their being. Whatever they do, they cannot stop the abuse, make their families safe, or bring relief to the persistent pain in their soul.

WHY BOTHER?

Eventually, those who experience an overwhelming sense of powerlessness get to the point of saying "Why bother? It's not going to make any difference anyway!" Some people become passive; others try to maintain control. Regardless of the external manifestation of powerlessness, they begin to practise the art of learned helplessness. The sense of powerlessness in major formational times of their lives has caused them to believe that they have no power at all in their lives.

Kelly had grown up in a home that seemed pleasant enough on the outside. Often she returned home from school to find her mother talking on the telephone to a neighbour or friend from church. It was often difficult to get her mother's attention. When she was younger she would wait politely for her mom to finish her telephone conversation, anxious to show off her latest art project or gold-star homework assignment. Regularly she would wait for forty-five minutes or an hour before her mom would join her in the TV room.

Eventually, she stopped waiting for her mother to get off the phone and took her time getting home from school. While she was a good student, she was working well below her capability. She managed to graduate from high school but saw little need to go to university or college. Kelly began working as a cocktail waitress at a local bar, to fill her time and gain enough financial independence to move away from home. Her high school boyfriend was pressuring her to get married. He did not deeply touch her heart, but he was pleasant enough, and it seemed like a good way to get away from home.

Within two years they had their first baby, then another. In addition to having two toddlers, Kelly had to work to supplement her husband's mediocre wage. She'd return home exhausted, desperate for some attention and encouragement from her husband. Frequently, once they exchanged pleasantries and details about the kids, he'd slip off to the garage to work on one of his projects.

Kelly's marriage was devoid of any emotional and, eventually, physical intimacy. But what could she do to change things? She simply sat and waited for her husband to connect emotionally. She began to distract herself from the pain in her soul by engaging in her own projects. Life became a hopeless void.

Early in her life Kelly had given in to the downward spiral of powerlessness. She had tried her best to get her mother's attention, but it was no use. "It must be my fault," Kelly thought to herself one day in early elementary school. "I shouldn't bother Mom with my school projects unless they are perfect!" So she worked harder, became a star student, and still waited for her mother's attention. Eventually she stopped trying, not just with her mom but also in many areas of her life. Life became a bland landscape devoid of risk and passion.

Like Kelly, when we are faced with the reality of the powerlessness of our lives, we generally begin a downward slide. At first, we try really hard to change the situation. If it doesn't change, we assume there is something wrong with us and so we increase our effort. Our effort, of course, cannot change someone else's heart—Kelly's efforts couldn't change her mom's heart. We become deeply discouraged and eventually we give up all together. "Why bother trying? It won't make any difference anyway," we tell ourselves.

Many people don't move beyond the first stage of the downward powerlessness spiral. They continue to work hard to change themselves. Often, in an attempt to not feel so powerless, they may also try to change you with equal fervour!

In North America, few of us truly face the angst of powerlessness. Generally speaking, we believe that if we work hard and do the right things, life will work out all right. But that is a lie. There are still diseases that our advanced medicine can't cure. People still lose their jobs unexpectedly, and children raised by godly parents still make bad choices with their lives. Dr. Dan Allender, in *The Wounded Heart*, sums up the reality of powerlessness. "When the pretense that the good life is a matter of hard work and fair play is stripped away through victimization, we are faced with the awful fact of how little, if anything, is in our direct control."[32]

Jake's dad was one of those alcoholics whom people at office parties and other social functions called a happy drunk. But Jake didn't find too much happiness in his dad's drinking. Dad would habitually arrive home after Jake, his mom, and his siblings had finished eating supper. Dad was loud and abrasive. Sometimes they were spared his rude remarks because he would pass out on the couch.

At the supper table, Jake would try to keep his younger sister and brother distracted from their father's drunken blunders and offensive comments by telling jokes and funny stories. He got to be pretty good at it. But one day the stories were not enough to distract the children from the shouts coming from the other room. As usual, Jake's mom had gone to try to quiet down his father. Lately, his mother's peacemaking efforts seemed to be less effective. Just when he was about to deliver the punch line on his latest joke, he heard his mother scream. Running to the living room, he saw his mother sitting on the floor, her right hand cradling her reddened cheek. She looked dazed and was crying. His dad was just standing there. Through her tears, his mom told him to take the other kids to their room and stay there.

Jake and his siblings were frightened. They went upstairs. Jake tried to finish the joke he had been telling, but all that his brother and sister could do was cry. He didn't know what else to do, so he just sat there with them, trying to deaden the fear and pain he was feeling. He had tried to do the right thing, but it wasn't working.

STATEMENTS OF POWERLESSNESS LEARNED IN CHILDHOOD

When people make statements like the following, it indicates that they have struggled with feeling powerless in their childhood or adolescence. The statements indicate that they are trying, in their own power, to change the reality of what happened.

❑ "If only I had been stronger, my dad would not have hit me."
False. It's a dad's responsibility to not use abusive force with a child (or with anyone else, for that matter).

❑ "If I had worked harder in school, my mom would have been proud of me."

False. Loving parents are proud of their children because of who they are, not because of what they do.

❏ "If I hadn't been so sexy, my uncle wouldn't have sexually abused me."

False. I have heard this statement said often by clients who are trying to come up with a way to understand why they were sexually abused. Victims of childhood sexual abuse try to minimize the powerlessness of being abused by convincing themselves that they had some power to stop it. I have yet to see a seductive preschooler. And even if they were uncommonly attractive, it is the adult's responsibility not to cross that boundary.

ADULT STATEMENTS OF POWERLESSNESS

People fall under the curse of powerlessness when they make themselves responsible for changing something that is outside of the true boundaries of their power, influence, and control. In doing this, they oversimplify situations by expecting that changing one factor will make things different. When adults make statements like the following, there are clear indications that they have struggled with an overwhelming sense of powerlessness at some point in their lives and have continued to try and take some control, albeit unsuccessfully.

❏ "It's too bad I didn't get that promotion, but when I finish another course I'll be able to get the next promotion."

False. There are no guarantees that taking another course will land you a promotion, especially if office politics comes into play. What is true is that if God is directing you to take the additional course you should do it.

❑ "If only I had been (smarter, prettier, more spiritual), my husband wouldn't have left me."
False. Healthy marriages are held together by each partner's commitment to each other and God. Self-improvement is fine, but on its own it will not keep a marriage together.

❑ "I just need to pray more for my wife, and then everything in our marriage will be fine."
False. Prayer for a spouse is a great thing. But people you are praying for have one of two responses to make to God: they can respond positively and repent and draw near to God and others, or they can respond negatively by hardening their hearts even more to the Holy Spirit. Praying more may make things worse before they get better. And remember, you might be part of the problem too!

❑ "I've just joined an on-line Christian dating club so I can meet more people. Like everyone says, you just need to meet more people. Hopefully, I'll soon have met the perfect mate."
False. It's good to meet people, but that, in and of itself, doesn't mean we'll find Mr. or Miss Right. There are just too many other variables—one of them being us!

There is nothing inherently wrong in taking a course, asking God to develop our character, praying more for people we care about, or using twenty-first-century methods of meeting new people. All of those actions may be part of God's process of changing us, but none has the power to change someone else or "solve" a complicated situation.

THE FRUIT OF POWERLESSNESS IN ADULT LIFE

If children experience that they cannot change their families or deaden the pain in their hearts no matter how hard they try, they will have the fruit of powerlessness in their adult lives.

1. Control Issues

People with control issues are trying, unsuccessfully, to deaden the pain of powerlessness with the anaesthetic of control. Whether they admit it or not, their failed attempts to control themselves, others, and the world around them merely reinforces the true nature of their powerlessness.

Controllers live with the illusion that they have more power than they really do. Unfortunately, controllers are adept at finding people who are willing to be controlled! For a controller to change, two things must happen. First, people must begin to challenge this illusion of control. Second, the controller must face the painful truth of the limits of his power in this world.

2. A Series of "Bad" Relationships: Revictimization

Most of us know someone who has drifted from bad relationship to bad relationship. If you did a survey of these individuals, you would find that they come from a wide variety of backgrounds socially and economically. Some of these people are highly intelligent; some would have average or below-average IQs. The group includes both men and women. Their socio-economic background, intelligence, or gender does not predispose them to continue in the role of victim, but their experience of powerlessness does.

Here's what happens: In the past they have tried to intervene in an abusive situation and found that their efforts did not make any lasting change. Remember Jake. His valiant attempts at humour did nothing to stop his dad's drinking or lessen the stress in the home. And Kelly's hard work was unsuccessful in catching her mother's attention.

As a result, they begin to tell themselves, "If only I had tried harder, been smarter, or not been as needy, then I could have made things different." As adults, they continue to connect with people who are open to this relational pattern of trying harder, being smarter, or doing whatever it takes to change them.

Revictimization can be obvious—for instance, a woman continues to get into relationships with men who have drug or alcohol addictions. Or revictimization can be more difficult to see—a person continually works long hours to make a company prosper, or has difficult bosses, or ends up in bad church situations.

People revictimize themselves when they have made an internal decision to continue in the pattern of helplessness. Internally, often not consciously, they have decided that this is what relationships are like. They need to work hard to change the other person; things will always be difficult.

I remember a man who was involved in our ministry many years ago. At the time, he was engaged and obviously looking forward to wedded bliss. However, even as a dating, engaged couple, their relationship was hardly blissful. They fought continually. He was far from perfect, but his fiancée was extremely controlling and manipulative. It seemed to be a match made in quite the opposite of heaven!

One day I tried to broach the subject with him. "Roland," I said, "you know that relationships aren't always supposed to be such hard work. It seems to me that you and Sylvia don't have too many good times together. You seem to bring out the worst in each other. Are you sure she's the one you're supposed to marry?"

Roland quickly responded. "She's had a lot of wounds in her life and, if I just keep loving her, she'll change." We talked a little while longer, with Roland continuing to assert that he could change his fiancée. I went to their wedding and then lost touch with him. When we did reconnect, he was divorced.

Roland placed himself in the familiar position of being a victim. And I suspect he will again, because he fails to acknowledge how powerless he really is to change anyone. He continues to believe that he has the ability to change another's sinful behaviour through his behaviour or good effort. If we live with that belief, we continue to enter into relationships with the hope that something we do can change the other person.

3. Life in a World of Fantasy

Powerlessness can lead us to live in one of two extremes of fantasy: optimistic delusion or despair, both aspects of denial. Optimistic delusion tries to paint a more pleasant picture of our current situation than is warranted by reality; despair tells us that not only is the current scenario bad, it is only going to get worse, and there is no use even hoping for things to get better. Both are equally deceptive and equally destructive.

The fantasy world that Jake created to cope with his dad's drunkenness was a world where humour reigned and any problem could be solved with the right punchline. While a merry heart is good medicine (Proverbs 17:22), laughter can never be used as a substitute for the truth.

The desire to "numb out" the pain of powerlessness by optimistic delusion has led some people to develop very good-looking false selves. These individuals often lie about themselves, others, or situations, because over the years their attempts to escape powerlessness by creating a false world have erased the line between reality and myth. In extreme cases, these individuals thoroughly believe that the lies coming out of their mouths are the truth, and no one can convince them otherwise.

Those who live in fantasy may rewrite the stories of their lives in ways that make the painful past much more palatable for others and themselves. It is pure fantasy to say that living in an alcoholic home didn't affect them. It is fantasy to believe that the bullying they experienced just made them a better person and didn't negatively affect their self-esteem.

Despair, at the other extreme, plunges hearts into darkness, self-pity and despondency. People who live in the fantasy world of despair have thrown up their hands and given up on life and themselves. Even those things within their realm of responsibility seem impossible to influence or tame. Nothing works. Why even try?

The deception of despair is this: despair removes from people any sense of true responsibility. God has made people stewards over certain areas of their lives; in despair, people drop their responsibilities, not doing their part so that God can do His. Despair deepens a sense of powerlessness, because it seems to reaffirm their assumption that the entire world is beyond their ability to understand and influence. This is a lie.

THE WAY OUT OF THE DECEPTION

The hard truth is that we are powerless to change many things. Then again, there are areas of our lives for which God holds us accountable.

God grant me the serenity
to accept the things I cannot change;
courage to change the things I can;
and wisdom to know the difference.

This Twelve Step prayer really says it all. We could probably stop there, but that would leave many of us wondering "What are the things I cannot change and what are the things I can?" Let's expand on what we have already touched on briefly.

Things I Cannot Change

❑ Anyone else—no matter what my relationship is to them. Wives, you cannot change your husbands, nor husbands your wives. Parents can, and should, influence their children, but they cannot force them to be someone they are not. Children cannot change their parents. Teachers, pastors, and other Christian leaders cannot change anyone. That's God's job.

❑ The condition in the world—near and far. It came as a great relief to me, post-September 11th, to realize that I did not need to figure out what needed to be done next. I could, and did, discuss the political ramifications of terrorism with my friends and colleagues. However, when it comes right down to it, all God has told me to do is to pray for those in authority over me (1 Timothy 2:1–2). That's it. While I believe we are called to be "salt and light" at all levels of society, I, personally do not have the power to change local, national, or world-wide social, economic, and political realities.

❑ Without God's help, I cannot change the things about me I want to change. I have been on enough diets in my life to know that willpower only goes so far. True behaviour change is the fruit of a changed heart. And only God can do that.

Things I Can Change, Really Change, On My Own

❑ Nothing!

The list of things we can change is pretty short, isn't it? While I am called to be a steward of many things, I cannot change anything with my own power, skill, or good intention. I cannot change the reality that my electrical and gas bills continue to increase significantly year after year. But, with God's help, I can learn to manage my financial resources better and use my finances in God-honouring ways.

Paul writes to the Christians in Philippi,

I am not saying this because I am in need, for I have learned to be content whatever the circumstances. I know what it is to be in need, and I know what it is to have plenty. I have learned the secret of being content in any

*and every situation, whether well fed or hungry, whether
living in plenty or in want. I can do everything through
him who gives me strength* (Philippians 4:11–13 NIV).

Paul had an understanding of what he could do and
what he could not. He could be strengthened, through
Christ, to be content in any situation!

POWERLESSNESS VERSUS OUR ABILITY
TO INFLUENCE AND STEWARD

To this point I have tried to make it clear that we, on
our own, really do not have any power to change anything
about others, our world, or ourselves. To stop there would
leave us with a deep sense of despair and hopelessness, and
that is not how God intended us to live. What we are called
to do is to influence others and to be good stewards of all
that God has entrusted into our care.

Our lives are to be led in such a way that we draw others
to desire to enter into relationship with our heavenly Father.
Here are a few Biblical examples of our power to influence:

*"You are the light of the world. A city on a hill cannot be
hidden. Neither do people light a lamp and put it under a
bowl. Instead they put it on its stand, and it gives light to
everyone in the house. In the same way, let your light shine
before men, that they may see your good deeds and praise
your Father in heaven"* (Matthew 5:14–16 NIV).

*Live such good lives among the pagans that, though they
accuse you of doing wrong, they may see your good deeds
and glorify God on the day he visits us* (1 Peter 2:12 NIV).

Wives, in the same way be submissive to your husbands, so that, if any of them do not believe the word, they may be won over without words by the behavior of their wives, when they see the purity and reverence of your lives (1 Peter 3:1–2 NIV).

Clearly, Scripture tells us that our lives can and should affect the lives of others. However, influence merely points them in a direction; they themselves must make the choice to follow. Someone once said to me that they saw me standing at the intersection of many paths. As people walked by, I would point them in the right direction. That's a great picture of what our role is in each other's lives. We can point people in a direction, but we must stand back and let them make their own choice.

God has given us stewardship over many things. We are to be responsible for how we use our spiritual gifts (1 Corinthians 12–14) and our natural abilities (Matthew 25:14–30). We are stewards of our relationships—most of the Epistles talk about this in one way or another. Controllers take note: at the end of the day, God looks at how I have lived my life, not how I have tried to control the way you live yours!

Helping Others Live Victoriously with Powerlessness

Powerlessness continues to keep people bound by having them believe lies. They believe that, if they try harder, do better, or are nicer, the people they care about or the difficult situations they find themselves in will change. The first thing they must do is make a break with the lie and embrace the truth.

1. *Help others acknowledge that they are not as powerful as they think they are.*

The lie of powerfulness must be renounced. It would be helpful to introduce them to something like the serenity prayer and begin to discuss the things they do have power over. Then, as you wait upon the Holy Spirit, ask Him to remind the individual of various situations where they have acted out of the lie of believing in their own power rather than in submitting to God. Say a prayer like the following:

> *Lord, I confess that I have trusted in my own power by believing I had power when I didn't. I acknowledge that it is Your power in me that changes me, and it is Your power in others' lives that changes them. Because I believed in my own powerfulness, I have sinned against You in the following ways: [name the ways you have tried to control situations]. I ask Your forgiveness now. Thank You for forgiving me and releasing me from the power of this deception.*
>
> *I now choose to believe the truth and ask You to give me your peace in all those situations I am powerless to change. And I ask You to give me courage to change the things I can. Amen.*

2. *Help them reframe their understanding of God's power and their responsibility.*

Facing situations of powerlessness, most people swing between the extremes of optimistic delusion or despair. Neither extreme is a helpful or holy way to address our lives.

One day I was writing on a whiteboard in my office, trying to explain this to a counselling client. I had written down the word *fantasy* (what I now call "optimistic delusion") on one side of the board and *despair* on the other.

Then I said to her, "The truth is somewhere in the middle," and with that statement drew a line through the middle, creating a cross.

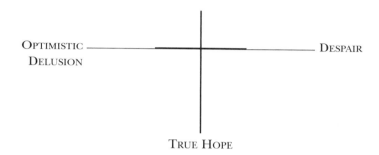

At that moment, it became abundantly clear that the only way out of the pendulum swing of fantasy and despair was to face the reality of the cross. But what does that mean in practical terms?

First, we must remember that Jesus promised that we would find freedom *by holding to and following* His teachings. Unfortunately, John 8:32 is often quoted without verse 31. *"To the Jews who had believed him, Jesus said, 'If you hold to my teaching, you are really my disciples. Then you will know the truth, and the truth will set you free'"* (NIV). It is only as we "hold to" Jesus' teachings that we know what truth really is, and then we have freedom.

So, people struggling with any aspect of powerlessness really need to develop a more Biblical understanding of control, power, influence, and stewardship. Use some of the references in this chapter to help them in this.

For example, the reality of the cross is that, as Paul said, it is only Christ who gives me strength to do anything

(Philippians 4:13). Like Christ, my role in life is not to seek to be in control. My role is to live with humility so that I will put down my desires for my life and for the lives of others and allow them to die on the cross (Philippians 2:3–8).

Ultimately, this death brings life, perhaps even the influence we had hoped to have all along. It is Jesus' death that took away the power of death and that gives us power to live our lives (John 12:24).

3. *Examine your own life and make sure you are not taking more authority than you should have in people's lives.*

Unfortunately, the effects of powerlessness are all too obvious. Not only are members of our congregation manipulative, but as leaders we too can try to take more authority for people's lives than God has given us. Spiritual abuse happens when spiritual leaders assume that it is their responsibility to change everyone in their fellowship.

God has created us all with a free will. Often leaders are frustrated by their inability to deeply influence those under their charge. Eventually they resort to a misuse of authority through some form of manipulation or control. The reality we must all face is that we can pray for hours on end and preach the best sermons, but ultimately everyone must make their own choice to respond.

4. *Empower people to influence, steward, and make wise personal choices.*

We must empower people in a godly way, rather than stripping them of any sense of godly self-identity and purpose. People who are struggling with a deep sense of powerlessness may be overly controlling or overly passive. Either they will be very manipulative, trying on their own to control the outcome of situations, or they will be very needy, constantly looking for your approval and guidance in any situation.

We must be able to paint a very clear picture of what is their responsibility and what is not. Are they trying to manipulate you or others in your church? You must remind them of the things discussed in this chapter and help them define what truly falls within their scope of power. For others, I have often found that the hardest thing is to allow people to come to their own conclusions about a life decision or situation without telling them exactly what to do. While I can guide them, I need to help them grab hold of the things that they truly need to take responsibility for.

In both situations individuals will need to face the powerlessness they have experienced in their lives. They will need to admit how lies have deceived them into living a life of fantasy or despair. Jesus will need to heal those traumatic memories, and in that process they will begin to live with true hope.

May God grant us all serenity and courage to live our lives with true hope.

Chapter Twelve

BETRAYAL

❋ ❋ ❋

Betray: (1) to place (a person, one's country etc.) in the hands of the enemy.[33]

"I feel so betrayed," she said softly, her head bowed so she did not have to look me in the face. "I thought he was trustworthy. I never thought my husband would have an affair."

"They betrayed me!" His words carried anger that had been bottled up for months. "I worked long hours to develop that project, and then when it was almost completed they replaced me with someone half my age, and she gets the credit for all my hard work!"

Her words carried a mixture of disappointment, anger, and disbelief. "I can't believe my mother didn't know something was going on. Did she sleep so soundly that she didn't hear her husband, my father, leave their bed and come to mine? What did she think he was doing all those nights? Why did she think I wanted to put a lock on my door? They were both supposed to protect me, and they didn't!"

INTO THE HANDS OF THE ENEMY

These, and other similar scenarios, are repeated every day in a variety of ways. We are betrayed. Someone whom we trust violates our trust. In breaking our trust, any safety in that relationship is removed. Before the betrayal, we believed that they would look out for our best interests. After we are betrayed, to minimize the pain we may deny that the betrayal has even happened or is significant. We are desperately hoping that it was simply a mistake. "If I give them another chance," we think, "everything will be fine."

Betrayal can only happen in a relationship where we view the other person as being trustworthy. We come to most relationships with certain legitimate expectations of trust. We assume that counsellors, pastors, and close friends will keep confidences. We expect parents, teachers, and others in authority to be safe people physically, emotionally, and spiritually. Also, we have a certain expectation that parents, teachers, and ministers will keep us safe from people who are physically, emotionally, and spiritually abusive. In the workplace, we have an expectation that we will be reimbursed fairly for our contribution to the company, and, provided we are good workers, that we will have a place of employment for years to come.

When trust is broken in any of these relationships, the act of betrayal puts us into the hands of the enemy of our soul. In the gospel of John, Jesus says about Satan, "*When he lies, he speaks his native language, for he is a liar and the father of lies*" (John 8:44 NIV). When someone betrays our trust, he has, either consciously or unconsciously, made a decision to lie to us. Even if no verbal lie about us was spoken, he has lied because he deceived us into believing that he was safe and worthy of our trust.

The following example, although extreme, clarifies my meaning. A spy for your country enters into a relationship with a political assistant from another country. The spy's intent is to win the person's trust so that he can gain information of value to his home country. The goal of this deception, ultimately, is to turn the foreign country over to its enemy.

Thankfully, most of us are not as intentionally deceptive as an abuser or a spy is. Regrettably, however, many of us betray another person's trust unintentionally by saying we are something we are not or by promising something we cannot deliver.

Over the past few years, a single mom and her three kids have been a part of our ministry. The mom became a Christian through one of our recovery groups and eventually began attending church. The children have had short but painful lives; they are needy kids. Many people have seen this need and responded. They began a relationship with the children. Unfortunately, most have betrayed the children's trust by not following through with their commitment. I've lost track of the number of men who have said, "I want to come alongside these kids and be like a father to them." After a few months the men realize that they do not have what it takes to be with such high-needs kids and eventually disappear from the scene. It's not just men either; couples, too, have offered to be there and regrettably have not. The failure of many people to follow through on their well-meaning words has left scars of betrayal on these kids' hearts.

I know the kids are desperately looking for a father who will love them unconditionally. I know this because we all are. It's part of how we are made. When these individuals failed to follow through on their words, their broken promises reinforced the lie these kids already believe: "I'm unlovable," or "I must be terribly wicked or difficult," or "I guess only smarter, better-looking, wealthier kids get fathers." And, as we have discussed throughout this book, once they begin to believe this lie, having it reinforced time and time again, they are trapped. The broken promises by some well-meaning but naive individuals have put these kids into the hands of the enemy of their souls.

Some day, when they are older and have lived more of life and have made their own choice to follow Christ, hopefully they will be able to forgive their birth fathers, their mom, and all the surrogate parents in between. In the meanwhile they will live with the effects of broken promises.

THE SHOCK OF BETRAYAL

The degree of shock we experience when we are betrayed has largely to do with the depth of relationship. The mechanic who says that repairs to my car will only be $300 and then gives me a bill for $2,000 may make me angry. His word is not trustworthy, but after the initial shock I will probably simply find a different mechanic and perhaps report him to the Better Business Bureau.

On the other hand, the shock and disbelief that sets in when marriage vows are broken or a deep friendship betrayed is at an entirely different level.

If an enemy were insulting me, I could endure it; if a foe were raising himself against me, I could hide from him. But it is you, a man like myself, my companion, my close friend, with whom I once enjoyed sweet fellowship as we walked with the throng at the house of God (Psalm 55:12–14 NIV).

King David may have written this psalm during the time of his son Absalom's attempt to usurp David's throne. Not only did Absalom betray his father, but someone who was part of David's inner circle, his advisor Ahithophel, was pulled into the plot as well (1 Chronicles 27:33; 2 Samuel 15). David's estrangement from his son Absalom must have been difficult enough. To have a trusted counsellor involved in the betrayal would have driven an arrow even farther into the wound in David's heart.

When we are betrayed by those closest to us, our heart utters the cry "How could you have done this to me?" What once had been a life-giving relationship has been killed by the act of betrayal. The experience of the betrayal brings with it such a strong sense of disbelief that often we may continue on in relationship as if nothing had happened, never facing the seriousness of the sin. Though the betrayal was devastating, we can hardly believe that our friend has sinned against us. Her betrayal calls into question her character and ours. If we had really seen our friend for who she was, we would have known that she was untrustworthy. Facing our own naivety is as difficult as facing the act of betrayal.

THE SET-UP OF BETRAYAL

Jesus reminded His followers that what we see in our lives comes out of our character. Using the analogy of a tree, He explained that good trees bear good fruit and bad trees bear bad fruit (Luke 6:43–45). Following this analogy, we see that part of our struggle with betrayal is realizing that the actual event of betrayal is only the surface problem. In the betrayer's heart is a deep pit of her own woundedness and sin. We begin to realize that she was able to pull us into her web of deception. Not only did she betray us but she set us up!

In his book *The Wounded Heart,* Dr. Dan Allender outlines the set-up that happens to those who have been sexually abused. (Please see his book for specific information on the set-up of sexual abusers.) While the pattern may not be as obvious with other forms of betrayed trust, it is useful in helping us understand that all acts of betrayal have some period of "set-up."

At the start, their families unknowingly set up sexual abuse victims. This set-up is generally not conscious. For example, in a home where they lack affection, warmth, affirmation, or attention, children become vulnerable to abusers who appear to offer the acceptance and love that they are missing. Since the vast majority of sexual abuse happens in a relationship of trust—a relative, parent, schoolteacher, coach, church leader—it is easy to see how the child's heart is drawn in by the illusion of affection he is missing. Often, looking back, abuse victims realize that their families were not warm nurturing places. Once the child is lured in, the actual sexual abuse takes place. The set-up process can happen in moments or months.

This same set-up and betrayal of trust happens to us all. Recently I worked with individuals who were sexually abused by a church leader. Here's how the set-up happened. This individual's charisma and spiritual giftedness gave him a place of recognition and honour in many churches. His spiritual gifts were powerful, impacting many people's lives in a positive way. Additionally, he always gave the appearance of propriety—never meeting with an individual without one of the pastors or elders present. As he gained favour with those in leadership, he was given more and more trust. When one of the victims finally came forward, a decade-long trail of manipulation and betrayal was revealed. Not only had he abused young women, he had taken advantage of the trust of numerous church leaders in the process. The betrayal was devastating.

As this betrayal was analyzed, inevitably people began asking "Why did this happen?" It became apparent, in hindsight, that the set-up of betrayal happened because the people in these churches were desperately looking for the tangible power of God in their midst. It is, of course, a good thing to desire to see and experience more of God. This man seemed to deliver just that.

As I have talked with numerous church leaders over the years, that aspect of broken trust seems common. Often those who have betrayed the trust of church congregations or movements have been able to do so because we—those of us who were betrayed—were so desperate for what they had to offer. The betrayer was an amazing preacher, a moving worship leader, or a merciful counsellor. Our unmet spiritual and emotional needs were filled, and we were unable to see the character flaws in other areas.

Take a look at those areas in your life where you have felt deeply betrayed. Can you see a similar pattern? Were there unmet needs in your own life that caused you to be unaware of the warning signs of betrayal?

Stephanie had a good friend named April. Stephanie was a believer; April was not. They had, Stephanie felt, a great friendship, connecting on many levels. Their friendship had spanned a decade, and they had talked about many personal issues. Then one day the relationship changed.

April had recently acquired a roommate. Stephanie never thought anything about it. However, soon April announced that her roommate was more than a roommate: she was her partner. April went on to say that some of the past relationships she had discussed with Stephanie had not been with men but with women.

Stephanie hardly knew what to say. While she believed that homosexuality was not God's best choice for her friend, there was something more chilling about the announcement. Over the years she had worked with, and been friends with, other women who were in homosexual relationships, and she had been able to interact with them without any problems. She had realized that they could not change without Christ and that their sin was not any worse than others. She respected them, and they respected her, even though their beliefs were different. But something was different here.

It took Stephanie a few days to figure out what was wrong. She realized that she felt betrayed by her friend. April had presented herself as someone she wasn't. She had lied about who she was, and it left Stephanie feeling that their whole friendship had been a sham. Additionally, Stephanie realized that there were warning signs that she ignored because she valued her friendship with April. Challenging those questionable comments or behaviour might have ruined their friendship. As it turned out, they were unable to resolve their differences. April was unable to accept responsibility for lying to her friend about her identity.

THE EFFECTS OF BETRAYAL

When trust is broken in any significant relationship, we are wounded more deeply than in more casual relationships.

Our disbelief or dismissal of the significance of the betrayal does not change that reality. It is a spiritual law that when we are sinned against we are wounded, whether we choose to consciously acknowledge the wounding or not.

Likewise, it is a spiritual law that when we are wounded we will react to that wound in a sinful way. Often, even if we speak forgiveness to the offender, we still resort to sinful ways of self-protection (instead of godly discernment) to protect ourselves from further pain. Our hearts are deceptive and quickly erect sinful walls of protection to ensure we will not be hurt again. Again, we may not even consciously acknowledge those walls, but they are there.

What's more, if we see the set-up that happened in the betrayal, we become suspicious of everyone's motives. Our self-protection analyzes and dissects even the most casual comment lest it be a set-up for further abuse. We are on high alert. Betrayal conveys two strong messages. "You can't trust anyone!" we emphatically tell ourselves. And then we reflect, "There must be some deep flaw in me that I am not worthy of their relationship."

No One Is to Be Trusted

To protect our hearts from further damage, we draw a wall of fortification around other people to make sure that the pain of betrayal never happens again. We will never again turn our hearts over to the enemy. Sometimes we are aware of this protective wall; at other times we are not. Frequently we erect subconscious walls to try to protect ourselves from the pain no one else could prevent.

Our sinful response to betrayal shuts down our hearts from being able to enjoy an open relationship with God and others. We become overly suspicious of others' motives, often going to great lengths to try and figure out the motivation behind a friend's special kindness to us. Every kind word or deed is questioned. We may say a pleasant "Thank you," but internally we are asking, "What do they really want? What do they really mean?"

The wounding of trust through betrayal may be evidenced in our lives in a variety of ways. We may become passively aggressive to others or become domineering and controlling. Or we may naively continue to trust everyone without discernment, desperate for intimacy and relationship in our lives.

Being Passive-Aggressive

It's a term commonly used but one which many of us fail to see operating in our lives. Simply put, when we are passively aggressive, we act out our distrust of others in indirect ways. We are aggressive to those whom we perceive to be untrustworthy, but not in an upfront, obvious way. For example, someone in the church may ask us to do something for him. We say, "Sure, no problem," but never get around to doing it. As an excuse, we say we were too busy or forgot. Or we may deep down inside dislike the person and so use this passive aggressiveness as our way of showing it. "After all," we reason, "he didn't support me in the last initiative I proposed to the church finance committee."

Passive people who actively distrust others will appear pleasant and compliant. They will take out the aggression, or mistrust of others, in "behind your back" ways. They give an appearance of doing everything they can to avoid conflict or issues that they perceive could lead to being wounded. They may physically avoid people they perceive to be untrustworthy, but it is more common that they will avoid any type of intimacy by emotionally detaching from relationships. They protect themselves through emotional distance, indirect aggression, and avoidance.

Mark had the reputation for being a nice guy. Ask him anything, and chances were good he could help you out. He had the reputation, as well, for failing to keep his promises to certain people. Mark did not like conflict. He never wanted to put himself in a situation where his refusal to help would put him out of favour with someone. He was dishonest with himself and with others, wanting to stay in control of relationships by keeping people at a distance with his good works. If he really didn't like someone very much, he would simply let the promise slip by unfulfilled. He was unaware that he was "getting back" at people by his inability to keep his promises.

In church or work situations, people who are passive-aggressive maintain control by being outwardly compliant while using gossip to maintain the upper hand in relationships. This is the method they have chosen to protect themselves against the possibility of betrayal. Gossip is always a form of passive-aggressive control: it always happens behind someone's back, and it always—yes, always—results in putting down a person in someone's eyes. Furthermore, gossip gives the participants a feeling of power, as they appear to know and understand something about someone that no one else does! Someone who is passive-aggressive uses words to control and manipulate behind the scenes. Their words are veiled and contorted.

Our words are to be a clear, open reflection of what is in our hearts. And our words are to be followed up by our actions. The apostle Paul, challenged by the Corinthians about his plans to visit them, said, *"When I planned this, did I do it lightly? Or do I make my plans in a worldly manner so that in the same breath I say, 'Yes, yes' and 'No, no'?"* (2 Corinthians 1:17 NIV).

My friend and I walked into her mom's kitchen, arriving early for supper so that we could visit before the other guests arrived. Mrs. Smith was talking on the phone. When she hung up the phone she greeted us, apologizing for the delay, and said, "Oh, that Mrs. Jones; she can be such a bother sometimes."

My friend replied, "Mom, I thought you liked her."

"Well, I do," Mrs. Smith said, and added, "but sometimes she just goes on and on. Since her husband had an affair she's become very whiny and self-centred. No wonder he cheated on her."

To her face Mrs. Smith was polite, friendly, and seemed to enjoy Mrs. Jones's company. However, when her back was turned, my friend's mom, Mrs. Smith, practised the favourite church practice of gossip. Gossip is passive-aggressive behaviour. We choose not to tell our friends the truth; rather, we show our displeasure of them behind their backs.

Here's an example of severe passive-aggressive behaviour. Extremely passive-aggressive people will tell you how much they like your new car; then, when you have left, they will take their keys and scratch a line down its side.

Control and Domination

When trust has been violated, we may protect ourselves by trying to actively control the relationship, ensuring that by our control we will not get hurt again. We may use our wit, social skills, rage, or anything at our disposal to make sure that we control how emotionally connected we become.

I have a good friend who is a quick thinker. Generally

speaking, I am not. I know my friend cares for me and values our relationship. When we get into a disagreement, he often uses this quick thinking to control and steer the conversation. Consequently, when I know we have to discuss something that might become a little heated, I have learned to write down my thoughts before we talk. On his part, my friend is learning to listen and wait for my thinking to catch up with his, but it is a lifelong pattern of staying in control, and it will take some time for him to be free of it completely.

Obviously, many people express anger to keep people at a distance. Angry words or actions are, after all, effective ways to scare people away. I have observed that people who have been wounded and have had their trust betrayed in significant relationships often exhibit their fiercest rage in their most significant relationships. Betrayal in key relationships, of course, would cause the greatest hurt. It is difficult for people who have been deeply betrayed to manage their anger until the underlying wound has been healed.

Ben and Nadine were both in their second marriage. Life had been challenging for both of them. Ben had used drugs and alcohol to cope with the turmoil of life; Nadine faced the disappointment she had experienced in life by working hard and spoiling her children. Ben and Nadine had become Christians about three years earlier and met and married at the church they had both begun attending. With God's help, and regular attendance at AA, Ben had managed to stop using drugs or alcohol to numb out his pain. He was beginning to face the truth about the trauma he had experienced in his life. The healing process was slower than he would have liked, but he was thankful for every small step.

Ben was a pleasant man, eager to redeem the years of pain. Married life had its challenges, but he refused to resort to drugs or alcohol to help him get by. The problems escalated when, concerned about Nadine's children's disrespect, he confronted their behaviour. The children had "run" the home prior to marriage and continued to treat their mom like a servant. Ben thought this behaviour was not appropriate and tried to correct the children. But Nadine didn't like his "meddling" in her family. In reality, Ben's desire to have the children honour their mom deeply touched a part of her heart that had been hardened for years. It was terrifying to feel vulnerable as this part of her began to come alive. She responded in rage every time she would overhear Ben's attempts to discipline the kids.

To avoid her rage, Ben tried to talk with the kids out of earshot of his wife. It didn't work, and her rage continued, overflowing into other areas of their lives. Increasingly, Ben retreated into himself to avoid Nadine's temper, saying less and less to his wife about anything important. Nadine had won. She had successfully used her rage to keep her husband at a distance and lessen the chance of betrayal.

Of course, like all our attempts at self-protection, Nadine's rage failed to protect her. Their marriage eventually ended with both Nadine and Ben feeling betrayed by the person they had loved.

Naïve Trust

Every once in a while I meet someone who seems to believe, without any question, anything I say. While I believe that I am a trustworthy person, I realize that I am far from perfect. People who naively trust refuse to believe the truth that we can all sin and make mistakes; therefore, everyone is capable of hurting another person, even if it is unintentional. They are unable to face the deep wounds that have been caused in their lives through broken trust. Afraid to face the pain of past betrayals, they refuse to use discernment in their relationships, hurting themselves time and time again by trusting people who are obviously untrustworthy.

Raymond thought he was a person of deep faith in God. He figured that everyone was created in God's image and therefore everyone deserved a chance. In his church, he gravitated to the people that others found difficult to be around, offering them friendship and access to his life. He loved the unlovely, something he believed to be a godly part of his character.

In order to minister to these individuals, he would open up and share his own fears and struggles. As far as he was concerned, his life was an open book. One day he was talking with one of his new friends, Ruth, about the struggles she was having. Men, starting with an uncle who had sexually abused her, had hurt Ruth once too often. As Ruth shared, she began to cry, and Raymond put an arm around her shoulder to comfort her.

Ruth began to yell, "Get away from me, you pervert!" among other things and ran from the room. The next day, Raymond's pastor called and asked that he come to the church office to meet with him. When he arrived, Ruth was sitting there too. She began to recite her part of the story, accusing Raymond of doing things that had never even entered his mind. Raymond was shocked. He hardly knew what to say.

Ruth was not a trustworthy person. If Raymond had been willing to face the truth about the reality of betrayal in his own life, he might have been able to see that Ruth was an unsafe person. She failed to share much of her own life or take an active interest in anyone else's. Ruth had bounced from church to church, generally leaving when someone challenged her behaviour. She was always critical of others but was never able to identify her own shortcomings.

Raymond had faced betrayal at an early age. His parents had left him with a female babysitter when he was eight years old. After the third evening of babysitting, she sexually abused him. But Raymond had difficulty even in identifying and admitting that what had happened was actually sexual abuse. Because he could not see the truth, he could not see how his babysitter had betrayed not only his trust but his parents as well. Because he denied and minimized the depth of woundedness in his own life, he could not see the depth of woundedness and sin in others either.

When, ultimately, our attempts to protect ourselves from further betrayal fail, we are left to conclude that we must not be worthy of being cared for or protected. As a result, we assume others are trustworthy while we, deep down inside, are flawed.

I Must Not Be Worthy

Children who are raised in abusive families struggle with a feeling of being betrayed by the non-offending parent. They may rage at the father who abused them, but they have difficulty facing the betrayal of the mother who was unable, or unwilling, to protect them.

The trauma of the physical or sexual abuse is devastating on its own. Children deal with feeling powerless, shamed and betrayed by the abusive parent. Their souls are so deeply wounded that it seems impossible to believe that the person who could stop the abuse, the non-offending parent, has not. Rather than face the betrayal from that parent, children begin to believe the lie that they are not worthy to be protected. To them, this is less painful to accept than to believe the betrayal of another parent.

Day-to-day betrayal may look something like this: Imagine you are up for a job promotion. It is a sure thing. Your boss has even said it is yours; all she needs is the approval from her manager, and that will come soon. You have a great relationship with your boss; she is more like a friend, and you feel confident about the promotion. Then one day you hear the devastating news: the promotion has been given to someone else in your department. You are distraught. You try to talk to your boss, only to find out she is in a meeting all afternoon.

You cannot believe that your boss did not stand up for you. "I must have done something wrong," you tell yourself. It feels like someone has punched you in the gut. "It was probably that last project I worked on. My part was fine, but John really did contribute a lot. I guess I'm just not ready yet."

As a Leader, How Can I Help Mend Broken Trust?

The reality is that everyone has had someone break a promise to them, big or small. And we all, intentionally or unintentionally, have broken our promises to someone. As a leader it would be naive to assume that, simply by keeping our word, we can help mend the broken trust and the pain of betrayal experienced by people who come to us. (We must, of course, be trustworthy; you may wish to review chapter 3 about safety to ensure you are being a safe and trustworthy person.) Only the Holy Spirit's healing can truly restore someone's ability to trust.

Here are some ways you can help people heal as they recover from the wounds of betrayal:

1. As a leader, remember that we are all commanded to love each other—but we are not commanded to trust each other. (See 1 John 4:7–8; 1 Corinthians 13:1–7.)

We inherit a certain level of "trust" with any leadership position. However, we should not take this inherited trust for granted. People do not need to trust others simply because they are in a leadership position. You are responsible to steward the implicit trust your position holds and to earn any extra trust.

Additionally, the Bible is pretty clear that our love for each other is to be a distinguishing factor in our lives. Even the "love chapter," 1 Corinthians 13, does not use the word *trust* as a definition of love (v 4–7). Trust is something we earn. Read over Paul's letter to the Christians in Corinth. Both 1 Corinthians and 2 Corinthians are Paul's recitation of why he is trustworthy and should be honoured. He earned trust by proving himself to the Corinthians in many ways, over and over again. He was not calling them to trust and honour because of his position in the early Church. He was reminding them of the trust and relationship that he had already proven to them.

Of course, love includes an element of trust. But it is never to be blind trust. It is trust that is developed over time through the process of discerning the trustworthiness of another. First John, a letter that is full of messages about love, reminds us in two separate passages about the importance of discerning the soundness of those who come into our midst (1 John 2:4-11; 4:1–6).

2. Help people learn how to discern trustworthiness.

People need tools to learn how to discern someone's trustworthiness. Discernment—on both a spiritual and an emotional level—is something that we learn in life. We learn to do it rightly or wrongly depending on the foundations laid in our childhood.

You can help those who come to you by giving people some tools in the discernment process. Books like *Safe People* and *Boundaries* ("see Suggested Reading") are a good place to start.

When I first began to meet regularly with a Christian counsellor, I remember the frustration I felt in learning how to develop healthy, trustworthy relationships. By that stage in the process, I had received healing for many of the significant wounds in my life. But I still did not know how to connect with people and build a healthy relationship built on mutual trust.

I began looking at how I initiated relationships. Basically, I lived behind an emotional wall—a mile high, and easily as wide! I was always pleasant—or at least superficially so—operating mostly in naive trust and passive-aggressive distrust. When I met someone whom I wanted to get to know better, I would take down the wall immediately. I would tell them everything about me in the first hour. All the wounds would be out and bleeding on the table. Usually, my new friend would nod and say "uh-huh" a few times, and I would think, "Wow, a new friend! Isn't it great how open and honest they are." However, what would often happen after this first meeting is that they would continue listening to my story without sharing any of theirs. Eventually the friendship would fall apart, and I'd be left wondering what went wrong.

Well, there were a few things.

We must, as leaders, teach people four basic keys for building a healthy relationship. Somewhere in my journey

I found these keys and have modified and adapted them for myself. You can teach these steps to those who come to you, too.

Keys to Building a Healthy Relationship

a. Honesty

To be honest simply means that we are real.

It was, of course, not wise for me to share everything about myself without developing a relationship with someone first. Honesty in relationship is something we develop over time.

I was being honest when I revealed my whole life story to a new friend. However, what I failed to see is that my new friend's failure to share her own story was a form of dishonesty.

We are to be truthful about who we are. Over time, I learned to share only a bit about myself and to allow the other person to respond in kind. If, after a reasonable amount of time, this person did not, I knew that the potential friendship could not go any farther until there was an equal amount of self-revelation.

Integrity means that who we are on the outside is the same as who we are on the inside. To really know if someone has integrity, if this person is honestly who she says she is, we need time and various interactions.

b. Affirmation

I had to learn that a friendship was based on mutual affirmation. While I wanted others to affirm me—"You're a great person...That was insightful...I've enjoyed our time together"—I realized it was difficult for me to say those affirmations back.

These are not words to speak lightly. They are to be true affirmations from our hearts. And we must learn to say them as well as receive them.

c. Affection

At some level a relationship that is growing in healthy trust needs to have a feel of affection or "warmth" to it. Maybe this is a hug, a pat on the shoulder, or kind words. Most people know true affection when they receive it. They feel appreciated, affirmed, and loved.

d. Commitment

A relationship is only as strong as the events that have tested it.

Commitment in any relationship is only tested when there is conflict. In the early stages of a friendship this may be a small issue, but it reflects both parties' willingness to take responsibility for their own issues and forgive the other. Ultimately, we only know whom we can trust when the chips are down.

I now look at conflict as the potential to grow things deeper in a relationship. As the conflict is resolved, we move to a deeper level of honesty, affirmation, and affection.

3. Extend forgiveness and break reactive sin patterns.

As people learn tools in discerning trust, they are able to enter into the process of forgiving those who have betrayed them. Ask them to write down the actual instance of betrayal, and then ask the Holy Spirit to show them the specific effects the betrayal has had on them. They will need to forgive the betrayer for the instance of betrayal and for how it has affected their lives.

Wounded people also need to ask God's forgiveness for

believing the lie that they were not worthy of being protected, cared for, and respected by the offending person. Statements like "I should have seen it coming" or "I should have know better" are indications that they believe this lie. In essence, they are minimizing the betrayers' responsibility for their actions.

The next step is to identify and ask forgiveness for the sinful relationship patterns they have used to protect themselves from the possibility of future betrayal. Whether they have been passive-aggressive, controlling and domineering, or naively trusting, now is the time to confess the sin and ask for God's forgiveness. Ask the Holy Spirit to clearly reveal to them these patterns of self-protection.

4. Pray for the healing of past wounds.

Often a betrayal in the present will open the door for healing for past wounds of betrayal. Ask the Holy Spirit to take the individual back to each and every instance of betrayal that he or she experienced. Go through the process of forgiveness and confession for each instance. This may have happened, to some extent, as you addressed self-protective patterns. Nevertheless, it is necessary to ask the Holy Spirit to specifically heal the wounds caused by betrayal.

AND REMEMBER

By the time we have reached adulthood, we have all been betrayed hundreds of times in big and small ways. Even those who have been raised in relatively normal families will have faced betrayal by family, friends, and others. Trust is something to be earned. Honour those under your leadership by not assuming that they should naively trust you simply because you are the leader. Be trustworthy. Even if your heart is in the right place, don't make promises you can't keep.

Chapter Thirteen

SEXUALITY, INTIMACY, AND IDENTITY

❊　❊　❊

"**D**oes God care about your sex life?" My colleague read aloud the words from a marriage brochure stuffed into our pamphlet rack at the office.

"Does God care about my sex life?" I chuckled sarcastically and said, "Apparently not!"

Of course, I know that is not the case. My understanding of God is that he cares about all areas of my life. However, it is a challenge, as a single Christian woman who believes that sexual intimacy outside of marriage is wrong, to wrap my head around the reality that God does care about my sex life. This is complicated by the reality that our society equates sex with sexuality.

Actually, more correctly, God cares about my sexuality. Through God's healing process in my life, I have come to understand that "sex" is an act; "sexuality" has to do with our identity as male or female.

On another occasion, during a recovery group for survivors of sexual abuse, two women began discussing the last time they had "been" with a man. One said something like,

"It's been over two years," another, "It's been eight months." Both women commented that the current lack of "sex" in their lives was a major struggle and disappointment. Both recently divorced, they weren't sure how much longer they could remain celibate. They professed to be committed evangelical Christians, but the need for sexual activity seemed to be a driving force in their lives that they did not want to leave unfulfilled. One woman said she felt like she would die without sex, and others seemed to agree.

We talked in that group about the many factors that affect our sex drive—hormones, triggers in brain chemistry, the need for the euphoric "fix" from sex, and a desire for intimacy. It turned out to be an interesting and healing time for many, but I left that meeting feeling disturbed. What was disturbing me was not what had been said and discussed in the group; instead, I was concerned about myself. I felt that there must be something wrong with me!

Given a world where sexual activity is fused to intimacy, I had momentarily fallen for the deception that my emotional health as a woman was based on the amount of sexual activity in my life. It is a common misconception, not only in our world but also in the Church.

Single, married, or divorced, it seems that most people struggle to understand their sexuality. The vast majority of the people with whom I deal in recovery groups or counselling sessions are adult survivors of sexual abuse. Their struggle to perceive "sex" in a healthy way is understandable. However, outside of this context, over my years in ministry I have been surprised at the number of committed Christian single adults who are sexually active. I have also heard too many stories of marital unfaithfulness. Clearly, whatever our state in life, we struggle to understand our sexuality.

Unfortunately, few Bible colleges or seminaries offer classes that teach a biblical view of sexuality. Yet, as citizens of our postmodern world, we are bombarded daily by sexual images and sexual philosophies that are false and deceptive. It is a confusing place to be, with little guidance given in Christendom for those beyond teenage or early adult years.

Resources are hard to find. There are materials for teens regarding abstinence, but they don't translate easily for separated, divorced, or otherwise single people over thirty. Likewise, material written for married couples is simply that, material for married couples; it does not, generally speaking, offer a Biblical world view of sexuality beyond the bedroom.

However, over the years I have managed to find a few Christian authors who have written about sexuality. This chapter is based on the half dozen books that deal in a Biblical way with this sensitive subject. Check out the "Suggested Reading" list for more information than this short chapter can provide.

Lewis Smedes begins his book *Sex for Christians* with the following words:

> The toughest problem Christians have with sex is how to feel about their own sexuality. On this subject, many of us are confused, confounded, and inconsistent. We may be sure that we know what is right or wrong about things people do with sex. Especially things other people do. But few of us really are sure within ourselves about how we actually feel and how we ought to feel about the sexuality that is woven into the texture of our very beings...Few of us totally deny our sexuality. But we cannot find the way into a happy celebration of it either. We carry a complex mixture of feelings.[34]

Despite our confusion, our sexuality—our distinct maleness and femaleness—is something God cares deeply about, whether we are married or not! It is the uniqueness of Himself that He put into each of us. Especially in these days we must as Christians do more than tell people what they should and should not do. We must be able to articulate and live out a Christian world view of sexuality.

CREATED IN HIS IMAGE

Then God said, "Let us make humankind in our image, according to our likeness; and let them have dominion over the fish of the sea, and over the birds of the air, and over the cattle, and over all the wild animals of the earth, and over every creeping thing that creeps upon the earth."
*So God created humankind in his image, in the image of God he created them; **male and female he created them*** (Genesis 1:26–27, emphasis added).

Our sexuality, our maleness and femaleness, is the one thing that God used to distinguish the pinnacle of His creation. Think about it. He could have given man one type of nose, and woman another. Or Adam could have had one eye, and Eve have two. But no, God choose to create us with different sexual organs and all the hormonal, physical, and soul characteristics that go with that decision.

It's also clear from the first two chapters in Genesis that femaleness and maleness are somehow unique expressions of God's image in us. Being male reflects the image of God; being female reflects the image of God. The image of God cannot be completely reflected without both male and female. Despite our great differences, the truth is that the only way the world will see God in us is through both male and female together. The implication of the truth revealed in Genesis 1:27 is that woman was not an afterthought. She was not simply created to be a companion to Adam. Without woman, there was something missing in God's revelation of Himself. We are not to despise our unique genders.

But we do. And we despise each other too. Writing in *Women of Destiny,* international speaker and leader Cindy Jacobs pinpoints this despising of our genders as the fundamental fault line running beneath all other human conflicts. She writes:

> I believe that the recent movement of reconciliation between cultures is a prelude to the biggest healing of all. The wounds inflicted by men and women on each other constitute the fundamental fault line running beneath all other human conflicts. If gender difference is used as the justification for the devaluation of one part of humanity, then the door is open for the selective devaluation of all of humanity based on some difference from the perceived ideal.[35]

So what does it mean to be male, what does it mean to be female, in the context of the reality that we are created in God's image? Unfortunately, most of our understanding of male and female is marred by the fall. As a result, our human tendency is to turn our discussions into debates about gender roles or brain functions or other physical attributes. In the process, as Cindy Jacobs points out, we manage to devalue each other. While discussions about roles or physical attributes can be significant, they are only external reflections of internal and spiritual realities.

SEXUALITY AND INTIMACY

Ultimately, a key component of our identity as human beings is our sexuality. It is an integral factor in how we relate to each other. A person who is whole must embrace his or her sexuality. It defines who we are and affects how we relate to each other.

Most Christians are aware that Eve and Adam's act of disobedience, in choosing knowledge over life, led to a break in their relationship with God and each other. That break in intimacy initiated a feeling of shame at being seen or exposed. That break in intimacy was a fall from our perfect maleness and femaleness.

In those first moments after they ate the forbidden fruit, they experienced something they never had before—shame. Instantly they were transformed from free, secure, unafraid, intimate partners in Paradise to humiliated, separate people. They were the first to be afraid of their own shadow and the growing shadows in their souls.

They were now separate people, separated from each other and also separated from their God. Intimacy on all levels—emotional, spiritual, and physical—had been broken. Today, living in this world that was so changed by our ancestors' choices, we can only, at best, catch tiny glimpses of the truth—that our sexuality is fused with intimacy.

INTIMACY

There are two words that cause participants in sexual abuse recovery groups the most discomfort. Those words are *intimacy* and *vulnerability*. If I mention that we are going to talk about anything related to intimacy, people begin to shift in their chairs, look at the floor, and shut down. For these individuals—in fact, for most of us—intimacy has only one meaning: sexual intimacy. When those who have been sexually abused are invited to talk about intimacy, they are also invited to look at an injury unfathomable to most of us.

However, they are not alone. Most people's definition of intimacy would undoubtedly include sexual involvement. In a world where "Sex in the City" is touted as the way relationships are to be, no wonder we have little concept of intimacy outside of sexual acts.

Intimacy is very simply knowing and being known. This is not knowledge predominately on an intellectual level (although understanding what someone thinks is a start). It is knowing someone on a deeply personal emotional level. It is allowing someone into your life and allowing him or her to have an effect on you. It is being in relationship with a person who reciprocates by giving you the same honour of knowing and influencing him or her.

Not all personal disclosures are intimate. For example, when I am teaching seminars, I will often share details of the areas of wounding where God has brought healing. Often, these disclosures can get pretty personal. However, even though I am sharing what appear to be intimate details, my relationship with the group of people in this seminar is far from intimate. Why? Because no matter how personal the issues I may share in a teaching situation, the other people do not have an opportunity to share at the same level with me. This relationship is not reciprocal.

However, if I were to share the same information in the small group I am part of at my church, there would be the potential for intimacy. In my small group, I have developed trusting relationships that allow others to speak into my life and vice versa.

At this point, it might be a good thing to define what I mean by *personal*. When I share personal information about myself, it goes beyond reciting of events; it also includes the emotional impact of those events on my soul. Sharing personal things about ourselves is not talking about what happened in our day but about how we feel about what happened in our day.

For example, the other day an error on my part resulted in an important cheque being returned NSF. When I found out about the mistake, I was upset and spent some time worrying about what would happen. Then, the next day I sat down and figured out what I'd done wrong, and the situation was resolved.

That last paragraph is not an intimate accounting of the event. To share this story with you in an intimate way would read more like this: Yesterday I found out that I had made a mistake and an important cheque had been returned NSF. I couldn't believe what had happened. I was so embarrassed and confused. When I came home, I managed to beat myself up for a good hour over the mistake. From there, I jumped to worrying about finances in the future and what people would think of me when they found out about the NSF cheque. I felt so ashamed. All I wanted to do was run away and hide. I know I'm not the best with finances and numbers, but it felt worse than just making a mistake; it felt like somehow I was flawed. It shouldn't have been a big deal, but it was. I felt such deep shame.

This is an intimate, though abbreviated, description of the event. Intimacy requires going beyond the information to the emotions.

Intimacy and sexuality are fused together. They were meant to be. Our sexual urges are meant to drive us "inexorably into a desire for personal, intimate involvement with another person."[36] In our woundedness this drive becomes distorted in one of two ways. Either we assume that intimacy and sexual acts are the same (and the only true form of intimacy) or we shut down any desire for intimacy, deflecting all relationships away from deep personal connections. Both choices keep emotional connection with another at arm's length. Often, those who struggle with emotional intimacy have been wounded sexually in some form.

WOUNDED INTIMACY

When we are emotionally, physically, or sexually wounded, our ability to be emotionally intimate with someone is diminished. A friend betrays a trust, and we wonder how we can trust that person again. Someone important to us uses their power in the relationship to entrap us. We decide we will never be so vulnerable with another person again. In both instances, whatever the external situation, we choose to detach ourselves emotionally and distance our hearts from the hurtful other.

Our ability to open our true self to another, our intimacy, has been wounded. In our hearts, we make a choice not to let anyone see our inner being; nor will we ever give anyone that degree of influence in our lives. We may continue physically in the relationship, but our hearts are distant and cold. If the wounding touches at all on our sexuality—our maleness or femaleness—the wounding impacts our identity at a much deeper level.

That is why any form of sexual abuse is so destructive. It is the form of evil most effective at shutting down our ability to love others and love God. Sexual abuse damages our soul at a level unparalleled by any other sinful action or trauma, no matter how minor the act of sexual abuse may seem.

Most people would define sexual abuse as forced sexual intercourse—what we would call rape. And most people would understand how horrific this experience would be, whether the victim was young or old, male or female. Sexual abuse, though, can be less physically violent and equally emotionally violent.

Sexual abuse happens when a defenceless person (usually a child or teenager) is used for the sexual excitement or pleasure of someone older, stronger, or with more authority.[37] Sexual abuse, then, includes touching, exposure, and even emotional or psychological abuse. I have counselled many men who were exposed to pornography at a young age—often preadolescent—and generally by a father or older sibling, friend, or relative. For these men, it is one of the roots of the sexual woundedness they struggle with. The exposure to pornography warped the development of healthy sexuality and a godly understanding of who they are and who women are. Although they merely viewed the pornography, because of its effect on them this exposure should rightfully be called sexual abuse.

In our sexually permissive society, I would suspect that few of us escape childhood or adolescence without some abuse, degradation, or confusion of our sexuality. Most of this sexual abuse would not be "criminal" in the sense of our legal system, but all of it is criminal when seen as a crime against our sexuality and personhood. It is an offence to the person God created us to be.

In our society, "sex" is understood as an act we perform. And in that context it is an act a person enters into to get his or her needs met. I remember watching a TV sitcom where one man was questioning his friend's real desire to be in a dating relationship. After all, he observed, his friend had seen the lady three times and they had not even been to bed. "How badly do you want to date this woman, anyway?" he wondered. Sex was seen as a way to establish intimacy in a relationship, not as an outcome of the intimacy that had already been established.

WOUNDED SEXUALITY

My family was not emotionally intimate. We very seldom expressed affection verbally or physically. I grew up starved for affection and male affirmation. However, my dad had a nickname for me. On one level I hated it, but on another level I treasured it because it was the only form of intimacy between the two of us. It was a goofy phrase with a sexual connotation.

I had bittersweet memories of those words. One day, I realized the full effect of the words. They had been a mockery of my sexuality and developing womanhood. I was devastated, but it was the beginning of the healing of my sexuality.

Being extremely overweight as a child and bullied by schoolmates, I grew up with a crushing sense of body shame. My father's sexually shaming nickname did not help matters much, nor did the lack of affirmation of my womanliness in high school. Always the wallflower, I never dated until I was in my early twenties. By then my desperation for physical affection and affirmation led me to look for love in all the wrong places! As a new Christian, my desperation for love overwhelmed any sense of moral rights and wrongs, and the few relationships I did have very quickly overstepped godly boundaries.

Through my twenties and early thirties, I remember very clearly feeling neither male nor female. It was as though my sexuality did not exist. It wasn't confused; it just didn't exist. I knew I was a woman, but that part of me had been shut down years ago. I felt genderless. My life experience had scoffed at my femininity. As a consequence, it was easier to shut off any emotional sense of my womanhood than to face the depth of the wounds to my sexuality.

This genderlessness helped me cope with life by numbing out the pain I felt from the lack of intimacy in my life. What's more, it gave me an illusion of protecting myself from more serious harm. For example, I never worried about being raped, because, I reasoned, who would want me? On an intellectual level I knew that rape was not about attractiveness but about power, so it could happen to any woman. However, it would not happen to me; I did not feel like a woman. I did not have any lesbian tendencies. I found men attractive and wanted to be with a special man. It was just...well, I didn't feel like a woman, or at least have any indication of what that meant.

My life experience to that point in time mocked my womanhood rather than affirming it. The lack of affirmation from my father, boys in school, and others was so painful that the only way I could cope with it was to shut down. I detached from the part of myself that seemed to be the cause of the pain—my identity as a woman. When I entered the career world in the 1980s, the work climate further reinforced my genderlessness by giving the strong message that only typically masculine characteristics would lead to success.

My female identity was wounded not only by my father but also by my mother. I first realized this when I was meeting with a counsellor. We had been spending some time talking about my likes and dislikes, in essence about my identity. At one point, my counsellor mentioned that I seemed to be a very nurturing person. My surprising response was that I wanted to leap out of my chair and punch him in the face! Sensing my obvious agitation, we talked about it. It took me a while to understand what was happening.

Mom was a psychiatric nurse. She took care of needy people, and she took care of me. This was good. But since, from my perspective, it seemed that she continually crumbled under my father's quiet rage and need to control, my conclusion was that to be nurturing—commonly thought of as a feminine characteristic—was a sign of weakness. When my counsellor said I was nurturing, I felt that he had put me down; I did not perceive the comment as a positive affirmation of my femininity. To be nurturing, to be feminine, was a weakness that I didn't want any part of.

It's ironic, really. What I do now—facilitating recovery groups, counselling, teaching about healing and wholeness—is nurturing to the max! By believing a lie about what it meant for me to be a woman, I shut down the very part of me that God wanted to be released as a blessing! While men can and should be nurturers too, my rejection of my mom's nurturing side closed the door to that part of my femininity.

Others I have talked to responded to the wounding of their sexuality by becoming promiscuous. The sexual woundedness they experienced seems to have left them with a sense that their identity is only sexual. Any significant relationship must move to a sexual level. This sexualization of intimacy never fills the need for true emotional intimacy—knowing and being known—that we all crave at the very depths of our being. Sexualization of intimacy is simply equating sex with intimacy.

A desire for intimacy can become sexualized with anyone. It is one of the reasons inappropriate relationships begin between pastors and church members, teachers and students. One or both of the parties have a deep desire for intimacy that has been wounded at some time. Consequently, an emotionally intimate relationship that may be very appropriate becomes sexualized, and one or both parties overstep a line. This is often a contributing factor in same-sex relationships too. People with wounded sexuality are still looking for intimacy. However, the depth of their wounding causes them to form intimate relationships only with members of their own sex.

EMOTIONAL PROMISCUITY

A few years ago a friend and I coined the phrase *emotional promiscuity* to describe what we saw going on in Christian single circles. Many of these men were deeply wounded but still seemed to be able to attract a regular following of single women. Eventually, a woman would desire the friendship to move to a deeper level of commitment. At this point, the man would distance himself, and the relationship would end. However, within a short period of time the individual would find another close female friend, and the pattern would start again.

Both the men and women in this scenario had intimacy problems. The women picked men who could not make commitments, thereby continuing the pattern of emotionally distant relationships in their own lives. The men in these scenarios were so deeply wounded that they did not even understand their gargantuan need for intimacy. Consequently, they could get their emotional needs met from these superficially emotional relationships without having to make the commitment that true intimacy requires. If they had not been committed Christians, and so emotionally detached, they would be sexually promiscuous. Instead, they were emotionally promiscuous.

Given the link between our sexuality and intimacy, emotional promiscuity is as dangerous to men and women as sexual promiscuity is. Both provide a taste of the intimacy we were created to enjoy with each other. Neither satisfies the longing, and both leave the participants with a growing emotional chasm that takes more and more to fill.

HELPING OTHERS FIND HEALING IN THEIR IDENTITY AND INTIMACY

At one point in my healing journey, I remember coming alive! The analogy of a flower beginning to bloom is somewhat trite but the best I can do to describe this experience. Something inside of me that had long been dormant was coming to life. It was at one moment exciting and at another moment frightening. I didn't understand it at the time, but I realize that through a variety of ways God had brought healing to my sexual identity. I was beginning to feel like a woman rather than some genderless being.

The healing process I observed in my own life, and in the lives of others, did not happen in isolation. It happened as I invited God and others into the deep part of my life. As a pastor or church leader, you too may become one of those others who help persons with a wounded sexuality to experience healing and wholeness in their lives.

Briefly, here is the information you will need to know and the key steps people need to walk through in this process.

*1. Be certain that you have established healthy internal sexual boundaries **yourself.***

As we have discussed, intimacy is a desire to be deeply enjoyed by another and to allow the other person's life to affect us. The more deeply this happens, the greater the intimacy. We also know that *intimacy* is not a word that is only applied to the sexual aspect of relationships.

However, we must have a better understanding of the link between physical and emotional boundaries in order to set healthy sexual boundaries in our relationships with people who come to us with wounded hearts. Relationships should be emotionally intimate before they enter into any level of physical intimacy. For example, I am uncomfortable when people give me a hug if our relationship consists only of polite conversation after a Sunday morning service. I don't feel that the emotional level of intimacy has reached a level where a hug is appropriate. I am able to articulate my boundaries. Others are not. They may want to give you a hug because, for them, physical intimacy comes before emotional intimacy. Hugs are really great, healthy ways of expressing affection. Just make sure they are always given, and received, with permission and clear boundaries.

In a pastoral counselling situation, it is not unusual for the "client" (for lack of a better term) to feel emotional intimacy from their pastor or counsellor. As Christians, that is really how it should be. Jesus extended His heart, His emotions, to those He spoke with. They would have deeply felt His love for them. Problems arise when the person with authority in the situation, the pastor or counsellor, cannot receive the emotional intimacy extended from the client in a godly way. Our sinful flesh links emotional intimacy with sex, and we can find ourselves in a dangerous situation. Please remember—as the pastor or counsellor, it is our response to emotional intimacy that is the problem, not intimacy itself.

At some time, if we are honest, most leaders have felt this struggle. Often, because we do not recognize emotional intimacy as a healthy part of life, we deflect the problem onto our client, blaming them for making advances on us or having a "spirit of lust." The only safe way to deal with this confusion between emotional and sexual intimacy is to establish internal boundaries in our hearts.[38]

So, what do internal boundaries look like? Simply, they are ways of putting safe, godly perimeters around the internal desires of my heart. If I have a lustful heart, that lust will surface somehow, somewhere, even if you can see through a window into my office and I am acting in an outwardly appropriate way.

Here are some guidelines to help guard our hearts:

a. Develop healthy friendships with members of the opposite sex. The more we understand that they are people like us, the easier it is to see them not simply as sexual beings or, worse, as the cause of the problems our sex struggles with. (In other words, as women we need to truly believe that men are not the enemy, and vice versa.)

b. Be honest about your sexual desires, not just to yourself but also to a trusted friend. When you do cross over an internal line, remember the power of confession. *"Confess your sins to one another, and pray for one another, so that you may be healed [or made whole]"* (James 5:16). Confession is one of the most powerful tools we have in dealing with our lust.

c. Have wisdom. It is true that there are some men I will not meet with in a counselling session or for a coffee appointment unless someone else is present. While I have well-defined internal boundaries, their internal boundaries are so weak that I can feel the pull. In these cases, I am open with my staff and take extra precautions. We are always to be asking God for wisdom, so don't take your own perception of a situation as wisdom; ask God, and ask your inner circle too.

d. Address your fantasy life. Men, if you have been attracted to pornography or are still addicted to it, you need to talk with a trained helper. Consult a Christian counsellor who may be able to direct you to more specific resources. Women, beware of the addiction of romantic fantasies. Reading too many romance novels—even Christian romance novels—can be an indication that you prefer "fantasy" relationships to real ones or that your real relationships are lacking true emotional intimacy.

e. If you were psychologically or physically sexually abused as a child, you have deeper issues to address. Talk to someone who can help you find healing for these deep wounds.

2. *A wounded person must have their masculinity or femininity affirmed by an authority figure.*

I've known some people to have this process initiated or completed through a formal prayer of blessing where a significant person in their life—most often of the opposite sex—blessed them as a woman, or as a man. This is important, but it is even more important that we, as a normal pattern in life, affirm people. Merely making comments on their appearance or behaviour, such as "You look very womanly today" or "You handled that in a manly way," does not do this. Rather, affirm them as persons. Since our sexuality is a main characteristic of our human identity, affirming someone for who they are will lead ultimately to an affirming of their sexual identity.

It is traditionally believed that Mary Magdalene had been a prostitute until she met Jesus. Throughout the Gospels, we get glimpses of her walk and journey with Christ, but they are simply that—only glimpses. How did she change so dramatically over a relatively short period of time to become one of the first witnesses of the resurrection? I believe it was because Jesus, the male disciples, and other women in Jesus' entourage treated her with the respect and dignity due to her as a woman.

3. *Ditch stereotypes.*

Intentionally ask God to help you see what it means for someone you are helping to be the person God created him or her to be. Some women are more nurturing than others. Some men are leaders, but some are not. Free yourself and free others to be who God has created us to be! Masculinity and femininity are not determined solely by our career choice or the clothes we wear!

4. Offer prayer ministry and counselling for the sexual wounds that have been inflicted.

A book and workbook like The Wounded Heart is a helpful tool to use to walk with someone through the process of healing from sexual abuse. However, it may be more appropriate to simply walk with the person in the process and refer them to a qualified counsellor or recovery group for further help. Nevertheless, learn all you can about sexual brokenness, and don't be afraid to address it.

5. Break spiritual bondages.

Whether or not the individual you are working with has been sexually abused, there is a need to be involved in prayer ministry. Any sexual abuse or sexual use of our body outside of marriage establishes a spiritual bond that needs to be broken and creates wounds that need to be healed. This includes any sexual relationship outside of marriage.

Ask the Holy Spirit to reveal all the areas that need to be healed or the bondages that need to be broken, and say this simple prayer:

Jesus, I confess that I have [state the sexual sin] *with* [name the person]. *Thank you for forgiving me and for breaking any bond that has been established through this sexual involvement.*

These bondages need to be broken for sexual abuse victims too. Use the following prayer:

Jesus, I acknowledge that I was sexually abused by [name]. *I ask that you break any bond that was established between my abuser and me through this sexual involvement. In your name, Jesus, I declare this spiritual bond broken.*

6. Model an appreciation for our physical bodies, no matter their shape or size!

In our society, both men and women are bombarded by the airbrushed Hollywood images of the perfect body. The sooner we can each accept the body God has given us, the freer we are. Make sure you model self-acceptance. While keeping our bodies healthy is important, no amount of dieting or exercise will ever give most of us the body of a superstar! Since our sexuality is reflected in our bodies, no one truly has been healed until he can accept his body for what it is.

God desires us to be free in all areas of our lives. And, as Christians, we need to freely declare that God's plan for our identity and sexuality is much better than the world's plan. It is time we saw our society's preoccupation with sex as a cry for something more than a physical experience. The gospel is good news for all aspects of our lives—not just spirit and soul, but body too!

Chapter Fourteen

Putting It All Together

At a recent home fellowship group, we were talking about forgiveness. One of my friends said, "I've forgiven the people who hurt me, but I can't seem to forget about it. The incident keeps coming back to my mind, and it hurts so much."

She was amazed and relieved when I told her, "There's a difference between forgiving someone and asking God to heal the wound." It was one of those "aha" moments for her. Slowly, she has entered into a deeper process of healing and forgiveness that is bringing to her the freedom that had eluded her for so many years.

One of the reasons I wrote this book was because I have met hundreds of people over the years who have been given well-intentioned but ultimately unhelpful counsel from a church leader. Often, rather than receiving counsel that led to healing and maturity, they have gone away feeling unheard, judged, or confused. Sometimes the advice worked—for a short time—but because the wound was left unhealed and the sin unconfessed, the problems soon returned. It wasn't because the pastor or leader intended to cause hurt; rather, it was because he or she didn't have the tools to help.

If I had a toothache, I would go to a dentist for help. My expectation would be that the dentist would have some specialized training to relieve the tooth pain. I have a great dentist. He has the requisite training and, I believe, being a godly man, he listens to the leading of the Spirit too. However, I would not see a dentist who, however well-intentioned and Spirit-led, did not have the basic training. Would you? Likewise, people come to church leaders every day with the expectation that they will be able to help heal the emotional and spiritual pain. Unfortunately, many of our church leaders do not have even an introductory course in prayer ministry or discipleship counselling and end up causing further damage.

Congratulations! Now that you've thoughtfully and prayerfully read this book, you are in a better position to be a person that brings healing rather than more pain.

Jesus' ministry began with the following announcement, recorded in Luke 4:18–19.

> *"The Spirit of the Lord is upon me, because he has anointed me to bring good news to the poor. He has sent me to proclaim release to the captives and recovery of sight to the blind, to let the oppressed go free, to proclaim the year of the Lord's favor."*

I believe that, as Jesus' followers, it is the mandate for all believers to be able to bring good news, release the captives, restore sight, and let the oppressed go free! Granted, the wounds in some people's lives may require more expertise than you currently possess. However, having read this book, you will understand some key concepts and how to apply them.

First, you will know that emotional healing and Christian maturity is a process. That process, at its root, involves identifying the emotional wound, asking the Holy Spirit to heal that wound, and confessing our reactive sin patterns.

Further, you will have a better working knowledge of the gift of confession and forgiveness. Now you can more effectively apply that cleansing tool to wounded hearts that come to you looking for hope and healing.

Third, you will understand the impact our past wounds have on our present relationships—both with each other and with God. You will have a working knowledge of the core wounds we all face: abandonment, rejection, shame, powerlessness, betrayal, and identity. More importantly, you will be able to point people in the direction of healing.

At the beginning of this book I introduced you to the picture of the tipped-over jar. The large jar full of gravel, sand, and water represents our lives. Somehow the larger stones—the foundation stones—were never placed in the jar. We missed key experiences and foundational truths or skills in our childhood development. God's desire is to replace these; but, in order to do that, He must tip over our jars. The role of leaders is to be part of the process of replacing those foundation stones.

We are to replace abandonment and rejection with safety and acceptance. Powerlessness is to be replaced with a godly understanding of influence and control. Learning to discern trustworthy from unsafe people replaces the wound of betrayal. And acceptance and affirmation go a long way toward healing the wound of shame and lack of identity.

I believe that, through reading this book, you will have been able to acknowledge how pervasive and deep the need for emotional healing is within the Body of Christ and society. Additionally, my intention was to help you identify some of the unhealed wounds in your own life and continue in your personal healing journey. Together, these two realizations will empower you as a healer of wounded hearts. May God grant you grace and wisdom in healing wounded and broken hearts.

MOOD DISORDER SYMPTOMS CHECKLISTS

✻   ✻   ✻

Compare yourself to the symptoms listed below. If you see yourself being described, you should take this list to your physician and discuss it with him or her.[39]

DEPRESSION

At least five of the following symptoms need to be present every day for at least two weeks when there is no other personal situation (like grief) or medical condition (like drugs or low thyroid) that may be causing the symptoms:

1. Persistent sad, anxious or "empty" mood most of the time most days

2. Feelings of hopelessness, pessimism and low esteem

3. Feelings of guilt, worthlessness, helplessness

4. Loss of interest or pleasure in hobbies and activities that were once enjoyed, including sex

5. Insomnia, early-morning awakening, or oversleeping

6. Loss of appetite and/or weight loss or overeating and weight gain

7. Decreased energy, fatigue, feeling "slowed down," or agitation that can't be controlled

8. Procrastination, since simple tasks seem harder

9. Thoughts of death or suicide, suicide attempts, constant feelings of "life isn't worth living like this"

10. Restlessness, irritability, bad temper, never relaxed or content

11. Difficulty concentrating, remembering, and making decisions due to persistent, uncontrollable cluttering of down, sad, negative thoughts that can't be kept out of the mind

Other common symptoms of depression are:

12. Persistent physical symptoms that do not respond to treatment, such as headaches, digestive disorders and chronic pain

13. Continuous anxiety that can't be turned off; uncontrollable worry about small things, including physical health

14. Social isolation or withdrawal due to increasing difficulty making small talk

15. Other relatives with depression, alcoholism or nervous breakdowns

16. In children, increased irritability, persisting complaints of physical problems, agitation and unwarranted anxiety or panic, social withdrawal

DYSTHYMIA

Dysthymia is a milder form of depression that is just as treatable as depression and with the same medications.

1. Depressed mood most of the time for most days for at least two years with at least two of the following symptoms:

   Poor appetite or overeating
   Insomnia or oversleeping
   Low energy, always tired
   Low self-esteem
   Poor concentration and difficulty making decisions
   Feeling hopeless

2. These symptoms interfere with social or vocational functioning.

ANXIETY

Do you have excessive or unrealistic anxiety and worry about a number of events or activities? Has it been noticeable on most days for at least six months? Is it difficult to control or "turn off" the worry? On most days in the past six months have you felt:

1. Restless, keyed up, or on edge

2. Tired frequently

3. Difficulty concentrating or mind going blank

4. Irritability

5. Muscle tension

6. Difficulty falling or staying asleep

Does the worry or anxiety cause significant distress (i.e., it bothers you that you worry too much) or significant interference with your day-to-day life? For example, the worry may make it difficult for you to perform important tasks at work, interfere with relationships, or get in the way of sleep.

Do you experience feelings of anxiety, fear, or panic immediately upon encountering a feared social situation?

Do you recognize that the fear is excessive, unreasonable, or out of proportion to the actual risk in the situation?

Do you tend to avoid a feared social situation, or if you can't avoid it, do you endure it with intense anxiety or discomfort?

OBSESSIVE-COMPULSIVE DISORDER

1. Recurring intrusive and persisting disturbing thoughts that cause anxiety and distress

2. The thoughts are unrelated to actual events

3. You try to stop the thoughts with another thought or action

4. You are aware that the thoughts are untrue and from your own mind

5. Repetitive meaningless behaviours (hand washing, ordering, checking) or thought rituals (praying, counting, repetitions) that you must do to neutralize the unwanted disturbing thoughts

6. The thoughts and resulting actions are time consuming, disruptive and embarrassing, but you have no control over them

MANIA OR HYPOMANIA (MILD MANIA),
INDICATING BIPOLAR DISORDER

1. Exaggerated elation, rapid, unpredictable mood changes

2. Irritability, impatience with others who can't keep up with you

3. Inability to sleep, not needing sleep, too busy to sleep and not being tired the next day

4. Big plans, inflated self-esteem, exaggerated self-importance, impulsive overspending

5. Increased talking, louder and faster and can't stop

6. Racing and jumbled thoughts, changing topics rapidly, no one can keep up

7. Poor concentration, distractibility

8. Increased sexual desire, uninhibited, acting out of character or promiscuous

9. Markedly increased energy, "can't be stopped," erratic, aggressive driving

10. Poor judgment, no insight, refusing treatment, blaming others

11. Inappropriate high risk social behaviour; brash, telling people off, overreaction to events, misinterpreting events, distortion of meaning of ordinary remarks

12. Lasts hour to days, usually ending with a crash into profound depression

13. Not caused by street drugs like "speed" or cocaine

ADULT ATTENTION DEFICIT DISORDER

1. Chronic forgetfulness
2. Problems with time and money management
3. Disorganized lifestyle
4. Frequent moves or job changes
5. Periodic depression, mood swings, or anxiety as in the mood disorders above
6. Chronic patterns of underachievement
7. Feelings of restlessness
8. Impulsive behaviour
9. Tendency toward substance abuse
10. Low self-esteem
11. May be over-or under-reactive
12. Easily frustrated
13. Difficulty concentrating
14. Difficulty maintaining relationships
15. Often labelled as lazy, immature, daydreamers, quitters, having bad attitudes

SCHIZOPHRENIA OR ANY PSYCHOTIC BREAKDOWN

1. Emotionally flat and withdrawn or very excited, hostile, or grandiose
2. Poor verbal communication; disorganized, unconnected thoughts

3. Delusional thinking, believing something to be true that is outside the realm or reason and for which there is no real evidence, often religious

4. Seeing things not visible to others or hearing things not audible to others

5. Feelings of being watched or followed by other individuals or organizations

6. There are many complex symptoms in psychotic illnesses needing professional assessment. Basically, during a psychotic episode a person loses touch with reality and is unable to function in his normal life activities. If you see this symptom, the person needs urgent medical attention.

The information contained in this chapter is for educational purposes only and does not replace the medical evaluation of a physician.

These checklists are adapted from *The American Psychiatric Association, Diagnostic and Statistical Manual of Mental Disorders,* fourth edition (Washington, D.C.: American Psychiatric Association, 1994).

Style of Relating Questionnaire

In *The Wounded Heart,* Dr. Dan Allender outlines some general patterns that are common for women and men who have been sexually abused. Over the years I have found that these patterns often apply to individuals who have either been emotionally, physically, or spiritually abused as well. A relational style, different than personality typing, is the way we choose to offer or protect our hearts in relationship with others.

Use the following checklists to identify your relational style.[40] Simply circle the numbers that apply to you. Keep a few things in mind as you go through this checklist. First, circle a characteristic if you do that often or very often. You may realize that you relate a certain way with men, or with women, or with authority figures versus your peers. Make note of that. In addition keep in mind that some of the features are not necessarily bad in themselves—it is the motivation behind the act that is of concern. It's good for people to find you pleasant (no. 9) but not if it's because you avoid conflict at all costs.

A key is provided at the end of the checklist.

Special note for men: Over the years I have found that the list in *The Wounded Heart Workbook* generally applies for men as well, though specific comments for men are listed at the end of this checklist.

Please circle all statements you feel would describe yourself often or very often in relationships.

1. I feel a lot of contempt (hatred, anger, or self-pity) for myself, but I try not to let others know about it.

2. I secretly struggle with sexual fantasies.

3. I'm fickle.

4. I'm easily hurt.

5. I place a high priority on helping other people.

6. I can be wonderfully pleasant, but people know they'll be sorry if they cross my line.

7. I have little or no interest in sex.

8. I'm more passive than assertive or aggressive.

9. I think people find me pleasant.

10. Nobody would dare call me cuddly or soft.

11. I feel lonely.

12. I like to be in control, especially of myself.

13. I really like a good time.

14. I don't like to impose on other people.

15. I take things out of context or mishear them.

16. I'm not good at delegating tasks to others (especially peers/adults).

17. I feel guilty if I'm angry at someone.

18. I can usually tell when people are being dishonest or untrustworthy.

19. I have trouble saying no.

20. I'm not good at keeping long-term relationships.

21. I tend to turn compliments aside with comments like "It was nothing," by giving the Lord credit, or by pointing out the flaws in what I've done.

22. I am critical of myself, especially as a woman/man.

23. As a child I was a great helper, even perhaps to my abuser.

24. I hate to be dependent on people.

25. I receive many advances from the opposite sex, and I'm surprised, wondering why the person is attracted.

26. I have trouble protecting my spouse or children from harm.

27. I have tended to view my longings as sentimental, sloppy, and/or weak.

28. People value me for my competence.

29. I avoid asking for help.

30. I like my environment to be organized, but I rarely feel I have the chaos in order.

31. I sometimes fantasize about dominating men.

32. I'd rather do something good for someone than give him or her a glimpse of my soul.

33. When people compliment me, I wonder what they're after.

34. I am highly competent at a variety of tasks.

35. I like to be in charge.

36. I enjoy being seductive.

37. When challenged, I am willing to go toe to toe with anyone to accomplish what I think is right.

38. I don't put much stock in compliments.

39. I feel uncomfortable with commitment.

40. One of my main goals is to keep peace and avoid conflict with others.

41. I have very strong opinions about women's rights.

42. As a child I was a good listener and generally quiet, not a troublemaker.

43. I lose my temper fairly frequently.

44. I am an energetic worker.

45. I'm hard to pin down.

46. Before I started dealing with my abuse, I recalled some events, but I didn't see it as all that important or blamed myself.

47. You can count on me to be unpredictable.

48. When I feel threatened or angry, I tend to be verbally aggressive or sarcastic to overpower the other person.

49. I tend to be busy up to, or often beyond, my real capacity.

50. I have moderate or wild mood swings.

51. I rarely lose my temper.

52. I tend to feel it's pointless to dwell on hurts.

53. I try not to let things bother me, but often they do.

54. I am whiny sometimes and bold at other times.

55. I often feel very afraid, but at other times I'm surprisingly brave.

56. I apologize a lot more than I receive apologies.

57. I feel enormous guilt about my fantasies, but I can't stop.

58. When a relationship starts to get too close, I want to end it, so I:

    a. Pull away

    b. Cause conflict

    c. Do something disloyal

    d. Get attracted to another man/woman

    e. Other—name it _____

59. My mind tends to go elsewhere during sex.

60. I get out of a relationship when the person demands too much time and energy.

61. I see myself as a take-charge, task-oriented person.

62. If I feel hurt, I tell myself I'm overreacting or push myself to forgive. It feels selfish to dwell on hurt.

63. I have trouble standing up to aggressive people or evildoers.

64. I flirt a lot.

65. When I feel sexual, I feel more powerful than desirable.

Key: Calculate your relating style by totalling up the numbers you have circled from the key below. Then you can calculate the percentage of each style

Good Girl, Nice Boy[41]

Numbers: 1, 2, 5, 7, 8, 9, 11, 12, 14, 16, 17, 19, 21, 22, 23, 26, 29, 30, 32, 40, 42, 44, 46, 49, 51, 56, 57, 59, 62, 63

Percentage: X/30 x 100 = _____ %

Tough Girl, Macho Boy[42]

Numbers: 6, 10, 18, 24, 27, 28, 31, 33, 34, 35, 37, 38, 41, 43, 48, 61, 65

Percentage: X/17 x 100 = _____ %

Party Girl, Seductive Boy[43]

Numbers: 3, 4, 13, 15, 20, 25, 36, 39, 45, 47, 50, 52, 53, 54, 55, 58, 60, 64

Percentage: X/18 x 100 = _____ %

Additional questions for men only. Please circle the numbers that apply.

M1. I place a high priority of being liked by other people.

M2. I see myself as a take-charge, task-oriented person.

M3. I really like a good time.

M4. People would consider me smooth.

M5. One of my main goals is to keep peace and avoid conflict with other people.

M6. I'd rather not make decisions.

M7. I hate to be dependent on people.

M8. I tend to be indifferent to the feelings of others.

M9. I can get out of trouble almost every time.

M10. I can convince others of almost anything.

M11. I am often cynical and suspicious.

M12. I feel a lot of contempt for myself, but I try not to let others know about that.

M13. I let others make choices so that I am not responsible for what happens.

Nice Boy

M1, M5, M6, M12, M13

Macho Boy

M2, M7, M8, M11

Seductive Boy

M3, M4, M9, M10

SUGGESTED READING

✳ ✳ ✳

Many, but not all, of the books listed here have been quoted in this book. The others are helpful resources as well and have been included for that purpose.

Allender, Dan B. *The Wounded Heart*. Colorado Springs, Colorado: Navpress, 1995.

Allender, Dan B., and Karen Lee-Thorp. *The Wounded Heart Workbook*. Colorado Springs, Colorado: Navpress, 1995.

Anderson, Neil T. *The Bondage Breaker*. Eugene, Oregon: Harvest House, 1990. See also www.ficm.org.

Anderson, Bill. *When Child Abuse Comes to the Church: Recognizing Sexual Abuse, Knowing What to Do About It— and Possibly Preventing It from Happening*. Minneapolis, Minnesota: Bethany House Publishers, 1992.

Bricker, Darrell, and John Wright. *What Canadians Think... About Almost Everything*. Canada: Doubleday Canada, 2005.

Brown, Tom. *How to Handle Rejection*. Nigeria, Africa: Asbot Graphics, 2000.

Cloud, Henry, and John Townsend. *The Mom Factor*. Grand Rapids, Michigan: Zondervan, 1996.

Cloud, Henry, and John Townsend. *Boundaries: When to Say Yes, When to Say No, to Take Control of Your Life*. Grand Rapids, Michigan: Zondervan Publishing House, 1995.

Cloud, Henry, and John Townsend. *Safe People*. Grand Rapids, Michigan: Zondervan Publishing House, 1995.

Eckman, David. *Becoming Who God Intended: A New Picture for Your Past, A Healthy Way of Managing Your Emotions, A Fresh Perspective on Relationships*. Harvest House Publishers, 2005.

Eldredge, John. *Waking the Dead*. Nashville, Tennessee: Thomas Nelson 2003.

Eldredge, John. *Wild at Heart: Discovering the Secret of a Man's Soul*. Nashville, Tennessee: Thomas Nelson, 2001.

Eldredge, John, and Stasi Eldredge. *Captivating: Unveiling the Mystery of a Woman's Soul*. Nashville, Tennessee: Nelson Books, 2005.

Friends In Recovery. *The Twelve Steps-A Spiritual Journey*. 1988 Recovery Publications, San Diego, California

Heitritter, Lynn and Jeanette Vought. *Helping Victims of Sexual Abuse*. Minneapolis, Minnesota: Bethany House Publishers, 1989.

Jacobs, Cindy. *Women of Destiny*. Ventura, California: Regal, 1998.

Lamott, Anne. *Traveling Mercies*. New York: Pantheon Books, 1999.

Matsakis, Aphrodite. *I Can't Get Over It: A Handbook For Trauman Survivors*. Oakland, California: New Harbinger Publications, 1996.

Mullen, Grant. *Emotionally Free: A Prescription for Healing Body, Soul and Spirit*. Tonbridge, England: Sovereign World, 2003. See also www.drgrantmullen.com.

Norris, Kathleen. *The Cloister Walk*. New York: Riverton Books, 1996.

Peck, M. Scott. *People of the Lie*. New York: Simon & Schuster, 1983.

Scazzero, Peter. *The Emotionally Healthy Church*. Grand Rapids, Michigan: Zondervan, 2003.

Seamans, David.*Healing of Memories* Victor Books, Wheaton, Illinois, 1985.

Smedes, Lewis B. *Sex for Christians*. Grand Rapids, Michigan: William B. Eerdmans Publishing Company, 1994.

Springle, Pat. *Trusting*. Ann Arbor, Michigan: Servant Publications, 1994.

van Dam, Carla. *Identifying Child Molesters: Preventing Child Sexual Abuse by Recognizing the Patterns of the Offenders*. New York: Hawthorn Press Inc., 2001.

Wholeness Through Christ see www.wholenessthroughchrist.com Contact: Jean Tibbles, Administrator Box 9, Hixon, British Columbia, Canada, V0K 1S0

Winner, Lauren. *Real Sex: the Naked Truth About Chastity.* Grand Rapids, Michigan: Brazos Press, 2005.

Wright, Norman H. *Always Daddy's Girl.* Ventura, California: Regal Books, 1989.

ENDNOTES

※ ※ ※

[1] The material we still use in these groups is from *The Wounded Heart: Hope for Adult Victims of Childhood Sexual Abuse,* by Dan Allender (Colorado Springs, Colorado: Navpress, 1995).

[2] Peter Scazzero, *The Emotionally Healthy Church* (Grand Rapids, Michigan: Zondervan, 2003).

[3] Peron et al., "Canadian Families at the approach of the year 2000" (1991 Census Monograph Series), Statistics Canada, 1999, pg. 51.

[4] "MIPC" Minister's Information Packet, flyer produced by the Pentecostal Assemblies of Canada, 2003, based on 1996 statistics.

[5] A Report on Mental Illness in Canada, October 2002, Ottawa, Canada, Public Health Agency of Canada.

[6] Raymond A. Lam, *BC's Mental Health Journal,* Fall 2000, 11:1.

[7] Carla van Dam, *Identifying Child Molesters: Preventing Child Sexual Abuse by Recognizing the Patterns of the Offenders* (Binghamten, New York: Haworth Press, 2001), p. 75.

[8] Ravi Prakash Tangri, *What Stress Costs: Executive Summary and StressCosts Formula* (Halifax, Nova Scotia: Chrysalis Performance Strategies Inc., 2002), p.1, http://www.teamchrysalis.com/WhatStressCostsExecSummaryandFormula.pdf.

[9] Lyle Larson, J. Walter Goltz, and Charles Hobart, *Families in Canada: Social Context, Continuities and Changes* (Prentice-Hall Canada Inc., 1994), p. 517–518.

[10] Aphrodite Matsakis, *I Can't Get Over It: A Handbook for Trauma Survivors* (New Harbinger Publications, 1996), p. 343.

[11] Scazzero, *The Emotionally Healthy Church,* p. 19, 50.

[12] David Eckman, *Becoming Who God Intended: A New Picture for Your Past, A Healthy Way of Managing Your Emotions, A Fresh Perspective on Relationships* (Harvest House Publishers, 2005), p. 45, 46.

[13] Darrell Bricker and John Wright, *What Canadians Think...About Almost Everything* (Doubleday Canada, 2005).

[14] Ibid., p. 49.

[15] For further information on the medical nature of depression, see *Emotionally Free: A Prescription for Healing Body, Soul and Spirit* by Grant Mullen (Tonbridge, England: Sovereign World, 2003). See also www.drgrantmullen.com.

[16] See chapter 5 for a further discussion on family of origin and what constitutes abuse and neglect. Chapter 11 contains a more detailed discussion of the effects of trauma such as car accidents, war and torture, and acts of nature such as earthquakes, etc.

[17] M. Scott Peck, *People of the Lie* (New York: Touchstone, 1998), p. 47–62.

[18] Dan Allender, *The Wounded Heart* (Colorado Springs, Colorado: Navpress, 1995).

[19] Grant Mullen, *Emotionally Free.*

[20] Reinhold Niebuhr, "The Serenity Prayer."

[21] The information on our "style of relating" is adapted from the work of Dr. Dan B. Allender, author of *The Wounded Heart.*

[22] A talent was worth more than fifteen years' wages for a labourer. So based on an annual salary of $20,000, this slave owed the modern day equivalent of 3 billion dollars! Knowing that, we have to acknowledge that it would be next to impossible for him to pay off his debt (text notes, NRSV).

[23] The denarius was the usual day's wage for a labourer. If this equalled $76 a day, it means he owed $7,600 (Ibid.).

[24] Anne Lamott, *Travelling Mercies* (New York: Pantheon Books, 1999), pg 213.

[25] Henry Cloud and John Townsend, *The Mom Factor* (Grand Rapids, MI: Zondervan, 1996), p. 28.

[26] Ibid., p. 21.

[27] BC Partners for Mental Health and Addictions Information, "Depression," http://www.heretohelp.bc.ca/publications/factsheets/depression.shtml.

[28] Kathleen Norris, *The Cloister Walk* (New York: Riverhead Books, 1996), pg. 54.

[29] Heather Carlini, *Adoptee Trauma: A Counselling Guide for Adoptees* (British Columbia, Canada: Morning Side Publishing, 1993), p. 24.

[30] Author's note: Identity diffusion is not to be confused with extreme dissociative disorders or what is still commonly referred to as Multiple Personality Disorder.

[31] Anne Lamont, *Bird by Bird: Some Instructions on Writing and Life* (New York: Anchor Books, 1994), p. 28.

[32] Allender, *The Wounded Heart*, p. 118.

[33] *Concise Oxford Dictionary*, 1990.

[34] Lewis Smedes, *Sex for Christians* (Grand Rapids, Michigan: William B. Eerdmans Publishing Company, 1994), p. 3.

[35] Cindy Jacobs, *Women of Destiny* (Ventura, California: Regal Books, 1998), p. 16.

[36] Smedes, *Sex for Christians*, p. 7.

[37] Dan Allender, *When Trust Is Broken: Native Christian Networking*),Project World Vision Canada, 1998 p. 5.

[38] For further information on the subject of boundaries, please see *Boundaries: When to Say Yes, When to Say No, to Take Control of Your Life*, by Henry Cloud and John Townsend (Grand Rapids, Michigan: Zondervan Publishing House, 1992).

[39] These checklists taken from chapter 12 of the book *Emotionally Free,* by Grant Mullen. See "Suggested Readings" for further information.

[40] This material is adapted from *The Wounded Heart: A Companion Workbook for Personal or Group Use* (Navpress Publishing Group, 1992) and is used by permission of the author, Dr. Dan Allender.

[41] Terms used in *The Wounded Heart.*

[42] Terms used in *The Wounded Heart.*

[43] Terms used in *The Wounded Heart.*

APPENDIX A

❋ ❋ ❋

GROUP MEMBER CONTRACT

Please carefully read the "Contract" outlined below. Everyone has different expectations – hope and fears – as they begin a group. The information outlined below can help you realistically approach your group experience.

A. GROUP CONFIDENTIALITY

I understand that every attempt will be made to guard my anonymity and confidentiality in this group, but that it cannot be absolutely guaranteed in a group setting.

I realize that the group facilitator cannot control the actions of others in the group. I realize that confidentiality is sometimes broken accidentally and without malice. I understand that the group facilitator is morally and ethically obligated to break confidentiality when:

- I communicate an intention to kill myself.
- I communicate an intention to harm another person.
- I reveal ongoing sexual or physical abuse.

I have been warned about consequences for communicating the above types of information: that reports will be made to the proper authorities, which may include the police and Child Protection services, as well as to any potential victim. I understand that the group facilitator's motivation in this action is for my well being and it will only be undertaken in cases of extreme personal danger or when other alternatives have proven unsuccessful.

B. GROUP PROCESS

I understand that the group operates by the following covenant for the overall healthy functioning of the group. I am aware that the group is only part of my healing process and that ultimately my healing process must move me toward being connected with others in community. (A community is a network of life-giving relationships.)

I understand that being a part of this group is a commitment and I will faithfully attend and complete weekly assignments.

I understand the need to be wary of establishing any exclusive relationship with another group participant. It has been explained to me that this pairing or sub-grouping can be detrimental to my healing process as well as the healing process for others in the group.

I understand that the group facilitator will make every effort to find additional help for me if my needs prove to be too great for the resources of this group.

C. GROUP BELIEFS & PHILOSOPHY

I understand that this group is based on Christian values and beliefs. I realize that I am not obligated to agree with any or all aspects of Christianity bur I am willing to explore, at my own pace, my relationship with Jesus as part of this group. I understand that group members may not be from my particular religious background and that the Bible may be discussed more (or less) than I would like it to be.

I realize that this group operates with a balance of professional training and "life experience" and is not facilitated by a trained psychologist or therapist. The leaders main role in this group is to create a climate where healing can occur, to support my personal work towards wholeness and health, and share her/his own experience, strength and hope.

OUR GROUP CONTRACT

1. Anything said in the group is considered confidential and will not be discussed outside the group unless specific permission is given to do so.
2. Reasonable time will be provided for each person to talk.
3. We will talk about ourselves and our own situations avoiding conversation about other people. We will use "I" phrases and take responsibility for our own thoughts and actions.
4. We will listen attentively to each other and will give each

person who shares our undivided attention.

5. We will not advise, analyze or 'fix' others. Each of us is free to find our own answers.

6. We agree to be here every week, unless an emergency arises. If we cannot attend we will inform the group leader prior to the meeting.

7. We will pray for each other and encourage each other.

D. WAIVER OF RESPONSIBILITY

I, _____, will not hold the Mars Hill Centre responsible for my emotional, mental, physical, spiritual, marital or family health.

I, alone, am responsible for my growth that takes place during the group process. I, alone am responsible for the choices I make.

Date signed: _____

Participant:

(print name) _____

(sign name) _____

Group Leader:

(print name) _____

(sign name) _____

Group Name: _____

Date & Time of Meeting: _____